APR 0 2 '00			

LITERATURE
AND
GERONTOLOGY

Recent Titles in
Bibliographies and Indexes in Gerontology

Home Health Care: An Annotated Bibliography
Ada Romaine-Davis, Aveliffe A. Lenihan, and Moira D. Shannon, compilers

Ethical Aspects of Health Care for the Elderly: An Annotated Bibliography
Marshall B. Kapp, compiler

The Image of Older Adults in the Media: An Annotated Bibliography
Frank Nuessel

Education for Older Adult Learning: A Selected, Annotated Bibliography
Reva M. Greenberg

The Older Volunteer: An Annotated Bibliography
C. Neil Bull and Nancy D. Levine, compilers

Gerontological Social Work: An Annotated Bibliography
Iris A. Parham, editor

Long Term Care: An Annotated Bibliography
Theodore H. Koff and Kristine M. Bursac, compilers

Employment of the Elderly: An Annotated Bibliography
John C. Rife, compiler

Alcoholism and Aging: An Annotated Bibliography and Review
Nancy J. Osgood, Helen E. Wood, and Iris A. Parham, compilers

Counseling Older Persons: An Annotated Bibliography
Valerie L. Schwiebert and Jane E. Myers, compilers

Research on Religion and Aging: An Annotated Bibliography
Harold G. Koenig, compiler

Psychology of Aging: An Annotated Bibliography
Bert Hayslip, Jr., Heather L. Servaty, and Amy S. Ward, compilers

LITERATURE AND GERONTOLOGY

A Research Guide

Robert E. Yahnke
and Richard M. Eastman

Bibliographies and Indexes in Gerontology, Number 29
Erdman D. Palmore, Series Adviser

GREENWOOD PRESS
Westport, Connecticut • London

Library of Congress Cataloging-in-Publication Data

Yahnke, Robert E.
    Literature and gerontology : a research guide / Robert E. Yahnke
and Richard M. Eastman.
        p.   cm.—(Bibliographies and indexes in gerontology, ISSN
0743–7560 ; no. 29)
    Includes indexes.
    ISBN 0–313–29349–X (alk. paper)
    1. Old age in literature.   2. Aging—Social aspects.   3. Aged—
Social aspects.   4. Old age in literature—Bibliography.
5. Gerontology literature.   I. Eastman, Richard M.   II. Title.
III. Series.
PN56.04Y35   1995
016.808′03520565—dc20   95–2462

British Library Cataloguing in Publication Data is available.

Library of Congress Catalog Card Number: 95–2462
ISBN: 0–313–29349–X
ISSN: 0743–7560

First published in 1995

Greenwood Press, 88 Post Road West, Westport, CT 06881
An imprint of Greenwood Publishing Group, Inc.

Printed in the United States of America

The paper used in this book complies with the
Permanent Paper Standard issued by the National
Information Standards Organization (Z39.48–1984).

10 9 8 7 6 5 4 3 2 1

Contents

Series Foreword by Erdman Palmore   vii
Preface   ix
Acknowledgments   xi
How to Use This Book   xiii

Part One: Essays on Topics in Gerontology

    Outline of Topics in Gerontology   1

    Aging and Society   3

    Aging and Relationships   15

    Aging and Physical Health   31

    Psychological Responses to Aging   39

    Life Events and the Search for Meaning   55

Part Two. Annotations of Literary Works

    Anthologies   73

    Autobiographies   79

    Novels   91

    Plays   111

    Poems   119

    Stories   145

Index of Authors and Their Works   203
Index of Topics in Part One   219
Index of Topics in Part Two   227

Series Foreword

The annotated bibliographies in this series provide answers to the fundamental question, "What is known?" Their purpose is simple, yet profound; to provide comprehensive reviews and references for the work done in various fields of gerontology. They are based on the fact that it is no longer possible for anyone to comprehend the vast body of research and writing in even one sub-specialty without years of work.

This fact has become true only in recent years. When I was an undergraduate (Class of '52) I think no one at Duke had even heard of gerontology. Almost no one in the world was identified as a gerontologist. Now there are over 6,000 professional members of the Gerontological Society of America. When I was an undergraduate there were no courses in gerontology. Now there are thousands of courses offered by most major (and many minor) colleges and universities. When I was an undergraduate there was only one gerontological journal (the *Journal of Gerontology*, begun in 1945). Now there are over forty professional journals and several dozen books in gerontology published each year.

The reasons for this dramatic growth are well known: the dramatic increase in numbers of aged, the shift from family to public responsibility for the security and care of the elderly, the recognition of aging as a "social problem," and the growth of science in general. It is less well known that this explosive growth in knowledge has developed the need for new solutions to the old problem of comprehending and "keeping up" with a field of knowledge. The old indexes and library card catalogues have become increasingly inadequate for the job. On-line computer indexes and abstracts are one solution but make no evaluative selec-

tions nor organize sources logically as is done here.
These annotated bibliographies are also more widely
available than on-line computer indexes.

However, this is no ordinary bibliography. In ad-
dition to the usual annotations of works in this field
(Literature on Aging), Part One presents a series of
useful essays which overviews the literary works relevant to a series of topics within gerontology. Therefore, as the authors point out, one can use this bibliography in four different ways: begin with the essays in
Part One, begin with the annotations in Part Two, begin
with the index of authors, or begin with the topical indexes.

In the past, the "review of literature" has often
been haphazard and was rarely comprehensive, because of
the large investment of time (and money) that would be
required by a truly comprehensive review. Now, using
these bibliographies, researchers, teachers, students,
and others concerned with a topic can be more confident
that they are not missing important previous literature
and reports: they can be more confident that they are
not duplicating past efforts and "reinventing the
wheel." It may well become a standard and expected
practice for researchers to consult such bibliographies,
even before they start their research.

In recent decades there has been a growing interest in literary work related to aging and the aged.
This is attested to by the numerous anthologies and collections listed in this book, as well as by the 350
annotations in Part Two. These works do something that
scientific reports cannot do: "show aging from the
inside as the intensified perceptions and feelings of
individual lives" (Preface).

The authors have done an outstanding job of
covering the literature and organizing it into easily
accessible form. They are exceptionally well-qualified
to produce this bibliography because they have already
produced a monograph on *Aging in Literature: A Reader's
Guide* (1990).

So it with great pleasure that we add this bibliography to our series. We believe you will find this
volume to be the most useful, comprehensive, and easily
accessible reference work in its field. I will appreciate any comments you care to send me.

Erdman B. Palmore
Center for the Study of Aging and Human Development
Box 3003, Duke University Medical Center
Durham, NC 27710

Preface

This is a book for gerontologists, about the ways in which literary works--autobiographical works, novels, plays, poems, and stories--can illuminate the problems and potentials of older people. The book is aimed at educators at various levels and health-care professionals, who may be interested in the ways literary works convey the complex nature of growing old in diverse social and cultural contexts. It is also a book for serious general readers, including older adults, who want to learn more about aging as shown in literature.

The relevance of literary works to the concerns of aging is by no means new. Besides such classics as Shakespeare's *King Lear*, Arthur Miller's *Death of a Salesman,* Ernest Hemingway's *The Old Man and the Sea*, and the poetry of William Carlos Williams, many contemporary authors have undertaken to show characters and themes of aging--writers such as Richard Bausch, Doris Lessing, May Sarton, Gina Berriault, and Donald Hall. They have done so because the swelling of the aged population invites literary attention. They have done so, in some cases, because the authors themselves, like May Sarton, are aging and therefore directly conscious of that stage of life.

What literary works can do beyond the disciplines of gerontology is to convey the *experiences* of aging. Gerontology properly focuses on research, case history, and theory. With possible exceptions it hardly tries to show aging from the inside as the intensified perceptions and feelings of individual lives. These are concerns of art, not science.

Much care has been taken in the last three decades to prepare guides to such literary works. Constance E.

Kellam provided the first reference text in her 1968 *A Literary Bibliography on Aging*. She has been followed by Walter G. Moss, Margaret E. Monroe, Rhea Joyce Rubin, Thomas Cole, and others, not to mention our own 1990 *Aging in Literature: A Reader's Guide*.

Anthologies of stories, poems, and other genres have appeared plentifully, noticeably beginning with Ruth Granetz Lyell's 1980 *Middle Age, Old Age: Short Stories, Poems, Plays, and Essays on Aging*. Later collections up to 1994 are described on pages 73-78 of the present volume.

Our attempt is distinguished, we think, by its direct address to gerontologists. Part One is organized around forty-four essays on seventy-seven topics often addressed in gerontology--topics such as ageism, elder abuse, dementia, life review. Topics were selected after consultation of numerous gerontological textbooks, reference books, and indices. For each topic a brief essay was prepared in Part One to generalize the topic and its major subdivisions, and to point to the explicit literary works in Part Two which would illustrate that topic.

For Part Two a large sampling of 343 literary works was selected: twenty-two autobiographical works, forty novels, fifteen plays, 112 poems, and 154 short stories. Among them are twelve anthologies that will provide a grounding for educators in gerontology and related fields. The possession of most or all of those collections will provide quick access to many of the works described in this volume.

The annotations of literary works in Part Two are meant to provide critical analyses of individual works. The average length of annotations is approximately 50-100 words for poems, 150 words for stories, and 200 words for autobiographies, novels, and plays. The expanded word length allows for detailed references to characters, plots, and themes in the literary works. Cross-references are provided to those essays in Part One which would generalize the topic and refer to other literary works of like concern.

A full survey of all relevant literary works would run to many times the size of our sampling. Not surprisingly, some important authors and works will have been left out. Nonetheless we are confident that the essays in Part One can profitably be applied to almost any work of literature which touches on aging.

Acknowledgments

I would like to thank Erdman Palmore, series editor, for his interest in this project, and Mildred Vasan, senior editor at Greenwood Press, for her support in the development of this bibliography.

I thank Richard M. Eastman for *mentoring*, Vivian Eastman for *friendship*, my Father for *wisdom* and *serenity*, my Mother for *legacies*, my sister Norma Jean for *family bonds* and *caregiving*, my brothers for *creativity* and *humor*, and special thanks to my wife Pat, for her gifts of *intimacy, patience, and caring*.

-- Robert E. Yahnke

Thanks to Vivian my wife.

Thanks to the American Library Association for permission to draw upon our earlier volume, *Aging in Literature: A Reader's Guide*.

Thanks to North Central College for encouragement and technical support.

Thanks to Nichols Library of Naperville for bibliographic support.

-- Richard M. Eastman

How to Use This Book

Relationships between gerontology and literary works are subtle and varied. This book is organized so that readers will have multiple ways to find useful and relevant information. Below is a quick summary of ways the text can be utilized effectively:

Begin with Part One: Readers who are interested in locating literary works that address specific topics--such as gender, sexuality, dementia--may scan the essays on topics in gerontology found in Part One. Each essay briefly describes those literary works--autobiographies, novels, stories, poems, plays--which illuminate that topic. Parenthetical references are to the numbers assigned works in Part Two. After readers have consulted the essays in Part One, they may turn to the fuller descriptions of those works in Part Two.

An outline of all essays on topics in gerontology which are treated in Part One is given in the section "Outline of Essays on Topics in Gerontology" which follows.

For example, readers interested in the topic "Sexuality" may read essay 13, Sexuality, Intimacy, and find a reference to the panicky breaking-off of a late romance in Isaac Bashevis Singer's story "Old Love." Under number 326 in Part Two, readers will find an extended analysis of that story, with suggestions as to what other topics the same story might illustrate. Readers will also find a bibliographic reference by which they can locate the full text of Singer's story.

Since that story also appears in a current anthology, readers will find that anthology referred to, and in the chapter "Anthologies" in Part Two, they will find the bibliographic reference to locate that anthology.

Begin with Part Two: Readers may want to scan the annotations of literary works found in Part Two. Entries are arranged alphabetically by author within each chapter. References to topics listed at the end of each annotation will lead readers back to the essays in Part One. Topics are listed according to the organization of the "Outline of Essays on Topics in Gerontology" which follows. Thus, four separate topics are listed under Singer's story, "Old Love": ethnicity, sexuality, suicide, and aspirations. Readers may turn to Part One, then, and find analyses of those topics in the essays for topics 7 (ethnicity), 13 (sexuality), 32 (suicide), and 39 (aspirations.) The example of Singer's story illustrates how a given literary work may appear in several essays in different contexts. This overlapping of various topics is a necessary and even desirable corollary of the wide relevance of certain literary works.

Begin with the Index of Authors and Their Works: Readers interested in finding literary works written by a particular author may consult the Index of Authors, at the end of the volume. For example, readers may find that two Isaac Bashevis Singer stories, "The Hotel" and "Old Love," are evaluated in Part Two on pages 188 and 189.

Begin with the topical indexes: Readers may consult the *Index of Topics in Part One* to find references to a variety of gerontological topics covered in the essays in that section. For example, consulting that index shows references to the topic "sexuality" are touched upon in Part One on page 22. A reference to "sexuality and alienation" can be found on page 45. Readers interested in identifying literary sources that relate to a particular gerontological topic will find the *Index of Topics in Part Two* a useful starting point. For example, readers will find the topic "sexuality" cross-referenced to thirteen literary works annotated in Part Two.

Complete bibliographic citations are given for entries, where available, in Part Two. *The Chicago Manual of Style* is followed for all citations. Information on the length of the various literary works is provided. The length of autobiographies, novels, and plays is noted at the end of citations. For instance, Pat Barker's novel *The Century's Daughter*, is 293 pages. For stories the citations include the page numbers of the story either in its original publication, a reprint, or an anthology. For example, Arturo Vivante's story

"The Orchard" appears in his collection *The Tales of Arturo Vivante*, pp. 35-42. In a few cases a story appears in more than one anthology. In that case, the page numbers of the story in only the most recent anthology will be cited. The length of poems is noted in two ways: for poems longer than one page, the length (in number of pages) is given at the end of its original source. For example, at the end of the citation for number 111, Robert Frost's poem "The Death of the Hired Man," the length of the poem is indicated as "7 pp." Readers may assume poems are no longer than one page in length when there is no reference to "pp."

Part One

ESSAYS ON TOPICS IN GERONTOLOGY

Outline of Topics in Gerontology

Note: Essays in Part One are organized according to the outline below. Each essay is numbered as indicated in the outline.

Aging and Society
1. Ageism, Stereotypes
2. Roles, Adaptation, Role loss, Role reversal
3. Economics, Poverty, Social class
4. Services, Housing
5. Rural Aging, Urban Aging
6. Race, Multicultural
7. Ethnicity, Culture
8. Gender: Men, Gender: Women

Aging and Relationships
9. Friendship, Neighbors, Community
10. Parent-Child Bonds, Family Bonds
11. Parent-Child Conflicts, Family conflicts
12. Older Couples
13. Sexuality, Intimacy
14. Intergenerational, Grandparenting
15. Caregiving
16. Elder Abuse
17. Rebellion, Enmity

Aging and Physical Health
18. Activity, Frailty
19. Disease, Disability
20. Mental Health, Dementia
21. Doctor-Patient Conflicts
22. Long-term Care

Psychological Responses to Aging
        23. Disengagement
        24. Autonomy, Coping
        25. Creativity, Humor
        26. Wisdom, Mentoring
        27. Alienation, Loneliness
        28. Anxiety, Isolation
        29. Mid-Life
        30. Deviance
        31. Depression, Suicide
        32. Vanity
        33. Courage, Endurance
        34. Serenity

Life Events & the Search for Meaning
        35. Employment
        36. Leisure
        37. Aging in Place
        38. Aspirations
        39. Retirement
        40. Grief, Widowhood, Loss
        41. Reminiscence, Life Review
        42. Religion, Spiritual Life
        43. Transmission of Values, Legacies
        44. Death

Aging and Society

1. Ageism, Stereotypes.

Ageism. Portrayals of ageism include the treatment of old people as washed up, useless, dispensable, even invisible. Examples include the salesman Willy Loman in Arthur Miller's play *Death of a Salesman* (83), the old man who is demeaned when he begins a much-needed job in J. W. Powers's story "The Old Man" (318), or the old people who are degraded in Julio Ricci's story "The Concert" (320). (See also story 205.) The younger generation may be repelled by the old, as in Ariyoshi's novel *The Twilight Years* (41). (See also story 350.) Two allegorical works, Bernard Malamud's story "The Jewbird" (287), and Edward Albee's play *The Sandbox* (75), illustrate the outright rejection and condemnation of the old.

Similar distaste for the old is reflected in Kingsley Amis's novel *Ending Up* where young couples dread the prospects of old age (37). (See also poem 156 and story 305.) A daughter looks at her old mother as "wreckage" in Gwendolyn Brooks' poem "Jessie Mitchell's Mother" (103). But a patronizing attitude toward the old can backfire when the old person becomes a worthy adversary, as in Wallace Stegner's story "The Double Corner" (327), or when the old person's resourcefulness surprises the young, as in Wendell Berry's story "Are You All Right?" (222). (See also story 295.)

Fears of "ending up" lonely and pathetic, or drooling and incontinent, are voiced by the family members visiting a nursing home in Rolf Jacobsen's poem "Part Song" (188) and in Philip Larkin's poem "The Old Fools" (137).

Faced with such negative images, the old often in-

flict ageist attitudes upon themselves: an old man in
Susan Dodd's story "Sinatra" resents any interactions
with other old people (239), and a woman feels betrayed
by her physical appearance in "I Hate the Way I Look,"
a poem by Lise Maclay (143).

Literary artists find the lives of ordinary older
people worthy of drama. An old woman's dull existence
is awakened by an angel that falls from the sky, in
Allan Gurganus' story "It Had Wings" (257). An old
woman is noticed by the poet in William Carlos
Williams's "To a Poor Old Woman" (195). A street person
freezes to death on a park bench, in John Ciardi's poem
"Matins" (106). A 92-year-old recluse is befriended by
a middle-aged woman in Doris Lessing's novel *The Diary
of a Good Neighbour* (56).

In Mark Van Doren's poem, "We Were Not Old," an
old man's neighbors wonder if he would be better off
dead rather than have to face the fury of a blizzard
(185). (See another Van Doren poem, 178.) In Elizabeth
Jolley's story, "Mr. Parker's Valentine," an old man is
regarded as a nuisance (271). In contrast, a young farm
couple is sensitive to the old hired hand who comes home
to die, in Frost's poem, "The Death of the Hired Man"
(111).

Stereotypes. In some literary works the old themselves defy being stereotyped as lonely, helpless, and
dependent. Examples include Maya Angelou's poem "On
Aging" (93), the active elders profiled in Berman and
Goldman's *The Ageless Spirit* (14), and the nursing home
residents who study poetry writing in Koch's I *Never
Told Anybody* (25). A group of old radicals, reunited in
John Sayles' story "At the Anarchists' Convention," are
shown full of vitality and passion (322). The feisty
Rocky Goodstein is active and engaged in family life at
the age of 103, in Max Apple's novel, *Roommates: My
Grandfather's Story* (40). (See also story 258.)

The main character in Wallace Stegner's novel *The
Spectator Bird* rages at society's negative attitudes
toward the old (69). The speaker in Philip Larkin's
poem "Old People's Home" complains that the old have
lost useful societal roles and have been warehoused and
abandoned in institutions (95). The poet Elise Maclay
wonders why the young can't relate to older people by
looking past their infirmities and seeing their individuality in "Infirmities" (144). (See also poem 102).

2. Roles, Adaptation, Role Loss, Role Reversal.

Roles. The lack of meaningful roles available to

the old is illustrated by the despair felt by recent re-
tirees in Barbara Pym's novel *Quartet in Autumn* (64),
Marjorie Dorner's story "Tree House" (243), and William
Trevor's story "The General's Day" (337). An old man in
Ernest Hemingway's story "Old Man at the Bridge" is left
behind in wartime to fulfill a pathetic role as tender
of animals (260). In contrast, a Native American grandmother's role is well-defined in Liz Sohappy Bahe's poem
"Grandmother Sleeps" (96). The indomitable Tante
Yvonne, in Michael Jenkins' memoir *A House in Flanders*,
exemplifies someone who maintains a consistent role
throughout a lifetime (22).

Sometimes old people feel the pressure to accept
the narrow roles prescribed by society. In Louis
Auchincloss's story, "Suttee," a widow accepts the roles
of dutiful wife and eternally grieving widow and fails
to risk new attachments (211). Or the old may fail to
assume expected roles. Examples include the father in
Edwin O'Connor's novel *I Was Dancing* (62) and the husband in Eudora Welty's story "Old Mr. Marblehall" (349).

The old may react with moral outrage at the limited
roles available to them in society. For instance, the
speaker in Yeats' poem "Sailing to Byzantium" rages
against the wretched state of old age (200). The
speaker in a poem by W. H. Auden, "Doggerel by a Senior
Citizen," rails against the absence of roles for the old
in the modern world (94). (See also story 295.) Their
outrage is contrasted to the poet's advocacy for new
roles for women in Denise Levertov's "A Woman Alone"
(142).

Adaptation. Examples of adaptation to new roles
late in life include the old woman in Angus Wilson's
novel *Late Call* (74) and the grandfather in Max Apple's
novel *Roommates* (40). Both find meaningful roles within
their extended families. In Bertolt Brecht's story,
"The Unseemly Old Lady," an old woman refuses to act the
role of conventional matriarch (224). The speaker in
Mark Van Doren's poem "We Were Not Old" praises the
adaptability of the old (185).

Failures to adapt to changing roles within the family include the grandmother in Neil Simon's play, *Lost
in Yonkers* (86), the old woman in Maya Angelou's poem,
"The Last Decision" (91), and the jaded husbands and
wives in Kingsley Amis' novel *The Old Devils* (38). The
father in Robert Anderson's play, *I Never Sang for My
Father*, never adapted to his children's need for a sensitive, nurturing father (76). (See also stories 246
and 317.)

Role Loss. Changed circumstances often displace
old people from accustomed roles. Political change dis-

rupts the role of Okonkwo, African tribal chief, in the
novel *Things Fall Apart*, by Chinua Achebe (36). The
displacement of an aristocratic family is featured in
Willa Cather's story "Old Mrs. Harris" (231). (See also
story 285.)

Role loss leaves old people adrift and uncertain
about their future. Examples include the aging butler
in Kazuo Ishiguro's novel *The Remains of the Day* (53);
an old man who loses touch with his race and with his
culture, in Paule Marshall's story "Barbados" (291); and
an old woman in Thyra Samter Winslow's story "Grandma"
(354).

Other examples of role loss include an old rancher
in Mark Van Doren's poem "Bay-Window Ballad" who feels
alienation and sadness at having to give up his former
role (177), and the former businessman who is reduced to
applying for a shipping clerk's job, in J. F. Powers'
story "The Old Man: A Love Story" (318).

Role Reversal. The aging process sometimes provides illustrations of the relativity and reversibility
of social roles. For example, in poems by Linda Pastan
(156) and Donald Hall (117), the speakers realize how
their perceptions of roles in old age have been altered
by their aging. (See another Pastan poem, 160.)

3. Economics, Poverty, Social Class.

Economics.   Ethical values as they relate to
economics are portrayed in the dispute between the owner
of a cannery and his handyman over the rights to a piece
of property, in Stephen Minot's story "Small Point
Bridge" (299).

Carol Wolfe Konek's memoir, *Daddyboy*, illustrates
the danger of predatory con men who swindle vulnerable
older adults (26). Economic constraints seen from a
broader societal perspective inform the science fiction
story "Tomorrow and Tomorrow and Tomorrow," by Kurt
Vonnegut (344).

Several poems include images of old people who are
homeless or who face serious economic crises as part of
their daily lives. Lance Henson writes about a Native
American woman who scavenges garbage bins (126), and
John Ciardi recalls a street person who freezes to death
on a park bench, in "Matins" (106). Society's failure to
"see" these old women is illustrated in William Carlos
Williams' poem "To a Poor Old Woman" (195). (See also
poem 107.)

In Doris Lessing's novel, *The Diary of a Good
Neighbour,* a woman befriends a 92-year-old recluse (56).
(See also story 221.) An insight into the crushing pov-

erty of old people who live alone can be found in Gina
Berriault's story "The Diary of K.W." (220).

Poverty. Old people often face poverty because of
changed circumstances or limited opportunities for advancement. For instance, the bleak lives of working-
class women are portrayed in two Pat Barker novels,
Union Street (42) and *The Century's Daughter* (43). (See
also story 232.) Hagar Shipley, an old woman who lives
on the Canadian prairie in Margaret Laurence's novel *The
Stone Angel*, never escapes poverty after a divorce (54).
An old man is only considered a source of additional income for the family in "Old Harry," a story by Josephine
Johnson (269). (See also autobiography 33, novel 72,
poem 152, and story 334.)
     Three sources expose old people's lives defined by
poverty and oppression. A freed slave and former servant toils her whole life for a white family, in
Katherine Anne Porter's story "The Last Leaf" (316). An
old black woman in Eudora Welty's "A Worn Path" is so
poor she has no money for transportation or medicine
(351). In "Marigolds" (234), a story by Eugenia
Collier, an old black woman barely scrapes a living during the Depression.
     Two stories, Louis Auchincloss' "The Cathedral
Builder" (209), and Arturo Vivante's "The Orchard"
(342), illustrate individuals using their economic resources to pursue ambitious projects.

Social Class. The topic of social class often assumes a critique of the upper-middle class and the upper
class. Such is the case in Muriel Spark's *Memento Mori*,
a novel about upper-middle-class Londoners whose wealth
and property offer them little aid against their fears
of mortality (68). In Leo Tolstoy's novella, *The Death
of Ivan Ilyich*, life is privileged but hollow for the
man who faces a horrible death from cancer (71).
Likewise, two representatives of New York high society
in old carriage days are caricatured in Edith Wharton's
"After Holbein" (352).
     In D. R. MacDonald's story "Of One Kind" (283) the
main characters, a widow and her handyman, are incom-
patible because of contrasting social classes. Another
widow's hard life as a laborer is the background for intimacy in Sandra Scofield's "Loving Leo" (324)

4. Services, Housing.

Services. Two stories illustrate provision of
services that satisfy the needs of elderly people. In
Arturo Vivante's story, "A Gallery of Women," a son

hires women who will provide companionship and emotional
support for his aging father (340). In the story "The
Tradesman," by Francis King, an old woman settles her
affairs and then awaits the arrival of someone skilled
in providing the service of assisted suicide (275).

Two stories suggest that service providers can be
insensitive to the needs of elderly residents. A London
widow in William Trevor's "Broken Homes" is terrorized
when her apartment is trashed by teenaged volunteers in
an intergenerational outreach program (336). A compa-
rable violation of an old person's privacy occurs in Sol
Yurick's "The Siege" (358).

Housing. A son's search for affordable housing for
his aging parents is the subject of Nick Taylor's memoir
A Necessary End (33). The difficulty of finding appropriate services and associations that support Alzheimer's patients is illustrated in Rosalie Honel
Walsh's *Journey With Grandpa* (21). Honel's frustrations
as caregiver are similar to those experienced by a Japanese woman who struggles to find appropriate services
for her demented father-in-law in the novel *The Twilight
Years* (41).

Two stories show contrasting responses of old
people to their housing needs. In "A Window Full of
Sky" (357), a story by Anna Yezierska, an old woman rejects a cramped dimly lit room in a nursing home in favor of her rooming house apartment. In "Old Man Minick," by Edna Ferber (247), an old widower chooses to
reside in a retirement home because he enjoys the warmth
and camaraderie of the other old men who reside there.

5. Rural Aging, Urban Aging.

Rural Aging. Often the attitudes and values of
characters in literary works are determined by forces
related to setting. A variety of rural settings are ex-
ploited by writers in order to establish their characters' social and cultural contexts. Self-reliance and
resourcefulness of characters dominate in the New England landscape. An old woman determines to winter in
her isolated cottage in Josephine Jacobsen's story "Jack
Frost" (265). A grandmother manages her declining farm
in David Updike's story "Indian Summer" (338). (See also
poem 112.)

The rugged and desolate Maine seacoast is the setting for two stories by Stephen Minot (299, 300). Two
poems by Donald Hall, 118 and 120, further explore the
New England character. Donald Hall's memoir *String Too
Short to be Saved* (20) recalls fondly the rural values
of his grandparents.

The rural South also provides writers with examples of idiosyncratic, stubborn, and moralistic characters. An old woman clings to her farm in the Appalachian mountains of northern Georgia in Susan Cooper and Hume Cronyn's play *Foxfire* (78). An illiterate but dignified black farm widow is the subject of Sterling Brown's poem "Virginia Portrait" (104). The novel *Littlejohn* (63), by Howard Owen, portrays a strong-willed and ethical North Carolina farmer. (See also stories 24, 255, and 277.)

Other rural settings in stories include Midwest farms in Will Weaver's two stories (347, 348); the expansive farm country of rural California, in Wallace Stegner's "The Double Corner" (327); and the flat rural landscape of Indiana, setting for Wallace Knight's "The Resurrection Man" (276). Homages to the values of the rural farm landscape of turn-of-the-century America can be found in stories by Theodore Dreiser (244) and Willa Cather (230) and the poem "Death of the Hired Hand" (111) by Robert Frost.

Rural settings outside America include the English rural village and its cast of elderly characters, in Ronald Blythe's oral history *The View in Winter* (15), and the Italian countryside, where an old Italian laborer finds odd jobs in Goffredo Parise's story "Beauty" (312).

Urban Aging. The urban settings of these literary works are usually associated with harsh living conditions, interpersonal conflicts, and despair. For instance, Doris Lessing's *Diary of a Good Neighbour* (56) illustrates the hard conditions in which needy old single persons live in the city. A slum tenement is the setting for a battle between a landlord and his tenant in Bernard Malamud's story "The Mourners" (288). (See also another Malamud story, 286, and stories 237 and 358.) A perilous Central Park in New York is the stage for interchanges between two old friends in Herb Gardner's play *I'm Not Rappaport* (80). Decaying, overcrowded, crime-ridden urban centers in England are settings for Pat Barker's novels *The Century's Daughter* (43) and *Union Street* (42).

6. Race, Multicultural.

Race. The evils of racism are portrayed in *Driving Miss Daisy* (88), a play by Alfred Uhry, and *Do Lord Remember Me* (57), a novel by Julius Lester. African-American men resist racial bigotry and intolerance in both works. An African-American man is paralyzed by the effects of racism when he returns to his native Barbados

in a story by Paule Marshall (291).   Avey Johnson, in
Marshall's novel *Praisesong for the Widow*, realizes her
husband was disabled by racism (58).

Several older characters, determined and proud,
persevere despite racism and oppression. An African-
American farm widow finds contentment in memories of her
family in "Virginia Portrait" (104), a poem by Sterling
Brown. A strong-willed old black woman endures a solitary trek, in Eudora Welty's story "A Worn Path" (351).
An old black woman overcomes the bigotry of the members
of a white church, in Alice Walker's story "The Welcome
Table" (346). (See also poems 93, 108, and 127, and
story 234.)

Oral history by two successful African-American
women is told in *Having Our Say*, by Sarah and Elizabeth
Delany (17).

African-American characters relate across the generations in the stories "To Hell With Dying," by Alice
Walker (345); "The Death of a Grandmother," by Gwendolyn
Brooks (225); and   "Presents," by John Edgar Wideman
(353).   (See also poems 113 and 189 and story 103.) An
old black woman's wretched state inspires militant determination in the speaker of "Miss Rosie," a poem by
Lucille Clifton (107).

Multicultural.   A breadth of multicultural relationships is explored in literary works. Katherine Anne
Porter's story "The Old Order" documents the long-time
relationship between an old white woman and her former
slave, Old Nanny (317). (See 316 for another Porter
story that continues Old Nanny's story.) The interracial
bond between a white woman in South Africa and her
"colored" servant Sofie is the subject of Hennie
Aucamp's story "Soup for the Sick" (208). In Alfred
Uhry's play, *Driving Miss Daisy* (88), the rigid working
relationship between an old Jewish woman and her
African-American chauffeur evolves into a special interracial bond.

Other stories reflect the struggles inherent in
forging multicultural bonds. When Mr. Watford returns to
his native Barbados to begin a commercial venture, in
Paule Marshall's story, he can not overcome a paralyzing
isolation from both white and black communities (291).
A young man selling burial insurance to poor blacks in
the South is drawn to a wise old African-American woman
in Alan Gurganus' story "Blessed Assurance" (255).   An
unconventional widower and an African-American woman
live together, and then go their separate ways, in
Bernard Cooper's story "Picking Plums: Fathers and Sons
and Their Lovers" (236).   An old woman finds herself
adrift in another culture in Mavis Gallant's story "His
Mother" (254). (See also novel 58.)

    Personal and familial conflicts test the wills of
an Indian widow and her Dutch lover, in Ruth Prawer
Jhabvala's story "The Man With the Dog" (266). In "Miss
Sahib" (267), another story by Jhabvala, an English
woman's years of devotion to India are undermined by the
coarseness and cruelty of her neighbors.
    The tragedy of colonial governments encroaching
upon African cultures at the turn of the twentieth century is shown in Chinua Achebe's novel *Things Fall Apart*
(36). Indians from the Pacific Northwest are deprived of
their way of life in the poem "Memories" (133) by Helen
Knopf.

7. Ethnicity, Culture.

    Ethnicity. The majority of the literary works de-
scribed in this volume refer to Jewish ethnicity. Relationships between Jews and Gentiles are featured in
Peter Harris' story "My Father-in-Law's Contract" (124).
There a Gentile son-in-law regards his Jewish father-in-
law with tenderness and affection. Daisy Werthan, a
Jewish widow from Atlanta, at first patronizes, and then
bonds with her African-American chauffeur Hoke in the
play *Driving Miss Daisy* (88). Susan Dodd's "Bifocals"
(237) shows the friendship between two grandfathers, one
Irish and one Jewish. (See a Linda Pastan poem, 159,
for a negative portrayal of Jewish-Gentile relations.)
    The importance of observing Jewish rituals and cus-
toms and of affirming one's Jewish identity is illustrated by the widow Rivke in Michele Lee's novel *Missing*
(51), the devout Jew Rocky Goodstein in Max Apple's
novel *Roommates* (40), the father-son relationship in
Philip Roth's memoir *Patrimony* (29), and the story of
Eva, a Russian Jew and immigrant in Tillie Olsen's "Tell
Me a Riddle" (310). (See poem 99 and story 287.)
    Jewish immigrants are main characters in two Isaac
Bashevis Singer stories: "The Hotel," about a Yiddish
colony in Miami Beach (325), and "Old Love," which portrays two Polish Jews on the verge of a late marriage
(326). Lively arguments mark the reunion of Jewish
liberals in John Sayles' story "At the Anarchist's Convention" (322). Compare the interaction between an Israeli doctor and his patient in Susan Dodd's story
"Subversive Coffee" (240). Changes within an entire Yiddish community in the Bronx are the subject of Lou
Myers' novel *When Life Falls it Falls Upside Down* (60).
    European immigrant communities are depicted in two
stories: Willa Cather's "Neighbor Rosicky" (230) and
Joanna Higgins' "The Courtship of Widow Sobcek" (261).
A Japanese-American ethnic community is portrayed in a
story by Toshio Mori (301). The handing down of ethnic

skills in a Native American culture is the subject of
Liz Sohappy Bahe's poem "Grandmother Sleeps" (96). (See
poems 126 and 153 for additional examples of Native
American elders.)

   Culture. Examples in other cultures of how families
respond to crises in long-term care are found in the
Dutch novel *The Big Ward*, by Jacoba Van Velde (72), and
in the Japanese novel *The Twilight Years,* by Sawako
Ariyoshi (41).
   Strict cultural assumptions about the roles of men
and women limit the helpfulness of a Zimbabwean grandfather in Charles Mungoshi's story "Who Will Stop the
Dark?" (303). Another Mungoshi story, "The Setting Sun
and the Rolling World," portrays cultural values in conflict between a father and son (302). Contemporary Chinese culture plays a role in a story by Lu Xin'er, "The
One and the Other," where a widow is unable to adapt to
changing cultural conditions in contemporary China
(356).
   Arturo Vivante's story "The Orchard" (342) is set
in Northern Italy and shows an old man's lifelong dedication to growing a peach orchard. French and Italian
cultures are featured in autobiography 22 and story 278.
   Cultural attitudes toward gay relationships are reflected in Goffredo Parise's story "Memory" (314).

8. Gender: Men, Gender: Women.

   Gender: Men. Rivalry, competition, petty jealou-
sies, and mean-spirited personal attacks are the basis
of the encounters between old male friends in Kingsley
Amis' novel *The Old Devils* (38). (See also story 299.)
Men may perceive other men to be a threat to their domi-
nance or control of family or work, as in Robert Anderson's play *I Never Sang For My Father* (76) or the
story "The Double Gap" by Louis Auchincloss (210).
   In contrast, an old man's dying is soothed by the
presence of women from the community in Arturo Vivante's
"A Gallery of Women" (340). An old man seeks contentment apart from a competitive environment in Goffredo
Pa-rise's story "Beauty" (312). Compare another Parise
story, "Memory" (314), about an old Italian's chance
meeting with a former gay lover.
   In only a few cases men are shown forming bonds
with other men based on sharing, trust, and intimacy.
Examples include the two nursing home residents in Tracy
Kidder's nonfiction account *Old Friends* (23) and the two
old men in Josephine Johnson's story "Old Harry" (269).
Compare the difficulty two laborers experience at the

termination of a long friendship in "Work" (285), a
story by D. R. MacDonald. (See also story 222.)

   Gender: Women. Many of the works in this text
feature images of strong African-American women. An
African-American farm widow in "Virginia Portrait," a
poem by Sterling Brown, calmly faces the rigors of winter (104). A strong-willed old black woman in Eudora
Welty's story "A Worn Path" overcomes numerous obstacles
with her keen wit and a loving heart (351). (See also
autobiography 17, poems 108 and 93, and story 234.)
   Women who find new independence in old age, freed
from traditional roles, include a widow in Bertolt
Brecht's story "The Unseemly Old Lady" (224); the
speaker of Marilyn Zuckerman's poem "After Sixty" (203);
the newly widowed Lady Slane in Virginia Sackville-
West's novel *All Passion Spent* (65); a widow in Angus
Wilson's novel *Late Call* (74); and the woman who de-
clares she will wear "purple" in old age in Jenny
Joseph's poem (131). (See also novel 39, poem 115, and
story 277.)
   Other women fail to embrace a new identity and
freedom in old age. Hagar Shipley's emotional blindness
plagues her old age in Margaret Laurence's novel *The
Stone Angel* (54). Agnes Lynn, a widow, retreats behind
a conventional role in Louis Auchincloss' story "Suttee"
(211). (See also story 254.) An old woman finds only
temporary respite from the constraints of family relationships, in the story "Appropriate Affect" by Sue
Miller (298).
   Several women resist the domination of the men in
their lives. A woman in her 70s leaves her husband and
establishes herself in a Montreal apartment in Constance
Beresford-Howe's *The Book of Eve* (45.) A middle-aged
woman, separated from her husband for fifteen years, rejects his entreaties to resume their relationship in
Doris Lessing's story "The Pit" (281). Eva, dying of
cancer, rebels against her self-centered husband in
"Tell Me a Riddle," a story by Tillie Olsen (310). (See
also novels 42 and 43.)
   A daughter resists domination by her father in
Carol Wolfe Konek's memoir *Daddyboy* (26), and an old
Italian woman resists manipulation by her children in
Betty Coon's story "Daisies" (235).
   The nurture and support offered by women to other
women who are in crisis is evidenced when an old woman
comforts a middle-aged woman in "Womb Ward," a story by
Doris Lessing (282). Other examples of such shared
trust include the dying women in a nursing home, in
Jacoba Van Velde's novel *The Big Ward* (72), and the el-
derly aunts in Michael Jenkins' memoir *A House in Flanders* (22). (See also story 304.)

A middle-aged woman's compassion and care for her demented father-in-law is revealed in Sawako Ariyoshi's novel *The Twilight Years* (41).

Several poets portray old women as creative, resourceful, and fulfilled. May Sarton suggests old women are perfect models of purity and strength in "Who has spoken of the unicorn in old age?" (171). Denise Levertov envisions old age for women as a time of wisdom and individuality in "A Woman Alone" (142). Rolf Jacobsen praises the mystery and complexity of old women's lives in "The Old Women" (129). (See also poem 114 and story 207.)

May Sarton's journal *At Seventy* (31) exemplifies one woman's strengths of character, identity, and potential.

Aging and Relationships

9. Friendship, Neighbors, Community.

Friendship. Friendships can be enjoyed at greater leisure by older people, as Alan Olmstead discovered in his memoir *Threshold: The First Days of Retirement* (28). They may also fill greater needs. The mutual dependence of life-long male friendship is celebrated in Edwin Robinson's long narrative poem, "Isaac and Archibald," in which each friend cares for the decline in the other's health (163).

In Susan Dodd's story, "Bifocals," one friend, a mortuary director, lovingly prepares his old friend's body for burial (237). Two new friendships are forged by Lou and Joe in Tracy Kidder's reportorial *Old Friends* (23). In Herb Gardner's play, *I'm Not Rappaport*, the quixotic liar Nat cons the city world to protect his helpless friend Midge (80). A retired professor and a museum guard form a close bond finally broken by the suicide of one to the deep grief of the other, in Josephine Johnson's story "Old Harry" (269). (See also stories 222, 321, and 329.)

Coworkers may form strong bonds, which may end painfully with retirement, as with the two fellow laborers in D. R. MacDonald's story "Work" (285).

Friendships among women are celebrated by May Sarton. (See memoirs 30 and 32). In Doris Lessing's novel, *Diary of a Good Neighbour*, Janna Somers leaves her glamorous world to befriend the aged pauper Maudie and to learn about the urban underclass (56). Two life-long friends pull through a nursing home crisis in Alice Munro's "Mrs. Cross and Mrs. Kidd" (304). (See also story 356.) Cross-gender friendships develop in Alfred Uhry's play, *Driving Miss Daisy*, in which a difficult

Jewish widow and her African-American driver painfully
and finally become fond of each other (88).   A retired
middle-aged farmer collaborates amicably with an old
neighboring woman in Marjorie Dorner's story "Tree
House" (243).

Neighbors. The "good neighbor" is exemplified in
Yetta Klugerman, who ministers to the retirement residents in Warren Adler's story "The Angel of Mercy"
(206). A quarrel between neighbors is finally resolved
in Ethan Canin's story "Emperor of the Air" (227), but
not resolved in Elizabeth Jolley's story "Mr. Parker's
Valentine" (271). (See also autobiography 31 and story
231.)

Community. A friendly community helps a widower
develop a new partnership in Raymond Carver's poem
"Happiness in Cornwall" (105). The inmates acquire a
strong sense of community in Kenneth Koch's account, *I
Never Told Anybody: Teaching Poetry in a Nursing Home*
(25). The women in Jacoba Van Velde's novel *The Big
Ward* support each other through illness, death, and dying (72). Residents of a nursing home form a mutual
support system in Tracy Kidder's account, *Old Friends*
(23). An invalid immigrant to Australia, Nora Porteus
is helped by neighbors and her doctor to move into a new
life, in Jessica Anderson's novel *Tirra Lirra by the
River* (39). (See also story 341.)
    Reunions can reinforce the self-assurance of older
people--whether school, service, professional, or whatever. So it works in John Sayles' story "At the Anarchists' Convention" where the old protesters reaffirm
their comradeship (322).
    A new interest may re-involve a lonely person with
friends and colleagues, as it does when Judge Man-
derville's daughter gives him a lovely plant which he
wants others to share, in Mary Ward Brown's story "The
Amaryllis" (226).
    What might be called a toxic community is seen in
the cottage residents of Kingsley Amis's novel *Ending Up*
(37). Two mutually exclusive communities both freeze
out the black entrepreneur in Paule Marshall's story
"Barbados" (291).

10. Parent-Child Bonds, Family Bonds.

(For marriages see Topic 12, Older
Couples; for grandparenting see Topic
14.)

Parent-Child Bonds. The father as role model is

attested to by two distinguished African American sisters whose father became the nation's first elected black bishop (*Having Our Say: The Delany Sisters' First 100 Years*, 17).

A full-length portrait of a courageous dying mother is given in Simone de Beauvoir's *A Very Easy Death* (13). (See also memoirs 19 and 27.) Mothers as role models are celebrated by the speaker of Denise Levertov's poem "The 90th Year" (141) and May Sarton in the poem "August Third" (165). The old African American mother of Langston Hughes' poem, "Mother to Son," spurs on her discouraged son by her own example: "I'se still climbin'" (127).

Role reversal can occur when the parent becomes helpless. Nick Taylor becomes the attentive "parent" of his declining mother in his autobiographical *A Necessary End* (33). Philip Roth assumes responsibility for his cancer-stricken father in *Patrimony: A True Story* (29). A demented old Japanese man becomes in effect the child of his caregiving daughter-in-law in Ariyoshi's novel *The Twilight Years* (41). William Wharton's novel *Dad* centers on John Tremont's parental care for his deteriorating father (73). (See also poem 139 and stories 216 and 294.)

The compassion of children for suffering parents finds an archetype in Cordelia's rescue of her mistreated royal father in Shakespeare's *King Lear* (85). A son grieves over his demented father in Gina Berriault's story "The Bystander" (219). A drab but loyal daughter fakes letters from her sister to the mother who could not accept that favorite sister's death, in Michael Cristofer's play *The Shadow Box* (79). The agony of choosing between a peaceful death for her father or the torture of radical treatment is faced by the daughter in Susan Dodd's story "Subversive Coffee" (240). (See also poem 105 and stories 239, 296, 330, and 348.)

Reconciliation and truer understanding between parents and adult children develop as the self-centered mother learns to accept her son's devotion to his new wife in Edna Ferber's story "Old Lady Mandle" (246). From a teenaged resentment of his father, Larry King grew to understand and enjoy him, as recounted in his memoir "The Old Man" (24). Annie Nations helps her son rediscover his Appalachian roots and his responsibility as a parent in *Foxfire*, a play by Susan Cooper and Hume Cronyn (78). The long bitterness between Willy Loman and his son Biff gives way to a final embrace in Arthur Miller's *Death of a Salesman* (83). (See also novels 49 and 63, and story 236.)

The adult child's grief for a lost parent is expressed in Galway Kinnell's poem "Goodbye" (132) and in Michael Blumenthal's "Elegy for My Mother" (97). A

father's misery over a lost son is the subject of
Chekhov's story "Grief" (232).
    A love-hate relationship between parent and child
is fully explored in Carol Konek's *Daddyboy: A Memoir*
(26) and in Dodd's strange story "Nightlife," where by
day the daughter finds her father a grouch and by night
a generous companion (238).

    Family bonds. A fierce argument for the family as
a vital institution is made by the widow who heckles a
cynical country club speaker in Jack Matthews' story
"Storyhood as We Know It" (295). A celebration of the
Bayard family as it richly endures from generation to
generation is provided by Thornton Wilder's play *The
Long Christmas Dinner* (90). The strong family life of
the immigrant Rosickys motivates the father's final sacrifice for his daughter-in-law in Willa Cather's story
"Neighbor Rosicky" (230). A dying woman happily remembers her family life in Mark Van Doren's poem "Sleep,
Grandmother" (182) and in Katherine Anne Porter's story
"The Jilting of Granny Weatherall" (315).
    Sibling bonds support Francis and Muriel Brimm as
they try to sort out their troubled lives in Dennis Mc-
Farland's novel *School for the Blind* (59). The two
Shattuck sisters successfully cling to their ruined cottage despite community efforts to institutionalize them,
in Mary Wilkins Freeman's 19th-century story "A Mistaken
Charity" (252). (See also story 262.)
    Bonds in the extended family are illustrated by the
benevolent uncle who welcomes his married nephew in Mark
Van Doren's poem "The Uncle I Was Named For" (184). Eccentric Tante Yvonne acts as Michael Jenkins' mentor in
his memoir *A House in Flanders* (22). Even the worn-out
farm laborer finds a home to die in with his former em-
ployers in Frost's "The Death of the Hired Man" (111).
(See also stories 207 and 297.)
    Special strength in surviving a family ordeal is
shown by Rosalie Honel's memoir *Journey with Grandpa:
Our Family's Struggle with Alzheimer's Disease* (21), and
again in Richard Bausch's novella "Rare and Endangered
Species" where the mother's suicide puts husband, children, and friends to severe test (214). A sense of
strong family roots in the past is conveyed by the
rancher's son in Thomas McGuane's story "Family" (296).

11. Parent-Child Conflicts, Family Conflicts.

    (For marriages see Topic 12, Older Couples;
    for grandparenting see Topic 14.)

    Parent-Child Conflicts. A generation gap between

mother and daughter ironically repeats when that daughter grows up and tangles with her own daughter, in Phyllis Bentley's story "Mother and Daughter" (218). A similar repetition of alienation is also the subject of Louis Auchincloss' story "The Double Gap" (210).

A self-centered, antagonistic father exploits his son in Edwin O'Connor's novel *I Was Dancing* (62). Another exploitive father has aborted his son Victor's future in Arthur Miller's play *The Price* (84). An insensitive, rigid father has become a major life problem for his dutiful son in Arturo Vivante's story "The Soft Core" (343) and again in Robert Anderson's play *I Never Sang for My Father* (76). A malignant, demented mother frightens her son and daughter-in-law in Wallace Stegner's story "The Double Corner" (327).

Parents who over-steer their children must include the tough domineering old mother who oppresses her children in Neil Simon's play *Lost in Yonkers* (86), and the hard-bitten Hagar Shipley who interferes with the life of her favorite son in Margaret Laurence's novel *The Stone Angel* (54). (See also poem 180.)

Of the parents who resent children, one of the bitterest is old Ben Brantley who explodes over a minor slight at the birthday party given by his own children, in Peter Taylor's story "Porte-Cochere" (333). Phil Doucet quarrels with one daughter whose conservative political views offend him, in Judith Freeman's novel *Set for Life* (48). (See also novel 74 and story 246.)

By contrast, adult children may exploit their parents, as do King Lear's evil daughters who crowd him out of all claims to power, let alone dignity, in Shakespeare's play (85). Son and daughter try to pressure Maria into selling her house, in Betty Coon's story "Daisies" (235). Grandma's children overload her with household drudgery in Thyra Winslow's story "Grandma" (354).

Or the children may simply write off their parents as burdens. So the widower Minick is merely tolerated by the children he stays with in Edna Ferber's story "Old Man Minick" (247). The two sons of an invalid mother shuttle her back and forth as a tiresome obligation, in Olga Masters' story, "You'll Like It There" (292). (See also story 270.) Such family dysfunction shades into elder abuse, which is treated under that title, below.

Children may oppress their parents by over-manipulating them with the best of intentions. Walter Brinkman is persecuted by an over-protective daughter in Anne Rosner's story "Prize Tomatoes" (321). For other such daughters see Richard Dokey's story "The Autumn of Henry Simpson" (241) and Joanna Higgins' story "The Courtship of Widow Sobcek" (261).

The resentment of children against difficult
parents is the subject of John Steinbeck's story "The
Leader of the People" in which a son loses patience with
his father-in-law's frontier reminiscences (328). A
caregiving son becomes hostile to the ungrateful father
who demands constant attention in Arturo Vivante's story
"The Bell" (339). A daughter's rebellion against a
bright but domineering father is recounted in Carol
Konek's *Daddyboy: A Memoir* (26). Chelsea quarrels with
her insecure father on finding that she is still picked
on as a little fat girl, in Ernest Thompson's play *On
Golden Pond* (87). The African-American Reverend Joshua
Smith is reviled by one son as an Uncle Tom in Julius
Lester's novel *Do Lord Remember Me* (57). (See also autobiography 29, play 83, and stories 103 and 331.)

Children may be shocked at a parent who chooses a
new independence, as in Bertolt Brecht's story "The Unseemly Old Lady" (224).

The break-up or discontinuance of a parent-child
relationship is the pathetic theme of Mavis Gallant's
story "His Mother" in which an expatriate mother virtually loses touch with a far-away son (254), and of
Robert Bly's poem "A Visit to the Old People's Home" in
which the son withdraws from his invalid mother (100).

Family conflicts. Sibling conflict is morbidly
illustrated by the sadistic-dependent relationship between Hattie and Alice in Patricia Highsmith's story
"The Cries of Love" (262). Ollie's brother Crater has
never forgiven her for damaging the family reputation
with her teenage pregnancy in Lisa Koger's story
"Ollie's Gate" (277).

General family strain runs throughout Rosalie
Honel's *Journey with Grandpa: Our Family's Struggle with
Alzheimer's Disease* (21), and in the Willis family's
difficulties with Munsey's retirement in Josephine
Lawrence's novel *The Web of Time* (55). Grandma Franny
learns, while convalescing from a stroke, how false has
been the pretense of family happiness in Sue Miller's
story "Appropriate Affect" (298). (See also novel 51.)

12. Older Couples.

Good lifetime marriages are often celebrated, like
that of the immigrant Anton Rosicky in Willa Cather's
story "Neighbor Rosicky" (230), or the fiftieth anniversary couple in Archibald MacLeish's poem "The Old Gray
Couple II" (147). A bedridden old husband reminisces
tenderly with his wife in Mark Van Doren's poem "The
First Snow of the Year" (179). A couple married 40

years faces an ultimate test when the husband begins an
inexorable decline toward dementia, in J. Bernlef's
novel *Out of Mind* (46). A highly literate husband and
wife have kept separate journals of their aging, but the
deaths of friends persuade them to unite their efforts,
in Hortense Calisher's novel *Age* (47). In Ernest Thompson's play, *On Golden Pond*, the courageous and sympathetic Ethel helps her husband Norman through the in-
securities of his aging (87). (Also see novel 69.)

Marriage ties going beyond the grave are the subject of the play *Foxfire* by Susan Cooper and Hume
Cronyn, in which the widow Annie converses regularly
with her dead husband (78). The old farmer Henry Reifsneider, lost after the death of his loving wife, hal-
lucinates her image and seeks her over the countryside,
in Theodore Dreiser's story "The Lost Phoebe" (244).
(See also autobiography 20, novel 57, and poems 145,
146, and 181.)

Husband and wife may differ deeply while staying
true to the marriage; so the African-American father
feels shame and despair over unemployment while the
mother remains the source of family strength in Eugenia
Collier's story "Marigolds" (234). The wife may resent
a parasitic husband, as Sylvia resents her alcoholic
moocher of a mate in Angus Wilson's novel *Late Call*
(74).

The new unions possible in later years is illustrated by John Jielewicz's discovery in "The Courtship
of Widow Sobcek," the story by Joanna Higgins (261).
(See also novel 61 and stories 245 and 311.)

Spouses may grow hopelessly apart, as the suffering
Ivan Ilyich becomes alienated from his shallow wife in
Tolstoy's novella, *The Death of Ivan Ilyich* (71). A
rigid insecure wife cruelly dominates her husband in
William Wharton's novel *Dad* (73). Actual break-up may
occur as when Eva simply leaves her loveless marriage
one morning in Constance Beresford-Howe's novel *The Book
of Eve* (45). A wife abandons her scholar husband for a
glamorous young poet in Alice Adams' story "Ocracoke
Island" (205). See also Chekhov's story of an old divorce revisited, "Old Age" (233).

Dysfunctional marriages also appear in the unhappy
reunion of Welsh couples in Kingsley Amis's novel *The
Old Devils* (38). Bitterly quiet evenings are recounted
by the conciliatory husband in Richard Bausch's story
"Letter to the Lady of the House" (213). (See also
story 228.) Dementia cracks the marriage of the Cohns,
in Richard Stern's story "Dr. Cahn's Visit" (330). (See
also story 217 and poem 101.) The wife's unexplained
suicide derails Harry Brewer in Bausch's novella "Rare
and Endangered Species" (214). The pathos of a lost
chance at marriage saddens the butler Stevens in Kazuo

Ishiguro's novel *The Remains of the Day* (53). (See also stories 253, 264, and 349.)

An unhappy but symbiotic union is that of the Indian lady who cannot give up her difficult Dutch lover, in Ruth Jhabvala's story, "The Man with the Dog" (266). May Darley wearies of her husband's curmudgeonly behavior but remains devoted, in Julian Gloag's novel *Only Yesterday* (49). (See also novel 52, and stories 204, 263, and 318.)

Marriages and friendships do not account for all old couplings. A lesbian relationship is mourned by the survivor in May Sarton's poem "Mourning to Do" (169). A gay dresser's care for the aging actor he serves is shown in Ronald Harwood's play *The Dresser* (81).

A cross-cultural companionship is featured in Katherine Anne Porter's story "The Old Order" (317). (See also story 208.) A widow so mourns the death of her poodle that she wants Mass said for him, in Frank O'Connor's story, "Requiem" (309).

Couples bound in hatred are described in Patricia Highsmith's story "The Cries of Love" in which two elderly sisters trade nasty tricks on each other but cannot live apart (262). Also see D. L. Coburn's play, *The Gin Game*, in which compulsive card-playing leads to intense quarreling and destructive character analysis (77).

13. Sexuality, Intimacy.

Sexuality. The sexual urge may stop, diminish, or continue in the later years, but such a basic element of human nature still commands attention, as represented in several sources.

Sex life may be happily given up as with Yvonne and Matthew, quite content in their retirement (though the wife still reflects on it), in Alice Adams' story "The Girl Across the Room" (204). The sexual drive can also remain strong, as in Yeats' ribald poem "The Wild Old Wicked Man" (201), or in the yearning of the old woman in Muriel Rukeyser's poem "In Her Burning" (164). (See also poems 98 and 108.) It can trickle out: the tired lecher Godfrey falls back on voyeurism in Muriel Spark's novel *Memento Mori* (68).

Sadly frustrated sexual desire is experienced by Simon Morris, humiliatingly rejected in Bernard Malamud's story "In Retirement" (286) and by the speaker in Thomas Hardy's poem "I Look into My Glass" (123). (See also poem 116 and stories 283, 291, and 337.)

A father's acceptance of his gay son is shown in "Picking Plums: Fathers and Sons and Their Lovers," a story by Bernard Cooper (236).

Intimacy. The richness of intimacy is lost when one lover escapes in panic, as in I. B. Singer's tragic story "Old Love" in which the widow Ethel on the day of her new engagement commits suicide, unable to risk independence from her dead husband (326). In Edna O'Brien's story, "Christmas Roses," a former cabaret dancer falls in love with a charming youth but flees rather than take the risk of a full relationship (306). (See also story 211.)

Or intimacy may be sacrificed, as Virginia Tyler decides to remain with a dull husband in William Humphrey's story "September Song" (264). Or lost by postponement, as in V. S. Pritchett's story "A Trip to the Seaside" (319). (See also story 253.) The pain of being abandoned is suffered by the husband whose wife has run off, in Alice Adams' story "Ocracoke Island" (205).

The reconciliation of alienated partners takes place subtly through poems left on the wife's window sill, in Ethan Canin's story "We Are Nighttime Travelers" (228). (See also story 213).

Homosexual intimacy figures in much of May Sarton's work, as in her elegiac poem "Mourning to Do" (169). (See also her novel 289, and poems 166 and 171.) The aging writer's infatuation for a beautiful youth becomes the fatal development of Thomas Mann's story "Death in Venice" (66). (See also play 79 and story 314.)

Short of marriage, new attachments can enrich the late years. The widow Deborah Holland, who has spent her life in the decorous shadow of her distinguished husband, discovers a deep new male friendship in which she is valued as herself, in Virginia Sackville-West's novel *All Passion Spent* (65). The main character in Constance Beresford-Howe's novel, *The Book of Eve*, abandons a loveless marriage and a respectable home to live in a basement apartment and find new values and a new life style with a warm but irresponsible younger lodger (45). The feisty trapeze artist Max Fried enters a contentious love affair with his neighbor Lettie in Lynn Sharon Schwartz's novel *Balancing Acts* (67). (See also novel 44, poem 105, and stories 245 and 324.)

An incestuous attraction nearly surfaces as a grieving father centers his emotions on his daughter in Stephen Minot's story "The Tide and Isaac Bates" (300).

14. Intergenerational, Grandparenting.

(For parent-child relations see Topics 10 and 11, Parent-Child Bonds and Parent-Child Conflicts.)

Intergenerational. An important contrast between the vision of youth and that of age is voiced in the poem "Hardy Perennial" by Richard Eberhart, who sees youth as romantically risking death but age as savoring each breath of life (109). Youth should overlook the "ugliness" of age, Lise Maclay pleads in her poem "I Hate the Way I look" (143). Relationships between young and old are given special attention in Ronald Blythe's documentary *The View in Winter* (15).

Old people can serve as mentors to the young. Phil Doucet takes in a runaway teenager and serves as guide and father just as she fills the void left by his grandson, in Judith Freeman's novel *Set for Life* (48). A wise old African-American woman becomes exemplar of life wisdom for the young insurance agent who deals with her, in Allan Gurganus' story "Blessed Assurance: A Moral Tale" (255). A young girl finds love and wisdom in a neighbor woman once disgraced for having an illegitimate child, in Lisa Koger's story "Ollie's Gate" (277). A maverick retired trapeze artist fascinates a rebellious teenage girl and helps her to find a way back to her conventional family and friends, in Lynn Schwartz's novel *Balancing Acts* (67). (See also novels 42, 43, 50, and 59.)

A misplaced generosity is wasted by the retired teacher in India, who befriends a lively girl who turns into a selfish slut, in Ruth Jhabvala's story "Miss Sahib" (267).

How the young can help the old is fantasized in Robert McEnroe's play *The Silver Whistle*, in which a mysterious young stranger helps to transform a drab old people's home into a rejuvenated community (82). An unattractive old hanger-on is offered hospitality by a young woman who can visualize her own future in this old woman, in Gina Berriault's story "Nocturne" (221). (See also stories 222 and 271.)

False motives can corrupt such assistance. Help miscarries horribly in William Trevor's story "Broken Homes," as a crew of volunteer students descend upon Mrs. Malby's apartment to paint it but actually vandalize it (336). (See also story 258.)

Old can be affectionately joined to young as in Alice Walker's story "To Hell With Dying" in which young African-American children cluster affectionately around the old guitarist Mr. Sweet (345). A rich philanthropist shares his dreams with an admiring young clerk in Louis Auchincloss' story "The Cathedral Builder" (209). The widow Laura Palfrey forms a warm friendship with a young writer in Elizabeth Taylor's novel *Mrs. Palfrey at the Claremont* (70). (See also story 301.)

The old may not always live up to expectations. In Leslie Norris' story "My Uncle's Story" the narrator's hero, once seen as a lively adventurer, turns out to have become a shrunken wreck (305). The young girl who idealistically visits an Old Ladies' Home is shocked to find two old cantankerous crones, in Eudora Welty's story "A Visit of Charity" (350).

The old in turn may fear and dislike the young, as in Raymond Carver's story "After the Denim" in which a retired accountant is outraged at the manners and misbehavior of hippie couple (229).

Grandparenting. At the earliest level grandparents and grandchildren enjoy their affection, as in John Crowe Ransom's poem "Old Man Playing with Children" (162). Duane Niatum's poem "Old Woman Awaiting the Greyhound Bus" (153) describes the wrinkled Native American woman happily remembering her grandchildren at play. (See also poem 99.)

Grandchildren like to hear stories, moralistic or not. So young Jody listens to his grandfather's frontier reminiscences in John Steinbeck's story "The Leader of the People" (328), and the narrator describes Grand's tales of the past in Allan Gurganus' "A Hog Loves Its Life" (256).

Grandparents can become role models. To the age of 106, "Rocky" Goodstein mentored and supported his grandson Max, in Max Apple's novel, *Roommates: My Grandfather's Story* (40). Tribute to his grandparents' influence is twice paid by Donald Hall: in his memoir *String Too Short to Be Saved* (20) and poem "Elegy for Wesley Wells" (118). The heroic self-sufficiency of his widowed grandmother in running the family farm is admired by the narrator of David Updike's story "Indian Summer" (338). In the Native American poem "Grandmother Sleeps," by Liz Sohappy Bahe, the grandchild vows to take up the weaving skills of her grandmother (96). (See also stories 287 and 353.)

The possible therapeutic benefits of this relationship are illustrated by the wonderfully tactful grandfather who supports his insecure fifth-grader in a personal ordeal, in Richard Bausch's story "What Feels Like the World" (215). (See also novel 63.)

A grandparent may work behind the scenes, as "Old Mrs. Harris" does in securing a university scholarship for her granddaughter in Willa Cather's story (231). Liza Jarrett spares her granddaughter a life of poverty by sending her to school in *The Century's Daughter*, a novel by Pat Barker (42).

A grandchild may in turn support the older person, as the nurse Jeannie cares for her dying grandmother in Tillie Olsen's novella "Tell Me a Riddle" (310). A "bridge" function is served by the granddaughter who

helps bring parent and grandparents together in Julian
Gloag's novel *Only Yesterday* (49).

The re-appreciation of grandparents is found in
Michele Murray's "Poem to My Grandmother in Her Death"
(152) and in Gwendolyn Brooks' story "Death of a Grandmother" (225).

Friction can divide the generations, nowhere more
pointedly than in Kurt Vonnegut's futuristic nightmare,
"Tomorrow and Tomorrow and Tomorrow" in which Gramps,
age 172 and virtually immortal, tyrannizes over his
roost (344). The unkempt talking black bird becomes a
controversial grandfather figure in Malamud's story "The
Jewbird" (287). A possessive grandfather resents and
opposes the marriages of his granddaughters in Doris
Lessing's story "Flight" (280). A grandfather is humiliated when his grandsons cause his driving privileges
to be withdrawn, in Will Weaver's story "From the Landing" (347). (See also play 86 and story 303.)

Quarrels may erupt between grandparent and child,
as in Flannery O'Connor's story "The Artificial Nigger"
(307). A solicitous grandmother fails to make contact
with an anxious child in Nikki Giovanni's poem "Legacies" (113). An embittered woman forced to marry a man
she did not love perpetuates the injustice with her
granddaughters, in Linda Pastan's poem "My Grandmother"
(159).

A grandparent may resign from the role, as does
"The Great-Grandmother" who announces her freedom from
the obligations of an aristocratic matriarch in Robert
Graves' poem (115). (See also 177.)

15. Caregiving.

The emotional burdens associated with caregiving
are illustrated in several sources. A son feels ambivalent in his role as primary caregiver for a father, in
the biographical account *Patrimony* by Philip Roth (29).
A nephew's caregiving is often resisted by a
tough-minded former radical in *The Old Left* (297), a
collection of stories by Daniel Menaker. A selfish,
mean-spirited old man resists his son's concerns for his
care and forces a bitter argument and eventual separation in the play *I Never Sang for My Father* by Robert
Anderson (76). (See also novel 49, play 81, and story
327.)

Examples of "hands-on" care are a son whose inten-
sive and unorthodox style of caregiving assists his
father's recovery from dementia, in William Wharton's
novel Dad (73), and a nephew who returns to his native
Nova Scotia and helps his uncle recover from a disabling

stroke, in D. R. MacDonald's story "Poplars" (284). (See also story 343.)

The daily burden of caregiving often falls on women when their husbands are unable to respond to the physical and mental decline of older parents. A Japanese woman is nearly overwhelmed with the responsibilities of caring for her demented father-in-law, in *The Twilight Years* (41), a novel by Sawako Ariyoshi. A similar burden is placed upon a daughter-in-law in Rosalie Walsh Honel's *Journey With Grandpa: Our Family's Struggle with Alzheimer's Disease* (21).

In Simone de Beauvoir's biographical account, *A Very Easy Death* (13), a daughter shares the caregiving burden with a sister and is able to resolve some of her ambivalent feelings about her mother. In the novel *The Big Ward* (72), by Jacoba Van Velde, a daughter's devotion to her mother, who is dying in a nursing home, extends to financial as well as emotional support.

When the primary caregiver in a family setting is also an older adult, that person's frailty or disabilities may complicate caregiving. For example, a frail old woman cares for her bedridden husband in Mark Van Doren's poem "The First Snow of the Year" (179). The burden of caregiving for an argumentative and spiteful 90-year-old woman falls on a daughter-in-law, 65, who suffers herself from a range of infirmities, in Margaret Laurence's novel *The Stone Angel* (54). (See also novel 37.)

Other complications arise when caregivers face multiple crises, as in Richard Stern's story "Packages" (331) where a family's care for a demented father is made more difficult because of their grief over their mother's recent death. (See also novel 59.)

The time caregivers can devote to caregiving is limited by pressures from their own work, by family responsibilities, or by lack of resources. A son caring for his dying father arranges for townspeople to provide additional caregiving, in Arturo Vivante's story "The Bell" (339). (See a similar arrangement in another Vivante story, 340.) Resistance to the responsibilities of caregiving is reflected in the unwilling care given to an old man by his children in Edna Ferber's story "Old Man Minick" (247).

The frustration of caregiving at a distance is felt by a daughter in two poems by Denise Levertov (139 and 140). A son's caregiving requires several trips to resolve medical and financial crises in Nick Taylor's autobiographical account *A Necessary End* (33).

Some families turn to health-care professionals to provide respite from the burdens of caregiving. In J. Bernlef's novel, *Out of Mind* (46), a woman hires aides to assist her caregiving for her husband, who suffers from Alzheimer's Disease. (See also poems 101 and 145, and collection of stories, 297.)

Caregiving as a symbolic activity is portrayed in "The Angel of Mercy" (206), Warren Adler's story about Yetta Klugerman, a mysterious old woman famous for dispensing solace and comfort to the old people in a retirement village.

16. Elder Abuse.

(For related topics see Topic 11, Family
Conflicts and Topic 14, Intergenerational.)

The classic mistreatment of the old is Shakespeare's *King Lear*, in which the retired old king is deprived of dignity, shuttled from cruel sister to cruel sister, and eventually driven mad (85). In May Sarton's novel, *As We Are Now*, a substandard nursing home becomes a veritable concentration camp (66). The old talking bird who assumes a place in the Cohen family, only to be resented, mistreated, and finally evicted symbolizes the unwanted grandfather, in Bernard Malamud's story, "The Jewbird" (287). (See also play 75 and story 292.)

Dysfunctional social service turns into cruelty in Sol Yurick's story "The Siege," as Miller, the Relief Inspector, spiritually rapes old Mrs. Diamond in his determination to invade her private room (358). In similar callousness, a party of delinquent teenagers descends upon Mrs. Malby's apartment, turning a charitable redecoration project into a shambles, in William Trevor's story, "Broken Homes" (336).

Elder abuse takes subtler forms in which the older relative is misunderstood, imposed upon, criticized, treated as a burden by the host family, as in Thyra Winslow's story, "Grandma" (354). To Old Man Minick in Edna Ferber's story of that name, this comes on only gradually after his son and wife take him in, but sooner or later he finds himself regarded as an interruption to their life, just an old geezer (247).

17. Rebellion, Enmity.

(See also Topic 11, Family Conflicts, and
Topic 14, Intergenerational, for other
illustrations of rebellion and hostility.)

Rebellion. Rage at death itself is commonly noted, nowhere more eloquently than in Dylan Thomas' poem "Do Not Go Gentle into That Good Night" urging his father to fight back all the way (176).

Cultural change may evoke the wrath of old people who are threatened. The African tribal chief Okonkwo kills the messenger from the white government which has weakened his people, in Chinua Achebe's novel *Things Fall Apart* (36).

Rebellion against the established order is maintained by the old radicals in John Sayles' story "At the Anarchists' Convention" (322). A one-person rear guard action against the evils of the big city is fought by the ingenious improviser Nat who cons his way past one danger after another, in Herb Gardner's play *I'm Not Rappaport* (80). Defiance of traditional expectations of aristocratic ladies is voiced by the matriarch who has spent her life in an artificial role, in Robert Graves' poem "The Great-Grandmother" (115). (See also story 348.) Theodora Bascomb, drunk as she is, puts up a spirited defense of the "family" against a cynical country club speaker, in Jack Matthews' story "Storyhood as We Know It" (295).

General feistiness, which may be thought of as taking an adversarial stance toward the world, is illustrated by the sharp-tongued, unconventional former trapeze artist in Lynn Schwartz' novel *Balancing Acts* (67). Feistiness is cheerfully anticipated by the speaker of Jenny Joseph's poem "Warning," who is resolved to wear purple in old age and to be unconventional in all sorts of ways (131). (See also poem 194).

Enmity. A generalized anger colors the hard-bitten old age of Hagar Shipley in Margaret Laurence's novel *The Stone Angel* (54).

Elder abuse and general helplessness may prompt a vindictive fury. For Caro Spencer, the spirited old woman victimized in an inhumane nursing home, this rage leads to her destroying the home by fire, in May Sarton's novel *As We Are Now* (66). An old drifter has fought against national leadership for a lifetime, drawing attention to his case by conspicuous self-torture, in William Wiser's story "The Man Who Wrote Letters to Presidents" (355). (See also poem 107.)

Hostility at the same age level erupts over a card game in D. L. Coburn's play *The Gin Game* (77). Hostility simmers between neighbors over an infested tree in Ethan Canin's story "Emperor of the Air" (227). It flames up between tenant and landlord in Malamud's story "The Mourners" (288). It becomes a sad rivalry between the two old men vying for the favor of children, in Toshio Mori's story "The Man with Bulging Pockets" (301).

Sheer spitefulness is expressed by the nasty hospital patient in Doris Lessing's story "Casualty" (279) and by several characters in each of Kingsley Amis' two novels *Ending Up* (37) and *The Old Devils* (38).

Aging and Physical Health

18. Activity, Frailty.

Activity. Physical strength and vigor are evident in an old man who plans a radical suicide, in Wallace Knight's story "The Resurrection Man" (276). Phoenix Jackson, an old black woman, walks the length of the Natchez Trace in Eudora Welty's story "A Worn Path" (351). The veteran stage actor known as "Sir," in Ronald Harwood's play *The Dresser* (81), moves from one crisis to another with boundless energy. (See also story 306.)

Constancy of activity is represented in the old man in Donald Hall's poem "Ox Cart Man" (120) and in Hall's portrait of his grandfather, a New England farmer in the memoir *String Too Short to be Saved* (20). (See also story 312.) Similar persistence and stamina are shown in the old man who devotes years of his life to establishing an orchard of peach trees, in Arturo Vivante's story "The Orchard" (342).

Activity in old age is portrayed metaphorically in the poet's depiction of busy small birds in a winter field, in the poem "To Waken an Old Lady" by William Carlos Williams (196). An old fisherman undertakes a vigorous competition with a great marlin, in Hemingway's *The Old Man and the Sea* (50). The adventurous spirit of old age is shown in the legendary figure Ulysses in Tennyson's poem (175). (See also story 257.)

The advice of more than forty older adults who have remained active in old age is central to the interviews in *The Ageless Spirit*, by Philip Berman and Connie Goldman (14). (See also poems 162 and 168.)

Frailty. The old are often portrayed as living a fragile existence, seeking a balance between health and

illness, activity and disability. A formerly active and
energetic woman admits to the difficulties of frailty
and dependence, in May Sarton's journal *Endgame* (32).
The difficulty of maintaining a household and completing
ordinary physical tasks is depicted in the old woman's
struggle to climb out of her bath, in Janet Frame's
story "The Bath" (250). An old woman barely finds the
energy to complete her daily ritual of making tea in
Mark Van Doren's poem "Spirit" (183). The concerns of an
old man living alone are expressed in Robert Frost's
poem "An Old Man's Winter Night" (112). (See also novels
39, 51, and 56.)

     The difficulty of managing a household when elderly
spouses are both frail is shown in Julian Gloag's novel
Only Yesterday (49) and in Nick Taylor's memoir *A Necessary End* (33). (See also poem 181.)

     Sometimes frail elders may be left behind in the
chaos of historical events, as in the old man too exhausted to join a column of refugees in wartime, in
Ernest Hemingway's "The Old Man at the Bridge" (260).
Or they may be broken by experience, as in the middle-
aged Welshman who returns home, his energy spent, after
years on the road in the Depression, in "My Uncle's
Story," by Leslie Norris (305). (See also stories 323,
347, and 352.)

     Other elders defy the constraints of their frailty.
An old woman struggles to rescue her flowers from a kil-
ler frost in Josephine Jacobsen's story "Jack Frost"
(265). Two old friends in Edward Arlington Robinson's
poem "Isaac and Archibald" are cheerful in the face of
their inevitable physical decline (163).

     Two poets, Lise Maclay in "Infirmities" (144), and
Rolf Jacobsen, in "Old Age" (128), describe negative
attitudes toward frail older adults. (See also story
346.)

19. Disease, Disability.

(See also Topic 20, Mental Health, Dementia.)

Disease. The devastating impact of cancer on an
older adult and that person's family is portrayed in
several sources. Two daughters are supportive of their
mother's suffering from cancer in Simone de Beauvoir's
memoir *A Very Easy Death* (13). A son shows understanding and insight when his father is stricken in Philip
Roth's memoir *Patrimony* (29). A son's personal account
of his father's cancer reveals strong father-son bonds
in "The Death of My Father" by Eric Lax (27).

     Autobiographical accounts of struggles with disease
can be found in two literary works. Anatole Broyard re-

lates his terminal battle with cancer in *Intoxicated by My Illness* (16). May Sarton's account of her struggle with diverticulitis and heart disease is detailed in her journal *Endgame* (32). An old man's life-threatening illness precipitates his descent into terrible isolation, in Donald Hall's poem "The Hole" (119).

Fictional portrayals of cancer include the stories of a brave woman who endures a painful dying in Arturo Vivante's "Last Rites" (341) and a cancer-ridden father whose daughter is shown in conflict with her Israeli doctor, in Susan Dodd's "Subversive Coffee" (240). (See also stories 229 and 289 for examples of older adults suffering from other diseases.)

Alcoholism is central to the experiences of characters in three stories: the desperate old man in a tavern in Hemingway's "A Clean, Well-Lighted Place" (259), the old officer in William Trevor's "The General's Day" (337), and the drunken Mr. Sweet, whose rapport with children is recalled fondly in Alice Walker's "To Hell With Dying" (345).

Disability. Disabilities caused by strokes are related in several literary works. In the journal *After the Stroke* May Sarton chronicles her six-month recovery (30). In Kingsley Amis' novel, *Ending Up*, a stroke afflicts an old man with aphasia (37). His determination to regain normal speech is at once heroic and humorous. Daisy Werthan's stroke, in Alfred Uhry's play *Driving Miss Daisy*, precipitates her mental decline and sends her to a nursing home (88). After suffering a stroke, a strong-willed old man receives therapy in a nursing home and returns home in a wheelchair, in "Poplars," a story by D. R. MacDonald (284). In "Appropriate Affect" (298), a story by Sue Miller, an old woman's true feelings about her family rise to the surface temporarily after her stroke.

A father's disability after an operation for bladder cancer is depicted in William Wharton's novel *Dad* (73). The poem "Letters from a Father," by Mona Van Duyn, shows a father whose complaints about numerous disabilities vanish after he receives a special gift from his daughter (186). A husband's concern for his wife, who has been in a coma in a nursing home for two months, is portrayed in the story "Winter Garden," by Janet Frame (251).

A blind widow retires to a cabin in Nova Scotia in D. R. MacDonald's story, "Of One Kind" (283). A nearly deaf old woman is the center of "Old Lady Chundle," a tragicomic story by Thomas Hardy (258).

Physical appearance may be perceived as a disability, as in the aging speaker in Thomas Hardy's poem "I Look into My Glass." who can not reconcile his feelings

of passion with the wasted face he sees in his mirror
(123). The speaker in Lise Maclay's poem, "I Hate the
Way I Look," also feels betrayed by her physical ugliness (143.) (See also poem 116.)

The infinite expansion of disabilities which would
be suffered by immortal persons is the curse of the
Struldbruggs, beings encountered by Captain Lemuel Gulliver in Swift's *Gulliver's Travels* (332).

20. Mental Health, Dementia.

(See also Topic 19, Disease, Disability.)

Mental Health. The figure of Shakespeare's *King
Lear* (85), raving wildly on the heath, is one of the
most famous depictions of mental breakdown in literature. Other examples of mental illness include the retired woman in Barbara Pym's *Quartet in Autumn*, who descends into obsessive behaviors (64), and the father in
a psychiatric hospital in Gina Berriault's story "The
Bystander" (219). Grief over the loss of a son drives
a father to the edge of madness in Thomas Hürlimann's
novel *The Couple* (52). The father in William Wharton's
novel *Dad* retreats into a fantasy life in order to find
solace from a dull marriage (73). (See also stories 274
and 358.)

Dementia. Three personal accounts of Alzheimer's
Disease illustrate the devastating effect of this dis-
ease on families and provide details on family history
and medical interventions: *A Woman's Story*, by Annie
Ernaux; (19), *Daddyboy*, by Carol Wolfe Konek (26); and
Journey With Grandpa, by Rosalie Walsh (21).

Dementia may be associated with tragedy, as in the
demented widower who falls to his death when he wanders
into the countryside looking for his dead wife, in "The
Lost Phoebe," a story by Theodore Dreiser (244).
Another tragic loss is shown in a confused elderly widow
whose deathbed memories return to a fateful jilting in
her youth, in "The Jilting of Granny Weatherall," a
story by Katherine Anne Porter (315). The wretched
suffering of the immortal Struldbruggs is recounted in
Swift's *Gulliver's Travels* (332). (See also stories 308
and 352.)

Disturbing contemporary accounts of dementia from
the point of view of the sufferers include the novel *Out
of Mind*, by J. Bernlef (46); Marisa Labozzetta's story
"Making the Wine" (278); the poem "Into the Nameless
Places," by David Wagoner (187); and Marjorie Dorner's
story "Before the Forgetting" (242). (See also poem 107
and story 217.)

Dementia is represented in institutional settings in Tracy Kidder's account of nursing home life, *Old Friends*, where demented residents are affectionately referred to as the "nudnicks" (23). In Lou Myers' novel, *When Life Falls it Falls Upside Down*, the lives of demented residents in a Jewish Old Age Home are depicted (60). (See also the poem 188.)

Demented older adults are sometimes shown as repulsive to those attending to them. A senile, grasping old woman disturbs a family, in Gina Berriault's story "Nocturne" (221). A dying grandmother in Gwendolyn Brooks' story "Death of a Grandmother" can only respond to questions with an incoherent "Hawh!" (225). (See also story 327 for an example of how demented persons may be a danger to their caregivers.)

Those attending the demented often feel embarrassed by their bizarre, unpredictable behaviors. A demented old man's wandering around a small town embarrasses family and friends, in "A Hog Loves its Life," a story by Alan Gurganus (256). A woman taking care of her demented father-in-law feels shame when he escapes her care and wanders away from home, in Sawako Ariyoshi's novel *The Twilight Years* (41).

In other sources a family's experience with dementia leads to insights into the underlying strength and resources of their relatives. For instance, a son comes to view his confused and demented father as a heroic figure in "First the Legs and Then the Heart," a story by Jack Matthews (294). In "Dr. Cahn's Visit" (330), a story by Richard Stern, a son witnesses a stunning moment when his father's severe dementia is reversed temporarily. (See also "Packages," 331, another Stern story.) Two stories by Arturo Vivante, "The Soft Core" (343) and "The Bell" (339) portray a son who feels a similar inspiration when he observes strong inner qualities in his father that have not been destroyed by his dementia.

21. Doctor-Patient Conflicts.

A misguided offer of medical intervention is shown in Lisa Mueller's poem "Monet Refuses the Operation" (151). Excessive treatments are detailed in Arturo Vivante's story "Last Rites" where doctors intervene repeatedly to treat a woman's cancer (341). In and Richard Stern's story, "Dr. Cahn's Visit," a barrage of diagnostic tests on a cancer patient triggers her stern rebuke of her doctors and other hospital staff (330). A daughter criticizes a haughty and insensitive surgeon who treats her dying mother, in the memoir *A Very Easy Death*, by Simone de Beauvoir (13). A son stands by his

father when the old man resists excessive diagnostic
tests and surgery in *Patrimony*, a memoir by Philip Roth
(29). (See also novel 54 and story 240.)

Other negative portrayals show the impersonality
and bureaucracy of health care. They include Gina
Berriault's story "Nocturne," which shows a hospital as
a warehouse for human wreckage (219), and a Doris
Lessing story, "Casualty," which depicts the noise,
pain, and indefinite waiting in a hospital emergency
room (279). (See autobiography 27, novels 56 and 59,
and poem 187.)

Cruel and insensitive staff in a substandard nursing home are the subject of May Sarton's novel *As We Are
Now* (66). The irritability of overworked staff is portrayed in the story "Death of a Grandmother," by
Gwendolyn Brooks (225). Doctors who routinize their patients so that the realities of death and suffering are
ignored are shown in Leo Tolstoy's novella *The Death of
Ivan Ilyich* (71).

An old woman returns to her native Australia and
regains strength and independence partly because of her
sensitive interactions with her doctor, in *Tirra Lirra
by the River* by Jessica Anderson (39). Other examples
of sensitive interactions between health care staffs and
older adults include Lou Myers' novel *When Life Falls it
Falls Upside Down* (60), and Kingsley Amis' novel *Ending
Up*, where a physician attends to a house of old people
in rural England (37). The sacred nature of the trust
between physician and patient is shown in John Stone's
poem, "He Makes a House Call" (174). (See also novel 48
and collection of stories 297.)

Autobiographical accounts and commentaries provide
insights into doctor-patient conflicts. May Sarton
shares her frustration with unsympathetic doctors, the
impersonality of the hospital, and the constant changes
made in medications, in *After the Stroke* (30). Her account of her illness-plagued seventy-ninth year and her
attempts to find relief through diet and holistic
medicine are featured in a later journal, *Endgame* (32).
Anatole Broyard's account of his doctor-patient relationship in *Intoxicated by My Illness* is fleshed out by
further study of other sources (16).

Two stories deal with the subject of active euthanasia. In "The Tradesman," by Francis King, a woman
seeks help from a "tradesman" to end her life (275). In
Arturo Vivante's story, "The Bell," a son considers euthanasia when his father suffers unbearable pain (339).

The folly of extending the life span indefinitely
through medical advances is examined in Kurt Vonnegut's
play *Fortitude* (89) and in two stories, Vonnegut's
"Tomorrow and Tomorrow and Tomorrow" (344), and "The
Immortals," by Jorge Luis Borges (223).

22. Long-term Care.

Drab and depressing portrayals of nursing homes and other institutions dominate this category. An old man flees a depressing retirement home in "The Autumn of Henry Simpson," a story by Richard Dokey (241). (See a similar response in stories 239 and 252.) A gallery of decrepit characters reside in a nursing home in Alice Munro's story "Mrs. Cross and Mrs. Kidd" (304). A lonely old man recalls happier days in order to escape the regimentation of a nursing home, in Elizabeth Jolley's story "A New World" (272).

The desperation, loneliness, and routines of nursing home life are overcome when residents find means for personal renewal, as in Robert E. McEnroe's play *The Silver Whistle* (82). (Other examples of renewal include stories 72, 245, and 251.) For a comic view of a geriatric hospital see "Dillinger in Hollywood," a story by John Sayles (323).

Several poets respond to the impersonality, dreariness, and feelings of abandonment that are the basis of nursing home existence. In W. H. Auden's "Old People's Home" (95) the speaker rages at the warehousing of the old in institutions. The nursing home is a symbol of hopelessness in "The Old Fools," by Philip Larkin (137). David Wagoner's "Part Song" (188) portrays a pathetic scene at a nursing home Thanksgiving party where residents and guests feel alienated. (See also poem 101.)

Autobiographical accounts of nursing home life can be found in Ronald Blythe's oral history *The View in Winter* (15), in Kenneth Koch's *I Never Told Anybody: Teaching Poetry in a Nursing Home* (25), and in Tracy Kidder's *Old Friends* which focuses on two male residents (23). Compare the enmity that breaks out between two residents in the play *The Gin Game,* by D. L. Coburn (77). (See also autobiography 26 for an example of a difficult nursing home placement.)

Retirement homes and their opportunities for "self-improvement" for older residents are shown in Elizabeth Gray Vining's autobiographical *Being Seventy: The Measure of a Year* (34) and in the novel *Balancing Acts*, by Lynn Sharon Schwartz (67).

Psychological Responses to Aging

23. Disengagement.

(See also Topic 39, Retirement.)

Downscaling, except for the most vigorous, seems inevitable for most people. As Emerson put it in his poem "Terminus" (110), "It is time to be old." The writer Elizabeth Vining, after a most productive and varied year, accepted her time to move into a retirement home, in *Being Seventy: The Measure of a Year* (34).

Retirement from a career is probably the commonest form of disengagement, involuntary as it may be. Disengagement also occurs through illness and disability which limit one's involvements. Such happens to the ageless but demented freaks in Jonathan Swift's "The Immortal Struldbruggs" (332). (See also poem 188.)

Disengagement from a role occurs when one leaves a function which has both determined and limited one's relationships. Deborah Holland, widow of a famous public servant, withdraws from celebrity to find her own peace in Virginia Sackville-West's novel *All Passion Spent* (65). (See also poem 115.)

One may disengage from close bonds. So Mr. Lomax leaves a selfish family to join an old Florida friend in Richard Stern's story "Arrangements at the Gulf" (329). In Galway Kinnell's poem, "Good-bye" (132), a son finds a way to release his dying mother. (See also stories 280 and 356.)

Despite the attractions of a late love, one may withdraw, nowhere more tragically than through the sudden suicide of Ethel Brokeles, in I. B. Singer's story "Old Love" (326). (See also stories 264, 283, and 306.)

King Lear gives up his world of political and military
strife--at first through madness and finally through his
daughter's love (85). A bitter quarrel with a neighbor
is relinquished in Ethan Canin's story "Emperor of the
Air" (227).
    There is the disengagement of involuntary defeat,
as with the glamorous uncle who ends up as a broken old
man in Leslie Norris's story "My Uncle's Story" (305).
    Imminent death can bring about the ultimate disen-
gagement, the preparing of oneself. Mrs. Masterson decides upon assisted suicide in Francis King's story "The
Tradesman" (275). Terminal illness drives an old man
into self-imposed isolation in Donald Hall's poem "The
Hole" (119). For the terminally frail, it may just
amount to giving up living, as in Maya Angelou's poem
"The Last Decision" (91). (See also play 75.)
    Most serenely, there is the calm readiness of those
ancient black women, their life functions behind them,
in Sterling Brown's poem "Virginia Portrait" (104) and
in Katherine Anne Porter's story "The Last Leaf" (316).

24. Autonomy, Coping.

    Autonomy. Several stories show older women deter-
mined to maintain their independence and their dignity
in familiar surroundings.   An old woman prefers a
cramped apartment to a dreary old people's home in Anzia
Yezierska's "A Window Full of Sky" (357). A woman is
determined to survive in her cottage through a long winter in "Jack Frost," a story by Josephine Jacobsen
(265). Two old sisters prefer life in their ruined cottage to the regimented life of a Old People's Home in "A
Mistaken Charity," by Mary Wilkins Freeman (252). (See
also stories 235, 250, and 336.)
    Several entries portray women who achieve an au-
tonomy they had lacked in their earlier roles as wife
and mother. A grandmother builds an independent life in
Bertolt Brecht's story "The Unseemly Old Lady" (224). A
woman walks away from her marriage in Constance
Beresford-Howe's novel *The Book of Eve* (45). Sylvia
Calvert, recently retired, discovers an inner resolve
that allows her to help her dysfunctional family, in Angus Wilson's novel *Late Call* (74). (See also novel 39
and story 257.)
    For men, too, autonomy is an important part of
self-fulfillment. For example, a widower struggles to
find his own identity and place in life in "Old Man Minick," a story by Edna Ferber (247). Rocky Goodstein, in
Max Apple's memoir-like novel *Roommates* (40), expresses
his autonomy through his commitment to his religion and
the emotional support he provides for his family.

The "Ox Cart Man" (120), a poem by Donald Hall, and "Beauty" (312), a story by Goffredo Parise, illustrate the autonomy of older men whose lives are defined by the meaningful routines of physical activity.

Several poets provide additional insights into autonomy. In May Sarton's poem, "The House of Gathering," the poet proposes the metaphor of ripening to suggest autonomy in old age (168). Autonomy is found in pursuing independence and self-fulfillment in Denise Levertov's poem "A Woman Alone" (142). (See also poems 93, 114, 173, and 194.)

Coping. Coping skills often relate to old persons maintaining a tenuous existence in their homes in the face of imminent physical decline. A widow maintains her farm alone in David Updike's story "Indian Summer" (338). Another old woman's simple routine of making tea is symbolic of her maintaining her home in Mark Van Doren's poem "Spirit" (183). (See another Van Doren poem, 185.) The capacity of the older person to rejuvenate and face new challenges is illustrated in May Sarton's poem "Gestalt at Sixty" (167). (See also poem 196 and story 284.)

Sometimes old people demonstrate remarkable, even heroic coping skills in the face of adversity. Santiago, an old fisherman in Ernest Hemingway's novel *The Old Man and the Sea*, latches onto a great marlin and struggles to fight off the sharks which eventually devour his catch (50). Nat, the quixotic hero of Herb Gardner's play *I'm Not Rappaport*, assumes numerous fictional identities in order to defy a heartless city and help downtrodden friends (80).

An old woman's lifelong pattern of coping skills serves her well when she is attacked on a dark street in Venice in Goffredo Parise's story "Fear" (313). An African-American minister in Julius Lester's novel *Do Lord Remember Me* copes with racism, bigotry, and intolerance (57). A grandson celebrates the lifelong coping skills of a grandmother in William Carlos Williams' poem "Dedication for a Plot of Ground" (193).

A woman becomes self-sufficient after her husband leaves her in Doris Lessing's story "The Pit" (281). Several older women cope with limited financial resources and family problems in Pat Barker's novel *Union Street* (43). A recent retiree learns to stand on her own in Barbara Pym's novel *Quartet in Autumn* (64). Two old brothers stay in their house and ride out a flood in Wendell Berry's story "Are You All Right?" (222). (See also stories 204, 254, 299, and 306.)

Sometimes coping means drawing upon a fantasy world, as in the old man who escapes the regimentation of life in a nursing home, in Elizabeth Jolley's story

"A New World" (272).   Maya Angelou's poem, "Old Folks
Laugh," suggests the power of laughter as a coping mechanism (92).

25. Creativity, Humor.

Creativity. An appreciation of the beauty of
flowers or gardening unlocks the latent creativity of
several characters in three stories: "The Amaryllis," by
Mary Ward Brown (226); "Christmas Roses," by Edna
O'Brien (306); and "Daisies," by Betty Coon (235).   (See
also story 321.)
       An old woman decides to continue giving music les-
sons to the students whose lives she has touched in
"Ashur and Evir," a story by Annabel Thomas (334).   An
old man's gift for playing sad songs on his guitar is
remembered fondly in Alice Walker's story "To Hell With
Dying" (345).   An old man recalls a childhood gift of a
guitar from his grandmother in John Edgar Wideman's
story "Presents" (353).
       Elizabeth Gray Vining continues to be creative and
productive in her old age as a writer, in her journal
Being Seventy: The Measure of Year (34).   An old couple
compiles a journal together as a means of reflecting
upon their later years in *Age*, a novel by Hortense
Calisher (47).
       May Sarton, the poet and novelist, wrote several
journals in her old age.   In *At Seventy* she maintains an
active schedule of poetry readings and seminars (31).
In *After the Stroke*, written when she was 76, she faces
months during which her creativity and imagination are
dulled by the effects of the stroke (30).   In *Endgame: A
Journal of the Seventy Ninth Year* Sarton struggles with
serious physical problems but still completes the journal and enjoys celebrations of her life's work (32).
       The residents of a nursing home study poetry writ-
ing in Kenneth Koch's account *I Never Told Anybody* (25).
       The ability to tell stories and inspire listeners
is related in two works about the bonds between grandfathers and grandsons: Donald Hall's memoir of New England
rural life, *A String Too Short to Be Saved* (20), and
Allan Gurganus' story of the rural South, "A Hog Loves
Its Life" (256).
       Storytelling is the basis of an old man's heroic
resistance to authority in *I'm Not Rappaport*, a play by
Herb Gardner (80).   An imaginative attempt to transform
the lives of the old is shown in Robert E. McEnroe's
play *The Silver Whistle* (82). There a young man disguis-
es himself as an old man to inspire the listless residents of a nursing home. An aging English actor during
World War II performs magnificently, if inconsistently,

the roles of *King Lear* and *Macbeth*, in Ronald Harwood's play *The Dresser* (81).

The sustained creativity of a diverse group of older adults, some of whom are well-known artists and writers, is featured in Philip Berman and Connie Goldman's *The Ageless Spirit* (14).

The relationship between the individual and the creative process has been examined by several poets. Old age is a time to be put in touch with regeneration and creativity in "On a Winter Night," by May Sarton (170). The creative process is reflected in Kenneth Koch's distillation of images gleaned from life experiences in "The Circus" (134). Linda Pastan compares the value of an old person to the timelessness of art in "Ethics" (156). A proposed medical intervention threatens the creativity of a famous Impressionist artist in Lisa Mueller's "Monet Refuses the Operation" (151). Three poems by William Butler Yeats (199, 200, and 201) celebrate creativity and imagination in old age. (See also poems 161 and 162, and story 243.)

Humor. Characters in literary works often use humor to ward off the pain and frustrations of old age. An old woman uses humor as a morale-builder in the story "Womb Ward," by Doris Lessing (282). The pain of long-standing feuds is assuaged by humorous interchanges among a group of old Leftists, in John Sayles' story "At the Anarchist's Convention" (322). A poet uses sarcasm to combat the pomp and formality of funerals in "Tract," by William Carlos Williams (197). Lise Maclay pokes fun at the condition of her aging body in her poem "I Hate the Way I Look" (143). (See also poems 92 and 93.)

A family's rejection of a grandfather figure is leavened with the sharp verbal sparring between the main characters in "The Jewbird," a story by Bernard Malamud (287). Laughter can be stress-provoking, as in the hypocritical laughter of fearful old people who are paid to laugh at comedians in Julio Ricci's story "The Concert" (320).

The repartee between an old Appalachian farm couple is one of the chief delights of *Foxfire*, a play by Susan Cooper and Hume Cronyn (78). The initial hostility between an old woman and her chauffeur yields to an evolving camaraderie and affection through many humorous interchanges, in *Driving Miss Daisy,* a play by Alfred Uhry (88).

26. Wisdom, Mentoring.

Wisdom. A dedication to learning and an inner resolve to resist oppression are strengths of the Delany

sisters, in their autobiographical *Having Our Say* (17).
Similar qualities are shown in an African-American woman
in "Blessed Assurance: A Moral Tale," a story by Allan
Gurganus (255).

A wealth of instructive experience can be found in
the interviews of more than forty older people in Philip
Berman and Connie Goldman's *The Ageless Spirit* (14).
Memories of a favorite aunt in Michael Jenkins' *A House
in Flanders* focus on her capacity for problem solving
(22). *Littlejohn*, a novel by Howard Owen, is about a
rural North Carolinian whose wisdom is based on his
well-defined values and a great capacity for love and
empathy (63).

Two works highlight the wisdom of old women.
Marilyn Zuckerman's poem "After Sixty" portrays old
women as ready for new learning and new adventure (203),
and Rolf Jacobsen's "The Old Women" shows old women as
complex, mysterious, and worthy of respect (129).

The wisdom of the old is also a function of their
willingness to come to terms with their own mortality.
Most of the older characters in Muriel Spark's novel
Memento Mori fear reminders of death (68). In contrast,
the old woman in "The Last Words of My English Grandmother," a poem by William Carlos Williams, confronts
death head-on (194). In "The Autumn of Henry Simpson,"
a story by Richard Dokey, an old man makes peace with
himself after at first fleeing in terror from a retirement home (241).

E. M. Forster's story "The Road from Colonus" (249)
and Richard Eberhart's poem "Hardy Perennial" (109) portray old age as a time for the attainment of special insights into the precious quality of life. (See also
poems 130 and 191.)

A realization of the timeless nature of life and
art is shown in two poems by William Butler Yeats, "The
Wild Swans at Coole" (202) and "A Prayer for Old Age"
(199). (See also poems 149 and 178.) In May Sarton's
poem "Who has spoken of the unicorn in old age?," the
speaker reflects on a state of completeness that can be
attained in old age (171). (See also poem 102.)

Mentoring. The title character in "Old Mrs.
Harris," a story by Willa Cather, is a mentor for her
family and especially for her granddaughter who is able
to attend college partly because of the old woman's
efforts (231).

A boy's grandfather teaches the values of educa-
tion, honesty, frugality, and self-sufficiency in Donald
Hall's memoir *String Too Short to Be Saved* (20). Uncle
Sol is a role model and mentor for his nephew in *The Old
Left,* a collection of stories by Daniel Menaker (297).

27. Alienation, Loneliness.

Alienation. Alienation often occurs within families. A grandmother endures a hypocritical role in the family in Sue Miller's story "Appropriate Affect" (298). After Sylvia Calvert moves in with her son's family, she feels adrift and out of place in *Late Call,* a novel by Angus Wilson (74). An old man's family is unable to comfort him when they learn he is going to die, in "Arrangements at the Gulf," a story by Richard Stern (329). (See also story 270.) In Eudora Welty's story, "Old Mr. Marblehall," a man is so alienated from his family and his community that he leads a double life of bigamy (349).

Three stories by Richard Bausch further illustrate alienation within families. An old man feels out of touch with his wife and family in "Evening" (212). In "Rare and Endangered Species" a woman's unaccountable alienation ends in suicide (214). In "Letter to the Lady of the House" a man seeks to recover intimacy with his alienated wife (213).

Alienation often is the consequence when the old are institutionalized. Examples include the poems "Old People's Home," by W. H. Auden (95) and "The Old Fools," by Philip Larkin (137). (See also poem 188 and story 350.) Feelings of alienation and separation from the outside world are shown in *Old Friends*, Tracy Kidder's account of life in a nursing home. (23).

Grieving creates feelings of separation and alienation. When an old woman's last surviving grandchild dies, she feels utterly abandoned and unable to cope with her suffering any longer, in Katherine Mansfield's story "Life of Ma Parker" (290). Grief leaves emotional wounds that do not heal in Linda Pastan's poem "The Five Stages of Grief" (157). The death of a son drives a husband and wife apart in *The Couple*, a novel by Thomas Hürlimann (52).

The old may feel out of step with the world, and frustrated because their dreams are thwarted or rejected, as in the anguish felt by an old man in Archibald MacLeish's "The Wild Old Wicked Man" (148). (See also poems 102 and 94.) MacLeish's poem bears comparison with William Butler Yeats' poem of the same title (201). (See also another Yeats' poem, 200.) The residents of an English village interviewed by Ronald Blythe in *The View in Winter* feel they have been left behind by the great moments of history which shaped them (15).

Mark Van Doren's poem "Bay-Window Ballad" shows an old man feeling left behind by the claims of a new generation (177). A retired war hero suffers repeated humiliations in "The General's Day," a story by William Trevor (337). (See also stories 229 and 234.)

The desperation of lifelong alienation is shown in
an old man's agony over having posed for a pornographic
book in his youth, in "The Eternal Mortgage," a story by
Jack Matthews (293). An ill-tempered old man who deserted his wife and children many years ago is the subject of Bernard Malamud's "The Mourners" (288). A be-
nighted loser engages in a lifelong protest against the
"system," in William Wiser's "The Man Who Wrote Letters
to Presidents" (355). (See also novel 150 and story
267.)

Other examples of lifelong alienation include the
characters Hagar Shipley, in the novel *The Stone Angel*
by Margaret Laurence (54), and Joe Allston, in *The Spectator Bird*, a novel by Wallace Stegner (69). The lives
of both characters were changed by the deaths of family
members and the loss of their dreams in middle age.

Alienation may result from one's perception of
physical unattractiveness, as in the old man who is dis-
mayed at the ugliness of his spouse and himself, in
Robert Graves' poem "Nightmare in Senility" (116). Alienation may be the result of the loss of mental func-
tioning, as shown in the terror felt by the aphasic
woman in "Into the Nameless Places," a poem by David
Wagoner (187).

Alienation from the natural order of things is reflected in the nightmare existence of people who are
granted perpetual life in Kurt Vonnegut's play *Fortitude*
(89).

Loneliness. Loneliness may lead to the creation of
a fantasy world. An old woman, never married, invents
a fantasy lover in order to gain status and acceptance
by her peers, in Laura Kalpakian's "A Christmas Cordial"
(274). A recent retiree in *Quartet in Autumn*, a novel by
Barbara Pym, becomes reclusive and fantasizes about
having a love affair with her surgeon after recovering
from breast cancer surgery (64). An old man's sexual
fantasy leads to his being rudely spurned in Bernard
Malamud's story "In Retirement" (286). (See also
stories 268 and 283.)

Loneliness may result from an individual's failure
to achieve a lasting relationship with another person,
as in the lifelong courting that never bears fruit, in
Mary Wilkins Freeman's story "The Old Lovers" (253).

Sometimes loneliness is the natural consequence for
characters who themselves are loners. An old man comes
"home" to die in "The Death of the Hired Man," a poem by
Robert Frost (111). A dreary old woman yearns for communion with others, but has no friends, in "The Diary of
K. W.," a story by Gina Berriault (220). The old man in
Ernest Hemingway's "A Clean, Well-Lighted Place" spends

an evening in a tavern engaged in desperate drinking
(259). (See also poem 161.)

The loneliness of widowhood is shown in the poems
"In Mourning for His Dead Wife," by Yueh P'An (155), and
"The Widow's Supper," by Mary Jane Moffat (150). A
widow dedicates her life to the memory of her husband in
"The One and the Other," a story by Lu Xin'er (356). A
widower's loneliness becomes self-destructive in "The
Lost Phoebe," a story by Theodore Dreiser (244).

Separation from friends devastates characters in
two stories, D. R. MacDonald's "Work" (285) and Josephine Johnson's "Old Harry" (269). May Sarton reflects
upon the loneliness of solitude, in her journal *After
the Stroke* (30). (See also poem 166 and stories 254 and
272.)

That loneliness can be overcome is the message of
several sources. Two old widowers find meaningful relationships which assuage their aching loneliness, in the
novel *The Last Good Time,* by Richard Bausch (44). An
old retiree, floundering in loneliness, finds new meaning in life, in "The Hotel," a story by Isaac Bashevis
Singer (325). Old man Minick, a widower, makes new
friends in Edna Ferber's story (247). (See also poem
172.)

28. Anxiety, Isolation.

Anxiety. Anxiety often results from fears of impending mortality. An old person lies awake at dawn and
is troubled by fears of death in Philip Larkin's poem
"Aubade" (136). An old man reaches out to an old friend
for support and comfort when he learns he will die soon,
in "Arrangements at the Gulf," a story by Richard Stern
(329). Anxiety is felt by a dying woman as she is moved
from her home to an ambulance in "The Last Words of My
English Grandmother," a poem by William Carlos Williams
(194). (See also novel 72 and story 276.)

Two old couples, anxious over their eventual separation by death, maintain loving and supportive relationships, in Hortense Calisher's novel *Age* (47) and in
Archibald MacLeish's poem "The Old Gray Couple, II"
(147). An old couple is anxious over an uncertain future
after the sale of the family farm in "The Hardys," a
story by William Humphrey (263).

Fear of dementia creates anxiety in an old woman in
"Horace and Margaret's Fifty Second," a story by Charles
Baxter (217). An old man, broken by grief, fears that he
is losing his mental faculties in Stephen Minot's story
"The Tide and Isaac Bates" (300). (See also story 336.)
An old woman realizes she is suffering symptoms of de-
mentia and will lose all associations with the past, in

Marjorie Dorner's story "Before the Forgetting" (242).
A sufferer of Alzheimer's Disease is aware that dementia
is slowly overtaking him, in *Out of Mind,* a novel by J.
Bernlef (46). (See also story 239.) Failing memory
causes anxiety in Norman Thayer, in Ernest Thompson's
play *On Golden Pond* (87).

Alan Olmstead examines anxieties associated with
retirement in his journal *Threshold: The First Days of
Retirement* (28). An old farmer survives a fire that
nearly destroys his home, but his resulting anxiety pre-
vents his entering an adventurous retirement, in "Ashur
and Evir," a story by Annabel Thomas (334). (See also
story 251.) The speaker in May Sarton's poem "On a Winter Night" fears an old age dominated by loss and despair (170). (See also poem 130.)

Intergenerational conflicts may create anxiety. A
father in Charles Mungoshi's story, "The Setting Sun and
the Rolling World" is overwhelmed with fears for the security of his son who is leaving home (302). An old
woman living in her children's home feels anxiety when
she realizes she is not wanted, in Olga Masters' story
"You'll Like it There" (292). (See also poem 113.)

Middle-aged children feel anxiety because of the
impending mortality of parents, in Robert Bly's poem "A
Visit to the Old People's Home" (100). A grandfather
rejects the anxieties associated with middle age in John
Crowe Ransom's poem "Old Man Playing With Children"
(162).

Isolation. Self-imposed isolation is shown in an
old woman's refusal to establish emotional links with
family members in Neil Simon's play *Lost in Yonkers*
(86). A widow isolates herself from new relationships
in "Suttee," a story by Louis Auchincloss (211). A widower feels increasing isolation after the death of his
wife, in "The Tide and Isaac Bates," a story by Stephen
Minot (300). (See also novel 62 and story 205.)

The effects of isolation on an old person's psychological state are shown in Wallace Knight's story of an
old man who lives alone in rural Indiana and concocts a
bizarre suicide plan, in "The Resurrection Man" (276).
An old man is alone in the confusion of war in Ernest
Hemingway's story "Old Man at the Bridge" (260). An old
man, alone in a farmhouse on a winter night, tries to
keep the darkness at bay in Robert Frost's poem "An Old
Man's Winter Night" (112). (See also novel 37.)

29. Mid-Life.

Mid-life crises are resolved in several literary
works. A man about to divorce his wife moves in with

parents, helps them resolve their health-care needs, and reconnects with a daughter, in *Only Yesterday,* a novel by Julian Gloag (49). A middle-aged woman, caught between the conservative generation she rebelled against and the licentious lifestyle enjoyed by her daughter, resolves her crisis in Phyllis Bentley's "Mother and Daughter" (218). A middle-aged man sees "The Wild Swans of Coole" for the first time in nineteen years and is soothed by their beauty and by his insight into all that happens in the passing of one's life, in William Butler Yeats' poem (202). But a woman of 40, when visiting the grave of her father with her mother, fears her own future role as widow in "Funerary Tower: Han Dynasty," a poem by Linda Pastan (158).

The pain of childhood events is resolved in middle age in Will Weaver's story "From the Landing" (347). The pain of middle age is resolved in old age in *The Spectator Bird*, a novel by Wallace Stegner (69). There a man in his 70s reviews his mid-life crisis twenty years earlier and gains insight into the precious quality of long-term supportive relationships.

A poet examines the experiences that helped him accept his turning from youth to middle age in Kenneth Koch's "The Circus" (134).

30. Deviance.

If age is commonly thought to bring ripeness and wisdom, it can also confirm lifelong maladjustments. The strains of aging may actually deepen these flaws into cruelty and crime.

Tom's father Daniel turns up as self-centered, dishonest, and predatory as when he disappeared twenty years ago, in Edwin O'Connor's novel *I Was Dancing* (62). A gallery of vices is displayed by the cast of elderly British upper-class characters in Muriel Spark's novel *Memento Mori* (68). Remorse over having acted in a pornographic film darkens the last years of a stranger in Jack Matthews' story "The Eternal Mortgage" (293).

The mutual dependence of sisters Hattie and Alice has turned into sadism as they play cruel tricks on each other in Patricia Highsmith's story "The Cries of Love" (262).

A neighbors' quarrel leads to a plan to infect the enemy's trees in Ethan Canin's story "Emperor of the Air"--a plan fortunately aborted on a better understanding of that enemy (227). Caro Spencer's rage against the inhuman conditions of her nursing home explodes in arson, in May Sarton's novel *As We Are Now* (66).

Such conspicuous cases of deviant behavior may be rare, but they reflect the maladjustments and aggres-

sions which may run at milder strength in the everyday
family and personal life of the aged.

31. Depression, Suicide.

Depression. The disappointments felt by those who
see too late what they have missed are briefly but mem-
orably described in Dylan Thomas' poem "Do Not Go Gentle
into That Good Night" (176).
Depression is a universal component of bereavement.
So the speaker remains distraught and fixed in memories
of his wife, in P'An Yueh's ancient poem "In Mourning
for His Dead Wife" (155).   (See also poem 198.)   Ma
Parker, after a lifetime of mutely borne miseries,
breaks into wild grief on the loss of her grandson in
Katherine Mansfield's story "Life of Ma Parker" (290).
A generalized loss of spirits is noted by May
Sarton in *Endgame: A Journal of the Seventy Ninth Year*
(32)--a depression brought about by myriad ailments,
pains, bereavements, fatigue, loss of energy. A sudden
apparently causeless gust of gloom penetrates William
Wallingham in Richard Bausch's story "Evening" (212).
What might be called a community depression darkens the
old people's home in Robert McEnroe's play *The Silver
Whistle* (82).   (See also poem 186.)
Perhaps no depression goes on as grindingly and
endlessly as that experienced by Lazarus, imprisoned in
immortality after being raised by Jesus from the dead,
in Alain Absire's grim fantasy novel *Lazarus* (35).

Suicide.   The ultimate exit from depression sometimes leads back to life, as with Wallace Knight's story
"The Resurrection Man" (276), where an old man shows
such creativity in working out an undetectable suicide
plan that he develops a new interest in life. (See also
story 321.)
Suicide to provide insurance for a loved one is
Willie Loman's supreme effort to show his love for his
reconciled son Biff, in Arthur Miller's play *Death of a
Salesman* (83).   Assisted suicide is planned and exe-
cuted by Mrs. Masterson who feels at the end of her pur-
poses in Francis King's story "The Tradesman" (275).
Simply giving up life at the end of exhausting difficulties might be considered suicide, as in Maya Angelou's
poem "The Last Decision" (91).
The enormous impact of suicide on others is the
theme of Richard Bausch's novella "Rare and Endangered
Species," in which the mother's unexplained suicide re-
verberates painfully through all her relationships
(214). The sudden challenge of a new love shocks Ethel
Brokeles into joining her dead husband, with correspond-

ing impact upon her new fiancé, in Singer's story "Old Love" (326). (See also poem 135 and story 269.)

32. Vanity.

The pompous conceits of old age are illustrated in "General" Tennessee Flintlock Sash, a 104-year-old Civil War veteran, a too frequent star of parades and stage appearances, in Flannery O'Connor's story "A Late Encounter with the Enemy" (308). The incurable vanity of an aging Shakespearean actor in World War II England is shown in Ronald Harwood's play *The Dresser* (81). A self-centered old man, who expects everything in his world to revolve around his own interests, makes it difficult for a son to break through, in Arturo Vivante's story "The Soft Core" (343). (See also story 319.)

Vanity in the face of mortality exacts contrary responses in two literary works. Ivan Ilyich's cold pride and his assumption that his comfortable life, so well-formulated, will go on pleasantly, are shattered when he suffers a terminal disease, in Leo Tolstoy's novella *The Death of Ivan Ilyich* (71). A gallery of conceited old people are hounded by an anonymous caller who intones, "Remember, you must die," in Muriel Spark's novel *Memento Mori* (68). But their aristocratic pride and self-absorption prevent them from grasping the implications of that message.

Vanity is often associated with one's physical appearance--especially as it is revealed when a person looks at his or her image in a mirror. Thus, the speaker in Thomas Hardy's poem, "I Look into My Glass," regards his face with dismay (123). Similarly, a woman is shocked by her physical ugliness when she examines her face in a mirror, in Lise Maclay's poem, "I Hate the Way I Look" (143). (See also poem 116.)

Two literary works suggest that vanity and self-centeredness may be overcome by hard experience. A woman's lifelong egotism and intractability yield to a more sensitive nature upon the deaths of friends and her husband, in "Nothing But Death," a poem by Mark Van Doren (180). An old woman who has been pampered and spoiled by a bachelor son eventually accepts her new role in the family after her son marries, in Edna Ferber's story "Old Lady Mandle" (246).

33. Courage, Endurance.

Courage. A striking statement of what courage can

be throughout life to the end is given by Anne Sexton's poem "Courage" (172). An impressive illustration is provided by the grim struggle of Mrs. Harraway to take a bath, in Janet Frame's story "The Bath" (250). Many individual examples of courage are given in the interviews in *The Ageless Spirit*, by Phillip Berman and Connie Goldman (14). (See also story 284.)

The courage to resist evil shows conspicuously in Caro Spencer's challenging the cruel inhumanity of the nursing home which imprisons her in May Sarton's novel *As We Are Now* (66). Another old woman faces off an assault by two thugs in Goffredo Parise's story "Fear" (313).

Although courage shows most conspicuously in confronting a specific challenge, it also appears simply as high morale, continued readiness, as it does with the old radicals in John Sayles' story "At the Anarchists' Convention" (322). Evir spurns the security of a retirement home in order to keep on with her beloved piano teaching, in Annabel Thomas' story "Ashur and Evir" (334). (See also poem 185 and stories 323 and 355.) Let go of drab security, urges the grandfather in John Crowe Ransom's poem "Old Man Playing with Children" (162): learn to play with life as children do. The same advice comes from the speaker who vows to do all sorts of eccentric things when she grows old, in Jenny Joseph's poem "Warning" (131).

Courage also shows in a more earnestly adventurous spirit. The legendary King Ulysses leaves his dull throne to hazard the high seas once again in Tennyson's classic poem "Ulysses" (175). More quietly, Edward Cakes risks loving the young woman who strays into his life in Bausch's story "The Last Good Time" (44).

Courage can enable one to relinquish a great treasure as a sacrifice. So the lonely grandfather lets go of his beloved granddaughter so that she can freely marry, in Doris Lessing's story "Flight" (280). Courage also enables one to resist temptation as Sarah resists her former husband's plea to rejoin him, in Lessing's story "The Pit" (281).

Endurance. Closely related to courage, self-reliance can pull one through the most daunting of trials. An old black woman trudges an epic journey to get medicine for her grandson in Eudora Welty's story "A Worn Path" (351). Singlehandedly, another old woman maintains the family farm despite increasing problems and worsening health, in David Updike's story "Indian Summer" (338). (See also novel 50.)

The nerve to hold fast no matter what comes is quietly illustrated by the gentlewoman who maintains her graciousness amid the confused boredoms of a retirement hotel in Elizabeth Taylor's novel *Mrs. Palfrey at the Claremont* (70). An aging Irish schoolteacher urges her students to have understanding for the terrorists and then calmly accepts her forced retirement, in William Trevor's story "Attracta" (335). (See also autobiography 17 and story 252.)

Perhaps endurance shows most bleakly in face of terminal illness. The Honel family coped for years with the gradual ravages of Alzheimer's Disease in their grandfather, as recounted in Rosalie Walsh Honel's *Journey with Grandpa* (21). Simone de Beauvoir describes her mother's gallant struggle with progressive cancer, in *A Very Easy Death* (13). (See also story 330.)

What might be called a happy endurance unfolds in Thornton Wilder's play *The Long Christmas Dinner*, which celebrates the lasting power of the Bayard family through ninety years of change (90).

34. Serenity.

Serenity can be attained when old people attune their lives to forces within the natural world. For example, a lonely old man recovers joy in life from the beauty of a flower in "The Amaryllis," a story by Mary Ward Brown (226). A daughter's gift of a bird feeder inspires her depressed father in Mona Van Duyn's poem "Letters from a Father" (186).

An old philosopher and novice agriculturalist delights in spending his adult years growing an orchard of peach trees in "The Orchard," a story by Arturo Vivante (342). (See also poem 161.)

Serenity is the outcome of seasoning, of resilience, and of the capacity to survive hardships. Phoenix Jackson, an old black woman, overcomes numerous obstacles in Eudora Welty's story "A Worn Path" (351). (See also poem 104.) The quiet serenity of an old Native American woman, an embodiment of the grandmotherly role, is shown in Diane Niatum's poem "Old Woman Awaiting the Greyhound Bus" (153).

Several poets portray old people as balanced, adaptive, and self-contained. An old woman faces her declining years with openness and self-control in Denise Levertov's "The 90th Year" (141). Another old woman finds wholeness and creativity in "The House of Gathering," by May Sarton (168). Rolf Jacobsen portrays old people as having achieved a sense of integration and serenity in "Old Age" (128). (See also poems 114 and 195.)

The harmony of longstanding relationships between older couples, characterized by unspoken happiness and contentment, is portrayed in Mark Van Doren's poem "Old

Man, Old Woman" (181) and in Archibald MacLeish's poem
"The Old Gray Couple I" (146).

An old man's heart is reopened to caring when he
befriends a young runaway in Judith Freeman's novel *Set
for Life* (48). An old woman resolves to live on in her
ancestral home, in Jessica Anderson's novel *Tirra Lirra
by the River* (39). An old person is comforted by recalling beloved people who have died before him, in John
Wheelock's poem "Dear Men and Women" (190). Finally, a
woman puts her house in order, settles her affairs, and
goes serenely to her death via assisted suicide in "The
Tradesman," a story by Francis King (275).

Life Events and the Search for Meaning

35. Employment.

Employment so fills and identifies one's life that it influences the later years whether or not one remains employed. The vocation may culminate in some major achievement in late life. So it does for the hard-working cleaning woman whose life earnings enable her to fulfill a long-held dream of owning a piece of land, in Elizabeth Jolley's story "Pear Tree Dance" (273). (See also novel 61.) Or the vocation may provide sustained enrichment over time, as in fulfillment felt by a heart specialist in John Stone's poem, "He Makes a House Call" (174).

The vocation may simply continue as the one thing which identifies and satisfies the worker, as in the old man who keeps repeating his annual cycle of raising and selling produce, in Donald Hall's poem "The Ox Cart Man" (120). (See also autobiography 31, and stories 216, 274, 312, and 325.)

Sadly, one's vocational skills may be slipping without a clear alternative to replace them, as with the aging actor in Ronald Harwood's play *The Dresser* (81). The career may turn out to have been a narcotic which prevented real life. Rarely has this been shown so grimly as in Tolstoy's novella *The Death of Ivan Ilyich* where Ivan has frozen his law practice into a deadly in-human routine (71). (See also novel 53, and stories 59, 210, and 268.)

Cut off from work, the retiree may languish in aim-less discontent and resentment, as does Munsey Wills, the mail-order clerk stranded in mandatory retirement, in Josephine Lawrence's novel *The Web of Time* (55). A partial return to work may humiliate one who learns how poorly valued are the aged in the work place, as in J. F. Powers' story "The Old Man: A Love Story" (318). (See also play 83.)

36. Leisure.

Failure to develop wide interests during the work life may well lead to aimlessness and discontent as leisure opens in retirement. So the dissolute retired army officer wanders in drunken frustration through William Trevor's story "The General's Day" (337). Dr. Simon Morris grows bored with studying Greek and walking the city streets, in Malamud's story "In Retirement" (286). So one falls into the trap of "filling the day more and more easily with less and less," as Alan Olmstead put it in his memoir *Threshold: The First Days of Retirement* (28). (See also novels 38, 55, and 70.)

Ideally, as the poet John Crowe Ransom writes in "Old Man Playing with Children," old age should find one ready to "play," to take chances, to enjoy (88).

Women especially can step away from traditional gender roles, like "The Unseemly Old Lady" of Bertolt Brecht's story, who shocks her family by plunging into new tastes and friendships (224). (See also poems 131 and 203.)

Retirement home activities are sometimes shown as conventional: dancing, musicals, play-acting, games are depicted--sometimes with dismal results, as in the quarreling over cards in D. L. Coburn's play *The Gin Game* (77); and sometimes with pleasant new contacts as with the chess game in Margareta Ekström's story "The King Is Threatened" (245). (See also autobiography 23 and story 239.) Growth through creative writing is the subject of Kenneth Koch's *I Never Told Anybody: Teaching Poetry Writing in a Nursing Home* (25).

Storytelling is traditionally a satisfaction of the elderly: both tedious for the listener as in John Steinbeck's story "The Leader of the People" (328) and enjoyable as in Allan Gurganus' story "A Hog Loves Its Life: Something about My Grandfather" (256). Regular lively discussion animates the old men of Grant Home in Edna Ferber's story "Old Man Minick" (247). (See also stories 322 and 340.)

Travel, another common recreation, tempts Mr. Lucas toward a discovery of ancient Greece in E. M. Forster's sad story, "The Road from Colonus" (249). It leads the African-American widow Avey Johnson into a reunion with her Caribbean roots in Paule Marshall's novel *Praisesong for the Widow* (58). (See also stories 24 and 204.)

Besides the common household puttering, one can engage in such projects as the tree house undertaken in the story of that title by Marjorie Dorner (243). The study of backyard birds is encouraged by the daughter's gift of a bird feeder in Mona Van Duyn's poem "Letters from a Father" (186). Gardening proves an engrossing and even a transforming occupation in numerous writings, as in Walter Brinkman's discovery of seed catalogs in Anne Rosner's story "Prize Tomatoes" (321). (See also May Sarton's journals 31 and 167, and stories 226, 234, 235, 251, 265, and 342.)

37. Aging in Place.

For many people staying in one's home is the preferred alternative to institutional life, or to the restless adventuring of King Ulysses, or certainly to being shunted from one relative to another, as happens in Thyra Samter Winslow's story "Grandma" (354). The home maximizes one's control over daily life. It continues secure and comfortable living arrangements. It embodies one's personal and family history.

Sometimes, of course, one stays rooted out of simple inertia, as Louisa lingers on in the old family house after all other family has left, in Laura Kalpakian's story "A Christmas Cordial" (274). (See also novels 42, 43 and 48 and story 250.) Or one stays rooted out of timidity, like Mrs. Malby in William Trevor's story "Broken Homes" (336).

A pathetic and almost pathological clinging to one's past occurs in Sol Yurick's story "The Siege," in which a mad slum welfare recipient grimly fights off the relief inspector's determination to examine her private-of-privates fourth room (358).

Farm people may feel closely bound to the earth which nourished their past, so strongly that in Will Weaver's story, "A Gravestone Made of Wheat," the old farmer buries his wife on the family soil in defiance of the law (348). (Also see novel 63, play 78, and stories 276 and 338.) The two sisters of Mary Wilkins Freeman's story "A Mistaken Charity" bolt from an Old Ladies' Home to resume their marginal crop-raising at their beloved cottage (252).

One may return to one's early home as a place to retire, as Francis Brimm comes back to Florida in Dennis McFarland's novel *School for the Blind* (59).

Simple affection for the home and its beauty (often its garden) can hold one to the old place. Thus Mrs. Travis refuses to leave her cottage flowers for the safety of the village in a harsh New Hampshire winter, in Josephine Jacobsen's story "Jack Frost." (See also May Sarton's journals 30 and 31, and stories 235 and 324.) A woman pressed to enter an old people's home de-

cides to stay on the top floor of her rooming house
where her window commands such a spectacular city view,
in Anzia Yezierska's story "A Window Full of Sky" (357).

A poignant illustration of home-love is furnished
by the old widower who pays nocturnal visits to his old
vacated home just to sit and smoke by candlelight, in
Elizabeth Jolley's story "A Hedge of Rosemary" (270).

Aging in place can extend beyond the individual to
generations of family, as in Thornton Wilder's play *The
Long Christmas Dinner* which celebrates ninety years of
the Bayards in this one home (90). (See also autobiography 22.)

38. Aspirations.

The generalized search for new adventure, new experience, is certainly embodied in Tennyson's restless
old King Ulysses (175). (See also poem 176 and biographical interviews of 14). More pathetically it appears in the hopeless yearning of K.W. as she lies
starving, in Gina Berriault's story "The Diary of K. W."
(220).

Some aging persons simply aspire to continue their
productive lives as do Gemma and Robert, architect and
writer in Hortense Calisher's novel *Age* (47). (See also
poem 120.)

Others fix on some new or final achievement, perhaps aimed at in earlier years. So John Lancaster will
spend his final years toward building a great church in
the story "The Cathedral Builder" by Louis Auchincloss
(209). (See also stories 273, 321, and 342.)

Sexual love can be thought of as a goal, especially
for those whom age has barred from opportunity, as in
Archibald MacLeish's poem "The Wild Old Wicked Man"
(148). (See also poems 116 and 123, and stories 283,
286, and 291.) The widower farmer who wanders the
countryside seeking his dead wife illustrates aspiration
gone mad, in Theodore Dreiser's story "The Lost Phoebe"
(244). And what is one to think of that decorous biga-
mist whose main hope is to shock the community when his
sins are found out, in Eudora Welty's story "Old Mr.
Marblehall" (349)?

To play the mentor to the daughter of his dead
lover is the final goal of Harry Bendiner in Singer's
story "Old Love" (326). Old Mr. Head aspires to mentor
his impudent grandson in Flannery O'Connor's story "The
Artificial Nigger" (307). Finally one may aspire to
find, at last, one's own identity. The speaker of
Randall Jarrell's poem "Aging" longs for a quiet time in
which to "make a life" (130). (See also poem 131 and
story 318).

39. Retirement.

Departure from the main career, whether chosen or not, can prove traumatic. One may be heartlessly dumped, like Willy Loman in Miller's play *Death of a Salesman* (83), or one may have been encouraged to take early retirement, or one may simply decide on one's own to leave the work place. But a grinding sense of being superfluous may result.

Alan Olmstead flounders in his first experience of freedom, in his memoir *The First Days of Retirement* (28). The retiree may suffer unaccountable stabs of depression, as William Wallingham does in Bausch's story "Evening" (212). (See also novels 55, 61, and 74, play 84, and stories 215, 228, 247, and 337.)

Simple stoicism may carry one through the first shocks of retirement, as it does Mrs. Palfrey in the frantic dullness of her retirement hotel, in Elizabeth Taylor's novel *Mrs. Palfrey at the Claremont* (70). (See also story 335).

Any retiree who has expected to continue enjoying the praise and honors of the retirement dinner will understand King Lear's shock at being discarded by the daughters to whom he had left his throne, in Shakespeare's play (85).

Others may disregard the pressure to retire and may continue or resume working, as Evir decides to go on giving music lessons whatever the risk, in Annabel Thomas' story "Ashur and Evir" (334). (See also poem 120 and story 325.)

Ralph Waldo Emerson in his poem "Terminus" urges older persons to "take in sail" but by no means to lie idle (110). Second careers attract many retirees, as do part-time work, or volunteer duties. Max Fried, a circus trapeze artist, becomes a school gymnastics coach in Lynn Sharon Schwartz's novel *Balancing Acts* (67). (See also story 311.)

A blessing for certain retirees is the sense of new life, new chances, as experienced by the speaker in Marilyn Zuckerman's exuberant poem "After Sixty" (203). (See also novel 64 and story 316.)

The sadness of failing to answer the invitation to new life is found in E.M. Forster's story "The Road from Colonus" (249).

Retirement can foster new friendships, as found by the old professor and the museum guard in Josephine Johnson's story "Old Harry" (269). (See also story 321).

Philip Berman and Connie Goldman's collection of interviews, *The Ageless Spirit*, reveals numerous older people who have remained active and creative (14).

40. Grief, Widowhood, Loss.

Grief. In his poem "Tract" William Carlos Williams urges honesty as a first consideration in treating grief--much preferable to the sham and hypocrisy which so often attend it (197).
Grief can be anticipatory, as with the speaker who attends her dying mother in Denise Levertov's poems "A Daughter I" (139) and "A Daughter II" (140). (See also poems 132 and 154, and story 300.) Grief can be circular, as in the process outlined in Linda Pastan's poem "The Five Stages of Grief" (157). Or grief can be divisive, as in the couple who mourn separately the death of their son in Thomas Hürlimann's novel *The Couple* (52).
Loss of a parent can be mourned through many years, as the son at sixty-four still feels the scars of his father's long-ago suicide, in Stanley Kunitz's poem "The Portrait" (135). A middle-aged son remains unhealed over his mother's death twenty-five years earlier, in Michael Blumenthal's poem "Elegy for My Mother" (97). Loss of a child is mourned by the coachman in Anton Chekhov's story "Grief" (232). (See also story 290.)

Widowhood. Many literary works describe the pain and depression of losing a spouse. P'An Yueh's poem "In Mourning for His Dead Wife" expresses a man's heavy heart after a whole year of bereavement (155). A circus performer carries his grief to his own death in Lynn Schwartz's novel *Balancing Acts* (67). Melancholy and guilt mark the empty days in Richard Dokey's "The Autumn of Henry Simpson" (241). (See also poem 125 and stories 214, 233, 286, and 321.)
A woman's grief is conveyed in Mary Jane Moffat's poem "Widow's Supper" (150) and in Williams' poem "The Widow's Lament in Springtime" (198). Sometimes a woman is so imprisoned in the role of mourner as to preclude new relationships as in Louis Auchincloss's story "Suttee" (211). (See also novel 51.)
What are the various exits from grief? The old grandmother in Neil Simon's play *Lost in Yonkers* hardens herself against all emotions (86). A demented widow denies death by inviting her husband to her bed in Marisa Labozzetta's story "Making the Wine" (278). The farm widow Annie Nations feels her husband's presence so fully that she consults him for advice in Cooper and Cronyn's play *Foxfire* (78). (See also story 244.) The African-American wife bids her dead husband farewell while expecting an eventual reunion, in Alice Walker's poem "Goodnight, Willie Lee, I'll See You in the Morning" (189).
On one hand, the widow may simply carry on with the

stiff upper lip, as in Elizabeth Taylor's novel *Mrs.
Palfrey at the Claremont* (70). At greater distance one
may celebrate the departed one, as in Donald Hall's poem
for his grandfather, "Elegy for Wesley Wells" (118).
(See also poems 158 and 193, and stories 250 and 251.)

Deaths may finally soften the callous heart, as in
Mark Van Doren's poem "Nothing But Death" (180). Or a
spouse may live on contented and fulfilled by memories,
as in Lise Maclay's poem "Occupational Therapy" (145).

Grief may give way to new interests and attachments. The conventional wife in India finds great happiness with an old admirer in Ruth Prawer Jhabvala's
story "The Man with the Dog" (266). The German widow of
Bertolt Brecht's story "The Unseemly Old Lady" plunges
into new tastes and friendships to the shocked surprise
of her children (224). Avey Johnson of Paule Marshall's
novel *Praisesong for the Widow* finds her
African-American roots in the Caribbean (58). The widower's children find him a housekeeper who becomes his
close friend in Raymond Carver's poem "Happiness in
Cornwall" (105). (See also novels 44 and 65, and
stories 226, 311, 319, and 356.)

Loss. Other losses would include that of a lover,
as in Thomas Hardy's poem "After the Journey" (121).
The death of a homosexual lover is lamented in May
Sarton's poems "Der Abschied" (166) and "Mourning to Do"
(169). (See also story 314.) A lifelong friend is prepared for burial by a mortuary director in Susan Dodd's
story "Bifocals" (237). Several types of loss are shown
in Michael Cristofer's play *The Shadow Box* (79). A husband bitterly loses his wife not by death but by des-
ertion in Alice Adams' story "Ocracoke Island" (205).
In Nikki Giovanni's poem, "The Life I Led," a young
woman acknowledges the losses she will experience as she
ages, and yet is determined to find meaning and self-
fulfillment in her old age (114). The real loss experienced by the death of a pet is expressed by the widow
who wants Mass said for her poodle, in Frank O'Connor's
story "Requiem" (309). (See also autobiography 30.)

Grief over a lost way of life is felt by the old
couple at the auction of their farm in William
Humphrey's story "The Hardys" (263). An Indian woman
feels the loss of her tribe's old ways in Helen Knopf's
story "Memories" (133). (See also novel 36 and stories
302 and 328.)

41. Reminiscence, Life Review.

Reminiscence. Reminiscence recovers and cherishes
the past for its own sake. A nursing home patient copes

with institutional existence by recalling cheerier days,
in Elizabeth Jolley's story "A New World" (272). The
old pioneer Grandfather dwells obsessively on the great
adventure of moving West, in John Steinbeck's story "The
Leader of the People" (328). In the shadow of eventual
separation, an old couple enjoys the memories of their
courting in Mark Van Doren's poem "The First Snow of the
Year" (179). A widow declines guided recreational activity because she would rather concentrate on her long
happy marriage, in Lise Maclay's poem "Occupational
Therapy" (145). In a comically demented delusion, two
old socialites reenact a brilliant dinner in Edith
Wharton's story "After Holbein" (352). (See also stories
103, 133, and 355.)

Sometimes reminiscence revives a powerful seminal
experience, one which re-invigorates the present--a
point made in Loren Eiseley's biographical piece "The
Brown Wasp" (18). So an old African-American recalls a
Christmas Eve when his grandmother opened creativity by
presenting him with a guitar, in John Wideman's story
"Presents" (353). (See also poem 117 and story 242.)

Reminiscence can be part of grief work. A
middle-aged son tries to resolve the long-ago loss of
his mother by recalling her last days in Michael
Blumenthal's poem "Elegy for My Mother" (97). The
feisty ex-circus performer Max Fried has to deal with
his prolonged heartbreak over loss of his wife in Lynn
Schwartz's novel *Balancing Acts* (67).

Life Review. Life review in its most structured
and formal sense is the full autobiography; and it is
well exemplified in *Having Our Say: The Delany Sisters'
First 100 Years*, by two distinguished African-American
centenarians (17). The autobiography appears in novel
form in Reverend Smith's account of his life in Julius
Lester's *Do Lord Remember Me* (57).

At the other extreme is the deathbed recapitulation
of one's life, like that which ends Tillie Olsen's
novella "Tell Me a Riddle" (310). A terrible early
trauma invades the proud memories of the dying grandmother in Katherine Anne Porter's story "The Jilting of
Granny Weatherall" (315). The dramatist Arthur Miller
uses flashbacks as a way of reviewing the conflicts
which surface in Willy Loman's last hours in *Death of a
Salesman* (83). An old man works through the pain of an
unresolved relationship by reading a set of notebooks
written twenty years earlier, on a trip to his family
home in Denmark, in Wallace Stegner's novel, *The Spectator Bird* (69). (See also novel 63, poem 182, and stories
278 and 296.)

In *Vital Involvement in Old Age*, Erik Erikson and
his coauthors have pointed out that life review is es-

sential toward the final wisdom and integration of one's life. Sometimes this step involves recognizing the misdirection of earlier years. Nowhere is this more poignantly shown than in the butler Stevens' learning how he served the wrong values and wasted his chance for love, in Kazuo Ishiguro's novel *The Remains of the Day* (53). The flint-hearted Hagar Shipley of Margaret Laurence's novel *The Stone Angel* learns what joy she has lost thanks to the rigidity of her character (54). Liza Jarrett recovers loving memories of the men in her life, in Pat Barker's *The Century's Daughter* (42). (See also novels 51 and 59, play 84, poem 115, and stories 255, 263, 268, and 293.)

Life review also prepares one for what is ahead. May Sarton's poem "Gestalt at Sixty" draws upon her past to ready her for old age (167). An immigrant farmer's memories of a struggling but happy earlier life prepares him for a final act of paternal love in Willa Cather's story "Neighbor Rosicky" (230). The recollection of their early passion puts their mortality in perspective for the golden anniversary celebrants in MacLeish's poem "The Old Gray Couple II" (147).

After reflecting on her smothered early aspiration to become a painter and her long secondary role as great man's wife, Deborah Holland can choose a quiet but genuine life of her own, in Virginia Sackville-West's novel *All Passion Spent* (65). (See also autobiography 28, novel 58, and stories 204 and 348.)

Life review includes the remembrance of others. In a full sketch of her mother, Annie Ernaux brings her back to life, so to speak, in her biographical *A Woman's Story* (19). The life of a whole Yiddish community is brought back by the narrator's reminiscence in Lou Myers' novel *When Life Falls It Falls Upside Down* (60). (See also autobiographies 20 and 256.)

General insights into life review are provided by Kenneth Koch's *I Never Told Anybody: Teaching Poetry Writing in a Nursing Home* (25) and Michael Cristofer's play *The Shadow Box* (79).

42. Religion, Spiritual Life.

Religion. Faith in God's plan for the afterlife is expressed by D. H. Lawrence in the poem "Shadows" (138). Faith in God's guidance during the last years is urged by Ralph Waldo Emerson's poem "Terminus" (110). John Lancaster has long saved up money to build a great church, in Louis Auchincloss's story "The Cathedral Builder" (209). The wide power of African-American religion is exemplified by Reverend Joshua Smith in Julius Lester's novel *Do Lord Remember Me* (57). (See also poem

189 and story 255.)   An Irish widow's faith that even
her poodle has a soul precipitates the conflict in Frank
O'Connor's story "Requiem" (309). The deep thoughtful-
ness of a devout Quaker runs through Elizabeth Gray
Vining's journal *Being Seventy: The Measure of a Year*
(34).
     A search for faith animates the late years of
Muriel Brimm in Dennis McFarland's novel *School for the
Blind* (59).   Faith is despairingly sought by the res-
urrected Lazarus who seeks the meaning of Jesus' mir-
acle, in Alain Absire's novel *Lazarus* (35). The African-
American widow Avey Johnson makes a pilgrimage to a
Caribbean island in search of her spiritual roots in
Paule Marshall's novel *Praisesong for the Widow* (58).
(See also poem 167.)
     One of the best-known religious conversions in lit-
erature comes to Ivan Ilyich on his deathbed in Leo
Tolstoy's novella *The Death of Ivan Ilyich* (71).   The
saintly ministries of a visitor to a retirement home
lead to her being seen by one resident as "The Angel of
Mercy" in Warren Adler's story (206).   King Lear's final
humility and discovery of love may be thought of as conversion (85).   A conversion resisted is the wonderful
revelation of beauty which vainly comes to Mr. Lucas in
E. M. Forster's story "The Road from Colonus" (249).
     A sustaining and comforting ministry is enjoyed by
the Catholic Honel family in Rosalie Honel's memoir
*Journey with Grandpa: Our Family's Struggle with Alz-
heimer's Disease* (21).   A priest's counsel to abandon
anger and seek love helps to change a parishioner's life
in Joanna Higgins' story "The Courtship of Widow Sobcek"
(261).   A dying Episcopal minister is both friend and
example to his son in Eric Lax's memoir "The Death of My
Father" (27). (See also poem 154.)   In a failed ministry, an old African-American woman is ejected from a
white church in Alice Walker's story "The Welcome Table"
(346).   (See also story 258.)
     Atonement for sin is sought by an old man remorse-
ful for his long-ago role in a pornographic movie, in
Jack Matthews' story "The Eternal Mortgage" (293).   A
grandfather suffers remorse for failing to stand by his
grandson, but feels restored to God's grace on making a
conciliatory gesture, in Flannery O'Connor's story "The
Artificial Nigger" (307).   (See also story 288.)

     Spiritual Life. Outside formal religion, spiritual
experience is expressed as joy in all of life and death,
in John Wheelock's poems "Song on Reaching Seventy"
(191) and "Dear Men and Women" (190).   (See also Walt
Whitman's poem "Song at Sunset," 192.)   The spiritual
serenity of the old is admired by the poet Rolf Jacobsen
in "Old Age" (128).

A dignified but secular funeral for a brave woman is described in Arturo Vivante's story "Last Rites" (341). An heroic and almost poetic stoicism carries the old fisherman through his combat with the great marlin in Hemingway's novel *The Old Man and the Sea* (50). A nihilistic Lord's prayer is spoken by the tired waiter in Hemingway's story "A Clean, Well-Lighted Place" (259).

Various religious testimonies appear in Ronald Blythe's oral history *The View in Winter* (15).

43. Transmission of Values, Legacies.

Transmission of Values. The universal human impulse to reproduce includes the hope of reproducing or even improving one's life values in the young so that the next generation may live with happiness and integrity.

Perhaps the most potent means of transmitting value is the force of personal example. Thus old Yetta Klugerman of Warren Adler's story "The Angel of Mercy" has a transforming impact on the convalescent patient who investigates her good works (206). An aunt with a zest for life inspires a young nephew in Hennie Aucamp's story "A Bridal Bed for Tant Nonnie" (207). The African-American mother holds herself up as an example to her discouraged son in Langston Hughes' poem "Mother to Son" (127). (See also poems 141, 163, 165, 190, and story 284.)

A special exemplary role is played by the mentor, the older person who teaches and encourages. The old woman Ollie befriends the young narrator of Lisa Koger's story "Ollie's Gate," and with her stories and companionship teaches the girl to be independent, to dream, to follow her heart (277). An African grandfather does all he can to prepare the young boy in the ways of nature and manhood, in Charles Mungoshi's story "Who Will Stop the Dark?" (303). The grandmother in Willa Cather's story "Old Mrs. Harris" encourages young Vicki to study toward university admission (231). (See also novel 65.)

The struggle to pass on vital values can meet indifference or hostility. The old pioneer of John Steinbeck's story "The Leader of the People" finds that adults will not listen to his tales of the epic migration to the West. He laments that "westering has died out of the people" (328). In vain the African chief Okonkwo tries to preserve the tribal way of life against the invading white culture, in Chinua Achebe's novel *Things Fall Apart* (36). (See also stories 301 and 335.)

While admiring her gifted, strong-willed father, Carol Wolfe Konek also rebelled in determination to be

her own person, in *Daddyboy: A Memoir* (26). The speaker
of Ann Stanford's poem "The Fathers" recognizes indebt-
edness to all "fathers" who came before but insists upon
finding her own way (173).

What might be called the negative transmission of
values occurs in Peter Taylor's story "Porte-Cochere"
(333). Here Old Ben Brantley, having resolved never to
imitate the cruelty inflicted by his father, ends in a
tantrum against his own children. Willy Loman, having
lived a flawed life, has bequeathed his womanizing to
one son, and his dishonesty to the other in Miller's
play *Death of a Salesman* (83).

The transmission of values over generations is celebrated in Thornton Wilder's play *The Long Christmas
Dinner*, which richly portrays the Bayard family continu-
ity over nearly a century (90).

Legacies. An old man reveals his love for his family by carefully arranging his estate, in Peter Harris'
poem "My Father-in-Law's Contract" (124). The farmhouse
passed on from Uncle Sol to his nephew Dave represents
a legacy of intimacy, caring, love, and trust, in *The
Old Left*, a collection of stories by Daniel Menaker
(297). Although a shaving mug is the tangible legacy
from a father to a son, in *Patrimony*, by Philip Roth,
that object represents the adult son's desire to understand how his identity and values were formed by his relationship with his father (29). (See also stories 243
and 353.)

A tangible legacy may reflect the pain of failed
relationships and unresolved conflicts, as in the actual
property left to two brothers and the human damage left
behind by their egotistical and exploitive father in
Arthur Miller's Play *The Price* (84). Nikki Giovanni's
poem "Legacies" shows the ambivalence felt when legacies
constrain self-expression and autonomy (113).

In many cases legacies have nothing to do with
tangible gifts. An old man's dedication to complete an
unfinished cathedral inspires a young man in Louis
Auchincloss' story "The Cathedral Builder" (209). The
poet Donald Hall recalls fondly the strong values and
commitment to neighbors and community that were passed
on from farmers like his grandfather to future generations, in "Elegy for Wesley Wells" (118). In Mark Van
Doren's poem, "The Uncle I Was Named For," the poet reflects on the ways in which being named after someone
represents a passing on of family history. (184).

The legacy of a mother to her son is her courage in
the face of a life-threatening disease in Richard
Stern's story "Packages" (331).

William Carlos Williams celebrates his grandmother's legacy of courage and love in the poem "Dedica-

tion for a Plot of Ground" (193). (See also stories 24 and 256.)

44. Death.

An extraordinary account of death as experienced from the inside is given by Anatole Broyard in *Intoxicated by My Illness* which besides describing his own terminal illness is deeply informed about the ethics and problems of dying (16).

Such a final and life-denying event as death can be ignored by the hypocrisy which often dominates bereavement and which William Carlos Williams attacks in his poem "Tract" (197).

Comedy also provides an escape--a thoughtful escape--from the more brutal aspects of death. An ironic look at how quickly the dead are forgotten is provided in Thomas Hardy's poem "Ah, Are You Digging on My Grave?," in which all the grave visitors have come for some other purpose (122). Would we really like to be immortal? Not if immortality meant the daily misery of Kurt Vonnegut's fantasy, "Tomorrow and Tomorrow and Tomorrow," in which the miracle drug gerasone has indefinitely postponed the final hour (344). (See also his play 89 and Jonathan Swift's fantasy 332.) An uncomic, even terrifying vision of immortality is projected in Alain Absire's novel *Lazarus,* in which the main character drags on into perpetual existence (35).

The unreadiness for death marks most of the aged characters of Muriel Spark's novel *Memento Mori,* who blithely pursue their various vices in spite of death's warning (68). Professor Revenant has so postponed his life that only when dead does he arrange a party for his long-neglected friends, in M.F.K. Fisher's story "The Reunion" (248). (See also story 289.)

The fearfulness of death is sharply conveyed in Philip Larkin's poem "Aubade" (136). It infects communities of invalids, who see their fellows constantly disappearing, as in the novel *The Big Ward,* by Jacoba Van Velde (72). (See also novel 60.) The thought of death clouds the affectionate companionship of "The Old Gray Couple I" in Archibald MacLeish's poem (146). It frightens the rich widower Lomax in Richard Stern's story "Arrangements at the Gulf" (329). (See also poem 140 and story 313.)

The courage to meet death, like the courage to meet life, is the subject of Anne Sexton's poem "Courage" (172). (See also poem 176.) Heroic nerve in a painful death is shown by Simone de Beauvoir's mother in the memoir *A Very Easy Death* (13). (See also autobiography

27 and story 341.)
    Faith in an afterlife supports D. H. Lawrence in
his poem "Shadows" (138). Excluded from a white church,
an old African-American woman sees Jesus and joyfully
follows him to her death in Alice Walker's story "The
Welcome Table" (346). Ivan Ilyich in the agonies of
death finds eternal salvation in Leo Tolstoy's novella
The Death of Ivan Ilyich (71).
    Death is seen by some as natural, as part of the
mysterious beauty of existence, as actually an enhancer
of life, as expressed by Walt Whitman in the poem "Song
and Sunset" and by the poet John Wheelock in "Song on
Reaching Seventy" (191) and "Dear Men and Women" (190).
(See also play 90.)
    Preparing for death not only may soften the final
shock but may enhance the life remaining. So Gemma and
Rupert, at the deaths of others, take stock of their
lives and resolve to share them more intimately, in
Hortense Calisher's novel *Age* (47). The Jewish
father-in-law arranges his estate in Peter Harris's
tender poem "My Father-in-Law's Contract" (124). (See
also novel 59.) Deathbed review, as a kind of summing
up, also prepares for the last moment, as in William
Carlos Williams' poem "The Last Words of My English
Grandmother" (194). (See also poem 182 and stories 310
and 315.)
    The need for some final contact with a key life ex-
perience is explained by Loren Eiseley in his memoir
"The Brown Wasp," in which he recalls the vivifying
example of a cottonwood sapling he had planted in
boyhood (18). Human contact at the end is needed by the
old father who is fortified by the presence of two
faithful servants in his last months, in Arturo
Vivante's story "The Bell" (339). In contrast is the
awful isolation of those who face death alone, as the
old starving woman must in Gina Gerriault's story "The
Diary of K. W." (220). (See also poems 112 and 119.)
    Death prompts the survivor to a special expression
of love. In this way the mortician Phil O'Dowd prepares
the body of his lifelong friend for burial, in Susan
Dodd's story "Bifocals" (237). The death of a bodily
repulsive grandmother opens up Maud's old vision of her
as loving Gramma, in Gwendolyn Brooks' story "Death of
a Grandmother" (225). At long recall, the death of the
speaker's mother evokes an extended lament and appreciation in Michael Blumenthal's poem "Elegy for My Mother:
The Days" (97). (See also story 207.)
    The possible shortcomings of health-care people in
dealing with death are suggested by the hospital staff
in Doris Lessing's novel *The Diary of a Good Neighbour*
(56). (See also story 225.)
    What might be called a sacrificial death comes as

Max Fried fatally risks his weak heart in the search for the runaway Alison in Lynn Schwartz's novel *Balancing Acts* (67).   Death in various aspects and reactions is the subject of Michael Cristofer's play *The Shadow Box* (79).

Part Two

ANNOTATIONS OF LITERARY WORKS

Anthologies

[Entries 1-12. Anthologies are listed in chronological order.]

1. *Middle Age, Old Age: Short Stories, Poems, Plays, and Essays on Aging.* Edited by Ruth Granetz Lyell. New York: Harcourt Brace Jovanovich, 1980, 390 pp.

An early anthology in this field but one of the most wide-ranging, Lyell's collection includes some seventy-five literary pieces: a score of short stories (with some folk tales), two-score poems, one play, and a half-dozen essays. Ruth Lyell, who has taught the psychology of aging, has also studied gerontology and draws upon it in the documented essays which introduce each of the seven sections. She is particularly concerned to get beyond the narrow view that the aging process of our time and culture holds true for all times and societies. Therefore she has drawn literary works from such cultures and periods as Biblical, Classical Greece and Rome, ancient and modern China and Japan, Renaissance, Arabic, Russia, India, modern France, Britain, and, of course, the United States. Middle age is also represented by a few pieces but not in an isolated way; it is seen as presenting some of the same challenges and difficulties that confront the later years. The length of selection ranges from extended--as for the whole two acts of Robert Anderson's *I Never Sang for My Father*--to brief poems and some excerpts. The seven sections bear these titles: Generational Relationships; Disappointment, The Life Review, and Unresolved Conflicts; Old Age as Wisdom and Peace; Loss; Dying and Death; Alone and with Peers; The Life Cycle. The decades after the 1950s are thinly represented. In other respects, Middle Age, Old Age may be said to set a high standard for such collections. A new edition should be looked for.

2. *Women and Aging: An Anthology by Women.* Edited by Jo
Alexander and others. Corvallis, Oreg: Calyx Bks, 1986,
262 pp.

This avowedly feminist collection opposes ageism,
especially as intensified for old women by sexism. It
will enlighten those who have supposed ageism to mean
the same thing for both sexes. It is comprehensive in
genre: essays, photographs, stories, journals, poems,
profiles, reviews, art works. Some hundred pieces are
here--a feature presumably expressing variety and the
gathered force of many voices. The writers, all American, with some exception do not have major literary
reputations, although many have published. They include
some amateurs and many who have credentials as teachers,
media workers, artists. An extensive bibliography lists
literary works about women and aging, as well as peri-
odicals, organizations, and art.

3. *When I Am an Old Woman I Shall Wear Purple: An Anthology of Short Stories and Poetry.* Edited by Sandra
Martz. Manhattan Beach, Calif.: Papier-Maché Press,
1987, 200 pp.

Like *Women and Aging,* this collection concentrates
on the female experience of aging. But it lacks the
militant tone of that volume; it includes eight contributions by men. Several pieces, including the title
poem, are delightfully light-hearted. Some fifty poems
are here, a dozen pieces of fiction, and a dozen photographs. As with *Women and Aging,* the contributors are
Americans not widely known to the general public, although many have published. Most have credentials as
writers, teachers, media workers, artists. No preface
or bibliography is provided.

4. *Full Measure: Modern Short Stories on Aging.* Edited
by Dorothy Sennett. Foreword by Carol Bly. St. Paul,
Minn.: Graywolf, 1988, 399 pp.

These twenty-three stories, published 1945-1985,
concentrate on recent and contemporary American and
British writers. Many are of preeminent literary reputation, for examples: Saul Bellow, John Cheever, Bernard
Malamud, Joyce Carol Oates. In her preface Dorothy
Sennett states that she wants the older people of these
stories "to be of our time. . . and yet to reveal
themselves . . . in all their extraordinary differences." Some stories deal with dying. Many deal with the
"renewal" by which older people survive. We variously
survive, Sennett suggests, through attachment to living
things, attachment to places, attachment to the things
we loved in the past, in the connectedness of generations, in those we love profoundly. The volume itself

eludes any special ordering; each of its five sections shows a range of theme and mood.

5. *Songs of Experience: An Anthology of Literature on Growing Old*. Edited by Margaret Fowler and Priscilla McCutcheon. Foreward by Robert Butler. New York: Ballantine, 1991, 379 pp.

An unusual range of genres distinguishes these sixty-odd pieces, which add journals, letters, interviews, essays, biographical and autobiographical sketches to the expected stories, poems, and novel excerpts. (Drama is not represented.) The overall emphasis is American, late 20th-century, and sensibly optimistic: "We wished to balance commonly held narrow definitions by concentrating on the positive, fulfilling, and rewarding prospects of aging." The eight sections explore such themes as what it means to age; the pleasures of freedom, contributing, loving, choosing, remembering; the acceptance of death. Except for the stories, most selections are brief. Most are by authors of established fame. Bibliography of contributions. No index. Both editors have worked closely with the National Council on the Aging.

6. *Trials, Tribulations, and Celebrations: African-American Perspectives on Health, Illness, Aging, and Loss*. Edited by Marian Gray Secundy with Lois LaCivita Nixon. Yarmouth, Maine: Intercultural Press, 1991, 308 pp.

The African-American experience of aging and death appears in roughly one-third of the fifty-odd poems, stories, autobiographical pieces, and novel excerpts of this anthology. Also presented are issues of health and bereavement. The stated aim of the editors is "to help those who provide care for black Americans to understand something of the experience of illness as it is shaped by African-American culture." An ample textbook apparatus implements this aim: introductory essays, section introductions, discussion questions for each of the three sections--Illness and Health-Seeking Behavior; Aging; Loss and Grief. Although the editorial guidance comes mainly from health care professionals, the authors carry solid literary credentials and include such well-known writers as Maya Angelou, Langston Hughes, James Weldon Johnson, Paule Marshall, Alice Walker. The collection can be valuable not only for health care professionals but for gerontologists and general readers both African-American and other. Notes on authors. Permissions. No bibliography or index.

7. *Vital Signs: International Stories on Aging*. Edited by Dorothy Sennett with Anne Czarniecki. Introduction

by Robertson Davies. St. Paul, Minn.: Graywolf, 1991,
230 pp.
     True to its subtitle, this collection includes 21
short stories, each from a different nation or culture.
They are grouped more or less geographically: I: Africa; II: U. S. minorities; III: East; IV: Middle East;
V: British; VI: European; VII: Caribbean and South America. At least in translated version, all stories date
from the 1960s or later. Headnotes identify the authors. A fine essay by the Canadian author Robertson
Davies heads the volume. The editor has furnished a
brief preface. No index. The present volume can serve
as a corrective to an America-centered view of aging.
It is a sequel to *Full Measure: Modern Short Stories on
Aging* (1988), also edited by Sennett, which concentrated
on American and British authors.

8. *The Art of Growing Older: Writers on Living and
Aging*.   Edited by Wayne Booth.   New York: Poseidon
Press, 1992, 349 pp.
     Here is not so much a collection as an eloquently
guided tour of over 200 pieces, most of them short,
often excerpted.   Its author, a well-known literary
scholar and cultural critic, has written an extended
personal essay, working from the challenge of aging
("Introduction: Feeling Older") through its darker side
("Part I: Facing the Facts: Losses, Fears, Lamenta-
tions") to its "Cures, Consolations, Celebrations" (Part
II), to end with an unmediated thirty-six-page anthology, mostly poems ("Part III: A Further Harvest").   Besides poems, the main text draws from the *Bible*, hymns,
diaries, letters, conversations, essays.   His writers
include gerontologists, statesmen, ordinary folk: these
from many countries and cultures from ancient Egypt and
China to the contemporary.   Booth, himself in the
seventies, favors authors who themselves have reached
the late years, but also considers reflections by the
young. An appendix lists ten books which "provide lists
of books about aging."

9. *Literature and Aging: An Anthology*.   Edited by Martin Kohn, Carol Donley, and Delese Wear.   Kent, Ohio:
Kent State Univ. Press, 1992, 434 pp.
     A remarkable feature of this collection is that
its   editors   combine   literary   and   medical   cre-
dentials--auspiciously for users who will come from both
fields. Its sixty-one pieces include twenty-seven short
stories, thirty poems, and four plays (a neglected genre
which invites active participation). Primarily modern
American writers were chosen to "represent the American
experience and vision of aging."   Two-thirds of the
pieces come from sources dated 1960 or later; and a

half-dozen come from outside the United States (Canada, Great Britain, Ireland, Russia). The authors range from famous literary figures to medical practitioners: again, an unusual feature. Organized by "concentric circles," the anthology starts with the individual search for identity (Part I), then moves outward to the family in its various forms (II), then to the community (III). Since the editors want the readers to experience these works directly and without mediation, commentary is limited to brief essays heading each section; but a reader's and instructor's guide is available. An appendix thumbnails the authors; another identifies sources; the index lists titles and authors. Of special interest is the sponsorship of this volume by the recently formed Center for Literature, Medicine and the Health Care Professions, a cooperative project of the Northeastern Ohio Universities College of Medicine and Hiram College.

10. *In the Midst of Winter: Selections from the Literature of Mourning.* Edited by Mary Jane Moffat. New York: Random House, 1982. Reprint, New York: Vintage Books, 1992, 274 pp.

Since bereavement comes to all ages, the old and their loved ones will find many voices in this volume, which includes over 160 selections. Some are only a few lines long, some are excerpts, all are short; but the resulting range is formidable. Nearly every culture and historical period is represented. The genres include short stories (four), poems, memoirs, journals, essays. An eloquent introduction evaluates the depth and variety of grief experiences, and using the analogy of nature's seasons, organizes the contents from shock (winter) through depression and groping (spring) to acceptance, wisdom, and readiness for one's own death (summer and autumn). Headnotes furnish occasional brief preparations. Table of contents has many helpful sub-headings. No index. The editor herself is a widow after "a long and contented marriage."

11. *Love in Full Bloom.* Edited by Margaret Fowler and Priscilla McCutcheon. New York: Ballantine, 1993, 381 pp.

"Love in old age is as varied, deep, and passionate as at any other time of life." Thus the editors announce the thesis for these sixteen stories. Love in old age is more possible than formerly, thanks to longer life-span and changing values. Based less on physical and economic appeal, such love can build on much more diverse assets. It brings both fulfillment and sorrow, both sexual and platonic affection. Published from 1956 through 1990, the stories range through many cultures:

American, Chinese-American, African-American, Jewish, Polish, Italian, British, Indian. The editors had previously entered the field of aging in literature through their 1991 anthology, *Songs of Experience*.

12. *The Oxford Book of Aging*. Edited by Thomas R. Cole and Mary G. Winkler. New York: Oxford Univ. Press, 1994, 419 pp.

Some two hundred and fifty pieces range through history and across globe and cultures. Concentrating on the traditional literary genres of fiction, poetry, and drama, this collection also includes religious and philosophical writings, interviews, diaries, essays, scientific and medical writings. To attain such breadth, much has been excerpted although poems and short stories remain largely intact. The introduction and chapter headnotes offer by themselves a coherent and illuminating view of the complexities of aging today. The nine chapters in turn consider aging as a journey, as change, as relating to youth, as solitude, as creative, as linking love and death, as linking celebration and lament, as related to spirit, and as the focus of remembrance. Credits and author index. Author of *The Journey of Life: A Cultural History of Aging in America*, Thomas Cole is also an editor of the newsletter *Aging and the Human Spirit*, and Graduate Program Director at the Institute for the Medical Humanities. Mary Winkler is Associate Graduate Program Director at that Institute.

Autobiographies

[Entries 13-34.]

13. Beauvoir, Simone de. *A Very Easy Death*. Translated by Patrick O'Brian. London: Deutsch, Weidenfeld, & Nicolson, 1966, 106 pp.

The emotional and psychological toll exacted upon adult children in their role as caregivers is revealed in this graphic record of the suffering and eventual death of Beauvoir's mother after her diagnosis of cancer. Beauvoir analyzes the contradictions that were the essence of her mother's character, reflects upon the ambivalence of their mother-daughter relationship, and examines the tensions that resulted from sharing the responsibilities of caregiving with her sister. The irony of the title is felt as Beauvoir captures the full range of her mother's response to her illness: fear, anger, denial, uncertainty, defiance, courage, loneliness, acceptance. The daughters were appalled at the magnitude of their mother's suffering. But they were impressed by their mother's unyielding courage in the face of unbearable pain and heartened each time she survived a crisis. TOPICS: Parent-Child Bonds, Caregiving, Disease, Doctor-Patient Conflicts, Endurance, Death.

14. Berman, Philip, and Goldman, Connie, Eds. *The Ageless Spirit*. New York: Ballantine Books, 1992, 282 pp.

Aging and the creative spirit is the major theme of this collection of more than forty interviews, based on Goldman's National Public Radio series, "I'm Too Busy to Talk Now: Conversations with Creative People over Seventy." Most of the old people interviewed are creative artists or performers. Some are well-known, such as Steve Allen, Norman Cousins, Hugh Downs, Maggie Kuhn,

Art Linkletter, May Sarton, Jessica Tandy, and Studs
Terkel. Others are known in their specific fields of
journalism, counseling, history, art, music, and enter-
tainment. These older adults consider aging a time for
identifying new goals, meeting new challenges, overcoming the setbacks of emotional and physical losses, resisting the ageism inflicted upon the old, ridding themselves of a reliance on materialism, maintaining a sense
of humor, and exploring the relationships between the
mind and body. They value experience, work, friendships,
wisdom. Their accounts accent the positive aspects of
aging. Several emphasize courage--also curiosity, affection, adaptation, and a strong self-image. TOPICS:
Stereotypes, Activity, Wisdom, Creativity, Courage,
Retirement, Goals.

15. Blythe, Ronald. *The View in Winter: Reflections on
Old Age*. New York: Penguin, 1979, 270 pp.
    Old age in myriad aspects is recorded by some
forty voices in this oral history done in England in the
1970s. The present and former vocations of the partici-
pants range across the population: mining, soldiering,
farming, homekeeping, medicine, teaching, ministry, and
gentry. Special attention goes to rural aging, to relationships between old and young, to old people's
homes, to the sense of being left behind by history, and
the testimonies of religious people. Blythe's own informed and compassionate but unsentimental commentary
enlightens these interviews. TOPICS: Rural Aging, Intergenerational, Long-term Care, Alienation, Spiritual
Life.

16. Broyard, Anatole. *Intoxicated by My Illness*. Edited
by A. Broyard. New York: Clarkson Potter, 1992, 135 pp.
    Broyard conveys an intense idea of what dying is like
from the inside, in this personal account of his own
terminal illness from cancer. Writing in early old age
after a brilliant career as writer and editor, he illuminates his own experience with illustrations from numerous authors, doctors, and gerontologists. Though he
eloquently describes many false ways of dying and of
tending the dying, he urges that the patient die engaged
in some creative project--in his case, writing the present book "to make sure I'll be alive when I die." Or
as he puts it elsewhere: "Inside every patient there's
a poet trying to get out." Broyard does not attempt a
systematic program for dying. Instead, he comes up with
insights and suggestions on nearly every page. The title
work is followed by an essay, "The Patient Examines the
Doctor." Another essay, "Toward a Literature of Illness," evaluates literary works which describe critical
illness. The death of his own father some forty years

earlier is movingly described by Broyard's "What the Cystoscope Said." TOPICS: Disease, Doctor-Patient Conflicts, Death.

17. Delany, Sarah, and Elizabeth Delany, with Amy Hill Hearth. *Having Our Say: The Delany Sisters' First 100 Years.* New York: Kodansha International, 1993, 210 pp.
     In this oral history two black women, 101 and 103 years old, reveal their individuality of character and their strong values, nurtured by strong family ties, which enabled them to surmount obstacles of racism and sexism and make a meaningful contribution to society. Their father, born into slavery, was educated at a mission school and became the nation's first elected black Episcopal bishop. Sarah and Elizabeth (known as Sadie and Bessie) never married. They were educated at Columbia University, and they dedicated their lives to their respective professions--teaching and dentistry. Each chapter, introduced by Hearth, provides an historical context for the women's experiences and then chronicles a different era in their lives. Each woman "has her say" in alternating chapters, often commenting on the same topic or shared experience. Through their stories the idiosyncracies and complementary natures of their characters are revealed. Bessie is openly defiant in the face of injustice; Sadie advocates compromise and political expediency. TOPICS: Race, Gender: Women, Parent-Child Bonds, Wisdom, Endurance, Life Review.

18. Eiseley, Loren. "The Brown Wasp." *In The Night Country.* New York: Scribner, 1971. Also in Anthology 5, pp. 313-19.
     The dying may desire to die not in isolation but in some contact with the world of the living. So Eiseley observed in the down-and-out old men who clung to seats in a railway station just to belong, however weakly, to the bustling world of travelers. So he had also noticed old brown wasps clinging to their deserted hive before winter dropped them off. In related observations, Eiseley notes the power of certain memories to give meaning and direction in old age. In boyhood he had planted a cottonwood sapling at his Nebraska home. Ever afterward that tree remained in his memory as a symbol of growth and permanence. In old age he went home to find that tree. It was gone, but not its reality for him. TOPICS: Reminiscence, Death.

19. Ernaux, Annie. *A Woman's Story.* Translated by Tanya Leslie. New York: Quartet, 1990, 92 pp.
     An unusual form of life review is the remembering of one's parent: here, the author's description of her mother, who died of Alzheimer's. Though Ernaux deals

touchingly and powerfully with her mother's last years,
she truly focuses on the whole life--the French village
background; the struggle to adulthood in a pinched,
deeply conventional community; the extraordinary force
of the mother's determination to rise into greater re-
spectability as shopkeeper; the vinegary affection between parent and child; the gentle unforceful father;
the later years of visiting and living with her educated
daughter; and of course the grim descent into dementia.
The full meaning of Ernaux's account is suggested in her
own words: "I believe I am writing about my mother because it is my turn to bring her into the world."
TOPICS: Parent-Child Bonds, Dementia, Life Review.

20. Hall, Donald. *String Too Short to be Saved.* 1961.
Reprint, Boston: Nonpareil Books, 1988, 188 pp.
     The nourishing role of grandparents in a teen-
ager's development is highlighted in this affectionate
memoir of summers the author spent on his grandparents'
farm in New Hampshire in the mid 1940s. A feeling of
nostalgia pervades this recreation of a gentle world
dominated by the values of education, honesty, frugality, self-sufficiency, pride in workmanship, tolerance,
being a good neighbor. Hall characterizes his grandfather, Wesley Wells, as a role model and mentor. The old
man's work ethic, his creativity and storytelling, his
pride in the farm and in his family all contributed to
the impact he had on his only grandson. Hall recreates
the high points of these summers: the experience of solitude, the blueberry picking, the haying, the rural
characters his grandparents knew, and the affectionate
bantering between his grandparents. The memoir includes
a final chapter written four years after Hall and his
wife took up residence in his grandparents' home.
TOPICS: Rural Aging, Grandparenting, Activity, Creativity, Mentoring, Life Review.

21. Honel, Rosalie Walsh. (1988). *Journey with Grandpa:
Our Family's Struggle with Alzheimer's Disease.*
Baltimore: The Johns Hopkins University Press, 243 pp.
     "Becoming a caretaker of a person with Alzheimer's
disease is a devastating experience. I believe, however, that it is within the power of the human spirit to
draw from that experience something good, something of
beauty..." So Rosalie Honel closes the account of her
family's seven-year trial with "Grandpa," her father-in-
law. A Czech immigrant, Grandpa had lived a good life in
factory work lightened by Bohemian dancing and singing,
until his disorientation brought him into the family's
home. His deepening disabilities are unflinchingly described: problems in eating, bathing, toilet, sleep,
hyperactivity, refractory behavior, wandering--all this

to the point where he seemed not a parent but a
two-year-old baby. The Honels and their six children
all found ways of coping, sometimes with anger, often
with affection. They learned what Grandpa could enjoy.
They learned to talk with each other about him. They
also learned to keep growing in their own lives. For
Rosalie this growth took place through her Catholic religion, her participation in such agencies as the
Alzheimer's Disease and Related Disorders Association,
and her writing. TOPICS: Housing, Family Bonds, Family
Conflicts, Caregiving, Dementia, Endurance, Religion.

22. Jenkins, Michael. *A House in Flanders*. London: New
York: Viking Press, 1993, 159 pp.
        The authority and wisdom of an elderly aunt is the
focus of this memoir about a boy's summer spent with
five eccentric aunts and uncles at the family estate in
Northern France after World War II. The eldest in the
family is the impressive Tante Yvonne, titular head of
the household, who held the family together after the
parents died when she was twenty. In her old age she devotes herself to the family's interests and resolves all
interpersonal conflicts. Tante Yvonne is the boy's mentor and guide. She blends wisdom with grace and a
deep-seated affection for her home and family. She even
shares some family secrets with the boy. Other residents of the house include Tante Yvonne's brother, two
sister-in-laws, and two of Tante Yvonne's younger sisters. The family has known tragedy: one of the younger
brothers died in World War I, and another died ten years
later. Now the estate is the center of their comfortable and circumscribed society, a place where propriety
and the social graces reign. The house was occupied by
Germans in World War II, but it survived because of
Tante Yvonne's courage and wiles. Before Tante Yvonne
dies, she makes plans for a granddaughter to become the
new head of the household. TOPICS: Roles, Culture, Gender: Women, Family Bonds, Wisdom, Aging in Place.

23. Kidder, Tracy. *Old Friends*. Boston: Houghton
Mifflin, 1993, 352 pp.
        What daily life is like for residents in a nursing
home is carefully observed and sensitively rendered in
the lives of two men, Lou and Joe, 90 and 72, roommates
in Linda Manor, a facility near Northampton, Massachu-
setts. One is recently widowed after a marriage of
seventy years, and the other suffered a stroke twenty
years earlier and now suffers from diabetes. Early in
their relationship the men appear to be a classic "odd
couple," with dissimilar tastes, attitudes, and social
and cultural backgrounds. At first Joe dreads living
with someone as "old" as Lou. But through their interac-

tion with the other residents and with each other Lou
and Joe become close friends and form a mutual support
system. Kidder also introduces a gallery of characters
who interact with Lou and Joe. The "nudnicks," is the
name residents give to those who suffer from dementias.
Other characters include a resident who leads other
residents in dramatic and musical performances and a
resident who has difficulty adjusting to life in a nursing home and dies a short time after entering Linda
Manor. TOPICS: Gender: Men, Friendship, Community, Dementia, Long-term Care, Alienation, Leisure.

24. King, Larry L. "The Old Man." *In "The Old Man" and
Lesser Mortals.* New York: Viking, 1974, pp. 4-30.
     How much the younger generation is bound to the
older generation by shared values, shared experiences,
and love based on family ties is the subject of this
memoir, written after the author's father died at the
age of 82. As a teenager, King felt constrained by the
barriers between father and son. Now middle-aged, he
acknowledges how much he has come to know and respect
his father over the years. He recalls a weeklong trip
to the Alamo and the State Capitol in Austin, taken a
few months before his father died. The old man had
proved to be a wide-eyed tourist, quick to engage in
conversation with strangers. The old man reminisced
about his childhood, his work experiences, and his
courtship of his wife. Father and son enjoyed each other's company. The trip affirmed the strong bonds between father and son based upon their resolution of
generational differences. TOPICS: Rural Aging, Parent-
Child Bonds, Leisure, Legacies.

25. Koch, Kenneth. *I Never Told Anybody: Teaching Poetry
Writing in a Nursing Home.* New York: Vintage, 1978, 259
pp.
     The twenty-five nursing home residents who were
students in Koch's poetry writing class reveal a willingness to confront ambivalent feelings and speak openly
about significant personal experiences through their
poetry. An accomplished poet, Koch taught the class in
1976 in New York City. When the older adults discovered
they could actually write poetry, they gained in self-
confidence and learned to analyze each other's work and
to respond to a diversity of topics. Koch learned that
some of his stereotypes about old people were inappro-
priate. His students were not preoccupied with nostalgia, and they had not lost touch with the intensity of
their emotional lives. The book is divided into two
parts: Koch's overview of the class and a summary of
eighteen lesson plans. He organized classes around topics, such as colors, music, touch, seasons, and compari-

sons. Some of the assignments: writing about quiet times, talking to the moon and stars, simultaneous events, and "I never told anybody" (self-disclosure). The latter section includes numerous student poems. The creativity, imagination, humor, and insight of the old is amply documented. TOPICS: Stereotypes, Community, Long-term Care, Creativity, Leisure, Life Review.

26. Konek, Carol Wolfe. *Daddyboy: A Memoir*. St. Paul, Minn.: Graywolf Press, 1991, 161 pp.
   A brilliant father's descent into Alzheimer's disease is chronicled by the daughter who had both loved and hated him. Leonard Wolfe, who ran the family car business, has been a fanatic for science and mathematics, a political radical, a freethinker, who pressed his daughter Carol (the author) to share these values. He made her, as a teenager, read Darwin, Freud, Marx. He has opposed her dating, her marriage to a Catholic, her choosing literature over science. He wanted her to be man-like, not weak and womanly. Carol has resisted, fought back, become her own person through she remains centered on this extraordinary man. What makes this account especially unusual is its linking the disease to the whole life of the man and his family. The mother's ordeal is clearly shown--especially the tragedy of her being swindled by con men (a danger to which the desperate members of an Alzheimer's family seem vulnerable). The account is also solid in medical detail, since the daughter, a disciplined professor, records the discussions of neurologists, nurses, sanitorium staff, Alzheimer's support groups. At the same time Carol's personal account is enriched with dreams, memories, scenes going back to infancy. TOPICS: Economics, Gender: Women, Parent-Child Bonds, Parent-Child Conflicts, Dementia, Long-term care, Transmission of values.

27. Lax, Eric. "The Death of My Father." In *Atlantic* 242 (1978): 75-78.
   This memoir, written by Lax after his father's death from cancer, reveals his father as a humorous, loving man who integrated the values of tolerance, compassion, and faith into the fabric of his life and passed those values on to his son. Jack Lax, an Episcopal minister, was also a practical joker who thrived on social interaction. The son writes, "He was funny and warm and does not seem to have burdened me with much of the excess baggage parents sometimes heap on their children." As his father's physical condition worsens, Lax records intimate moments between father and son. These interactions allow the two to speak honestly about their feelings for each other without becoming sentimental. Even Lax's description of the funeral reflects the

sense of completeness and resolution that was the hall-
mark of his father's life. TOPICS: Parent-Child Bonds,
Disease, Doctor-Patient Conflicts, Religion, Death.

28. Olmstead, Alan H. *Threshold: The First Days of
Retirement*. New York: Harper, 1975, 399 pp.
    The first shocks and some of the opportunities of re-
tirement are documented in this journal of the first
half-year of retirement, kept by a New England editor.
Olmstead works his way through the anxiety of not being
vocationally needed and not feeling financially secure
to the satisfactions of watching nature, of reminiscing,
of enjoying friends, and of acquiring a new independence. He learns the great retirement sin "of filling
the day more and more easily with less and less." He
joins his wife in housework. He tackles household maintenance. He takes new looks at his former career, at
patriotism, at war and peace. This book is not a profound analysis of aging but a personal account by a decent and observant person who finds retirement a new
country to explore. TOPICS: Friendship, Anxiety, Leisure, Retirement, Life Review.

29. Roth, Philip. *Patrimony: A True Story*. New York:
Simon & Schuster, 1991, 238 pp.
        Roth's memoir, a record of a son's caregiving re-
lationship with his cancer-stricken father, examines
some of the contradictions, frustrations, and ambivalent feelings inherent in familial caregiving relationships. Roth's experience as a caregiver begins
shortly after his mother dies in 1981. When he realizes
that his father's grief is affecting his emotional
well-being, Philip intervenes. Spurred by his son's
care, Herman Roth begins to adjust to his widowhood. But
seven years after the death of his wife, Herman is di-
agnosed as having a cancer. Now he faces a crucial decision: should he at the age of 86 undergo an operation,
which is likely to be successful, and yet will re-quire
a lengthy and difficult convalescence? Philip helps his
father gather information, supports his father's decision not to have the operation, and acts as a primary
caregiver when his father's condition worsens. Before
his father dies Roth gains insights into his
patrimony--his inheritance of the personal, familial,
cultural, and religious qualities that characterize his
father. In doing so, he gains insights into his Jewish
heritage and discovers a purpose in his activities that
transcends the stresses and burdens of caregiving.
TOPICS: Ethnicity, Parent-Child Bonds, Parent-Child Conflicts, Caregiving, Disease, Doctor-Patient Conflicts,
Legacies.

30. Sarton, May. *After the Stroke*. New York: Norton, 1988, 280 pp.

The author's recovery from a stroke is chronicled in her journal. Sarton suffered the stroke in February, 1986, when she 74, and began the journal (her seventh) two months later. Although the stroke does not leave her permanently disabled, Sarton--who lives alone--finds her recovery slow and often exasperating. She suffers recurring pains from a fibrillating heart, severe discomfort from medications to prevent another stroke, and long periods of loneliness and anxiety. She finds solace in her pets and the many friends who visit, bring food and flowers, or help with the house and garden. She is hospitalized three times between May and August. During her last hospitalization she rages at the staff and her doctors for their impersonality and inattentiveness. But after she returns home she is revived by a change in medication and resumes active and creative pursuits: she begins to write poems again, finds joy in Mozart, plans several poetry readings, and visits friends. She is her former self--not the "old" person she was when disabled by the stroke. She resumes her many correspondences. Her journal provides numerous insights into the strength and endurance required of an older person facing chronic pain. Sarton ends her journal on the one-year anniversary of her stroke. TOPICS: Friendship, Disability, Doctor-Patient Conflicts, Creativity, Loneliness, Aging in Place, Loss.

31. Sarton, May. *At Seventy: A Journal*. New York: Norton, 1984, 335 pp.

Spanning her seventieth year, beginning in 1982, Sarton's journal illustrates the ways in which she strives for a balance between her need for solitude and the stimulus of social contacts. To Sarton solitude is respite from the demands of her busy social calendar; it provides renewal of her personal energies, and fosters a context in which she completes her writing projects. In one entry she names the priorities in her life: "First friends, then work, then the garden." Sarton writes about her neighbors and friends as people who matter to her, not as people who relate to her only as a famous poet who gives numerous public readings. The journal often refers to mundane activities like shoveling a path through the snow to the bird feeder or taking her animals for walks. At 70 Sarton does not consider old age as part of her own experience. Her friends who are in their 80s and 90s represent old age to her. The deaths of two older friends are reminders of her mortality, but when she considers her own age, she concludes, "It is plain that I am not ready for old

age!" TOPICS: Gender: Women, Neighbors, Creativity, Employment, Leisure, Aging in Place.

32. Sarton, May.   *Endgame: A Journal of the Seventy
Ninth Year*.   New York: W. W. Norton, 1992, 347 pp.
    The indignities of chronic illness, frailty, lone-
liness, loss, and recurring bouts of depression dominate
a year in the life of a famous poet and journal writer.
Sarton chronicles her suffering from lung disease, severe diverticulitis, and a possible diagnosis of cancer.
She is hospitalized, progressively loses weight, and
finds little relief from her pain through medical interventions.   Sarton is distressed by her frailty; she
lacks the energy to work in her beloved garden, and she
tires after only an hour or two of creative activity.
She suffers several losses during the year: the deaths
of old friends and lovers, a diminishment of creativity,
a loss of independence and autonomy, and a loss of
identity--she feels that the May Sarton people have
known has become a stranger, someone "very old, wrinkled, and ill." She finds respite and renewal through
the unflagging assistance of many friends who run er-
rands for her, help maintain her beloved garden, and
provide an emotionally supportive network.   TOPICS:
Friendship, Frailty, Disease, Doctor-Patient Conflicts,
Creativity, Depression.

33. Taylor, Nick.   *A Necessary End*.   New York: Nan A.
Talese, 1994, 194 pp.
    The strain of eight years devoted to caregiving
for aging parents is recounted in this memoir by a
middle-aged son.   For many years Nick's parents live a
tranquil and fulfilling retirement in a small village in
Mexico.   The "days drift by," and their retirement is
golden. Inevitably the son, who lives in Atlanta, faces
the responsibilities of caregiving because of the
gradual physical and mental decline of his mother. Nick
wants to protect his parents and respond to all emergencies; yet he struggles to free himself from the excessive burdens of caregiving: the need to make snap de-
cisions regarding medical care in emergencies, to find
suitable living arrangements for parents with a low income and little savings, and to locate adequate health
care and long-term care services. Nick also becomes a
mediator between parents who are themselves responding
to new stresses in their relationship. Despite the difficulties associated with caregiving at a distance, Nick
maintains close ties to his parents and conveys his
close bonds with them.   His parents die months apart,
and Nick is with them either near or at the end of their
lives. TOPICS: Poverty, Housing, Parent-Child Bonds,
Caregiving, Frailty.

34. Vining, Elizabeth Gray. *Being Seventy: The Measure of a Year*. New York: Viking, 1978, 289 pp.

"An old lady who has a genuine joy in living is an old lady who draws people to her." This eloquent reflection is only one of many in this journal of an extraordinarily productive and happy year in the life of a sensitive and disciplined writer. Vining completes a major work of biography. She attends writers' meetings. She enjoys global friendships. She also lives a vigorous and varied inner life marked by curiosity, wry humor, religious thoughtfulness, and kindliness. A longtime widow, she happily remembers her marriage. Her observations of nature express an admirable contentment in simply *being*. She ends this year preparing, despite hesitations, to move into a retirement home. TOPICS: Long-term Care, Disengagement, Creativity, Religion.

Novels

[Entries 35-74.]

35. Absire, Alain. *Lazarus*. Translated by Barbara Bray.
New York: Harcourt Brace Jovanovich, 1988, 227 pp.
Originally published as *Lazare, ou, le grand sommeil*
(Paris: Calmann-Levy, 1985).

The horrors of immortality are realized in
Lazarus, the man raised from the grave by Jesus in the
New Testament miracle. "Long life" is not the same as
true living, as Lazarus learns through the decades of
his post-grave existence. Once a husky carpenter with
an ardent young wife, Lazarus now stinks of the grave;
his skin is corpse-like gray; he cannot make love or
sleep or even saw wood. Trying to discover the real
meaning of this miracle, he first seeks Jesus, only to
find him at the Crucifixion. He seeks out Jesus' dis-
ciples as well as Jair, the once-blind man whom Jesus
restored to sight. He wanders through the violent years
of Jewish unrest; the priestly tactics to crush the new
religion (seen as incitement to a disastrous uprising
against Rome); and finally, the Roman crushing of the
city. Lazarus has seen his young wife grow old and die,
as well as his old comrades. The novel ends bleakly as
this animated corpse finds that his "resurrection"
brought no joy nor, as far as he can see, significance.
TOPICS: Depression, Religion, Death.

36. Achebe, Chinua. *Things Fall Apart*. London:
Heinemann, 1958. Reprint, London: Everyman, 1992, 135
pp.

An African tribal chief, strong in traditional
values, vainly resists the cultural revolution which
threatens those values. Okonkwo is an aging but strong

Ibo leader who sees the white man taking over his tribal
culture. First the white missionaries enter to absorb
the marginal natives, then an occasional person of im-
portance. Any resistance is crushed by the armed might
of the nearby white government. At a climactic tribal
meeting to oppose the whites, a white messenger comes
with an order to disband. Okonkwo, enraged at the weak-
ening of his own people, single-handedly kills the messenger and then takes his own life. The time is presumably late 19th or early 20th century; the place is
Nigeria. Similar invasions by the surrounding culture
might be experienced in the United States by leaders of
conservative or ethnic values who feel threatened by
radical activism or by growing secularism. TOPICS: Role
Loss, Multicultural, Rebellion, Loss, Transmission of
Values.

37. Amis, Kingsley. *Ending Up.* New York: Harcourt Brace
Jovanovich, 1974, 176 pp.
       Mutual antagonisms, petty jealousies, boredom and
loneliness, physical and emotional disabilities, and
fears of dependency and death undermine a sense of community among a gallery of maladjusted older people whose
life together depends upon a shared past and shared
needs in the present. The five adults, all in their
70s, are residents of a remote cottage in rural England,
"far from a bad place to end up," as one of the characters muses. The cottage is owned by Bernard. Lacking affection and self-respect, Bernard delights in acts of
malicious mischief against everyone in the house. His
sister Adele, who never married, is in charge of the
household. Marigold, a widow and Adele's childhood
friend, is terrified at the first symptoms of her own
dementia. George, Bernard's brother-in-law, who recently
suffered a severe stroke which left him paralyzed and
aphasic, struggles to overcome his disability. Shorty
is a retired quartermaster, alcoholic, and Bernard's gay
lover from 35 years ago. Visits by Marigold's grandson
and family offer insights into the ageism and stereotypes of the younger generation. TOPICS: Ageism, Community, Caregiving, Enmity, Disability, Doctor-Patient
Conflicts, Isolation.

38. Amis, Kingsley. *The Old Devils.* London: Hutchinson,
1986. Reprint, New York: Summit Books, 1987, 294 pp.
       The extent to which petty jealousies, longstanding
disputes, and unresolved relationships persist into old
age is depicted in the adventures of a group of Welsh
married couples in their 60s who have known each other
for most of their lives. When two of their former
friends, Alun and Rhiannon Weaver, move back to Wales
after thirty-five years' residence in London, new jeal-

ousies and intrigues are added to this mix of relationships. These older adults are reluctant to face the
physical and psychological consequences of aging. The
women spend their days eating, drinking, and gossiping
at the houses of the other wives. The men withdraw daily
to the neighborhood pubs to seek solace in eating,
drinking, and gossiping. Alun is a writer and television
personality, the inheritor of the Welsh literary tradition. But his mean spirit and selfishness undermine
his popularity. When Alun dies suddenly at the end of
the novel, his wife completes final arrangements for the
marriage of their daughter and finds trust, affection,
and intimacy when she revisits an old friendship with
her son-in-law's father, a former lover. TOPICS: Adaptation, Gender: Men, Older Couples, Enmity, Leisure.

39. Anderson, Jessica. *Tirra Lirra By the River.* 1978.
Reprint, New York: Penguin, 1984, 141 pp.
     Through her life review an old woman relives sev-
eral deeply felt experiences that illuminate the
strengths of her character and provide a restorative
perspective on a life that has been lived primarily for
others. Nora Porteus, in her 70s, moves from London,
where she has lived most of her life, to take occupancy
of her mother's home 600 miles from Sydney, Australia.
Her memory brings to the surface unexpected, compelling
revelations about past feelings, relationships, and
griefs. Nora defines the stages of her life as periods
of "waiting": she married to escape her mother's control; she survived a bad marriage by working outside the
home and establishing a support group of coworkers; and
eventually she divorced. Nora's inward, psychological
journey is complemented by her outward, physical progress. Upon arrival she is bedridden, but with the aid
of neighbors and her doctor, Nora begins to establish
some familiarity with her environment and eventually
control over it. There are answers for Nora in these
physical and psychological journeys; some are tentative,
others more complete. Her story offers a refreshing view
of one character's movement toward insight and integration. TOPICS: Gender: Women, Community, Frailty,
Doctor-Patient Conflicts, Autonomy, Serenity.

40. Apple, Max. *Roommates: My Grandfather's Story.* New
York: Warner Bks, 1994, pp.
     A special intergenerational bond between a Jewish
immigrant and his grandson is the subject of this
memoir-like novel, inspired by the author's relationship
to his grandfather. When Herman Goodstein came to America in 1914, he worked sixteen-hour days in a bakery to
earn the money to bring his wife and two children to
America. Then his only son died in a car accident in

1936. Herman, nicknamed "Rocky" by his coworkers, became a defender of the family, a feisty and tenacious
father-figure; and he poured his energy into encouraging
and mentoring his grandson Max, the only surviving male
child in the family. Rocky became Max's "angry opinion-
ated fairy godmother/godfather." A devoted Jew, Rocky
hoped Max would become a rabbi but accepts grudgingly
the idea that Max wants to become a writer. When Max
goes to graduate school in the late 1960s, Rocky, 93,
joins him as his roommate. Rocky's strength and resourcefulness take a new emphasis in the middle section
of the book, as he supports Max's marriage to Debby, the
birth of their two children, and Debby's physical decline after contracting multiple sclerosis. At 103 he
is called upon to help Max raise his children and support Max in his efforts to care for Debby. Rocky dies
at 106 of natural causes. TOPICS: Stereotypes, Adaptation, Ethnicity, Family Bonds, Grandparenting, Rebellion, Autonomy.

41. Ariyoshi, Sawako. *The Twilight Years*. Translated
by Mildred Tahara. Tokyo: Kodansha International, 1984,
216 pp. Originally published as *Kkokotsu no hito* (Tokyo:
Shinchosha, 1972).
     The daughter's almost universal burden of care-
giving appears in this story of a Japanese woman's devotion to her demented father-in-law. Akiko, her husband
Nobutoshi, and their adolescent son live in Tokyo. When
Nobutoshi's mother dies suddenly, the couple discovers
that his father, Shigezo, is severely demented. Nobutoshi is repelled by his father's dementia and equates
his father's decline with the inevitability of the aging
process. He buries himself in his work. Although Akiko
works full-time and is in charge of all household tasks,
she accepts caregiving responsibilities as her duty and
strives to maintain his dignity and quality of life.
She takes Shigezo to a senior center daily. Details of
Shigezo's dementia are clearly presented, including his
limited verbal ability, bizarre behaviors (including
several episodes of wandering), and incontinence. Akiko
overcomes repeated crises, but when she seeks to place
him in a nursing home, she is frustrated at the shortage
of appropriate facilities. Eventually, Akiko accepts
the bond that has grown between the old man and herself.
Shigezo dies at home, and Akiko prepares his body for
the required Buddhist rites. The novel provides insights into Japanese societal and cultural attitudes
toward aging. TOPICS: Ageism, Housing, Culture, Gender:
Women, Parent-Child Bonds, Caregiving, Dementia.

42. Barker, Pat. *The Century's Daughter*. London: Virago,
1986. Reprint, New York: Ballantine, 1987, 293 pp.

The struggle of three generations of women to improve their chances for a good life and the power of intergenerational relationships to transcend the barriers
of age differences are primary themes in this novel.
Liza Jarrett, 84, born at the turn of the century, lives
an isolated existence in a run-down street in an urban
center north of London. Into her world comes Stephen,
a young social worker assigned to inform her that her
house will be torn down as part of an urban renewal project. At first Stephen views Liza from the perspective
of the detached professional. But soon her honesty, wry
humor, and insights into life win him over. Their
friendship offers resolutions for both characters: Liza
helps Stephen, who is gay, recover feelings of love toward his father after the latter's death; and Stephen
stimulates Liza to review her tragic life and recover
loving memories of the men in her life. Liza sends her
granddaughter to school as a means of helping the young
woman escape a life of poverty. TOPICS: Poverty, Urban
Aging, Gender: Women, Intergenerational, Grandparenting,
Aging in Place, Life Review.

43. Barker, Pat. *Union Street*. London: Virago, 1982.
Reprint, New York: Putnam, 1983, 265 pp.
The "stages" of a woman's life are represented in
the interlocking stories of women who live on Union
Street, a lower-class neighborhood in an industrial city
in the North of England. Each of the seven chapters
portrays the experiences of a woman older than the primary character in the previous chapter. The world of
this novel is a woman's world; and the women in it are
often trapped by poverty, by narrowly defined sex roles,
by physical limitations, and by children who have lost
a sense of filial piety. The old feel abandoned or displaced. But each chapter portrays the strength of character of the women, who either survive their personal
ordeals or gain some measure of dignity in the attempt.
The experiences of the younger women provide a context
for the crises that the older women face in later chapters. The interaction between an adolescent girl and an
old woman, featured in the opening and closing chapters,
is particularly significant. TOPICS: Poverty, Urban Aging, Gender: Women, Intergenerational, Coping, Aging in
Place.

44. Bausch, Richard. *The Last Good Time*. Garden City,
N.Y.: Dial Press, 1984, 227 pp.
Two lonely old widowers each has a "last good
time" in a loving relationship, though their lives are
generally bleak. Edward Cakes, a retired symphony vio-
linist in his seventies, has never enjoyed full love.
When a young woman stumbles into his flat looking for

the man who abandoned her, Edward befriends her, comes
to sleep with her and love her--only to discover that
she is hopelessly promiscuous and unable to return his
love. He then finds a minimal friendship with a gar-
rulous old woman who lives upstairs. His friend Arthur,
who is dying in a nursing home, finds comfort in fan-
tasizing about the "last good time" he had enjoyed with
a woman when both were about seventy. In this somber
novel the capacity for affection is what carries each
man through the deepening difficulties of their age.
TOPICS: Intimacy, Loneliness, Courage, Widowerhood.

45. Beresford-Howe, Constance. *The Book of Eve*.
Toronto: Macmillan of Canada, 1973, 170 pp.
   The break-up of a long marriage may signal the desperate desire of at least one partner to find a truer
life. Eva, the narrator, seventyish, simply packs up
and leaves her Montreal home one morning without ex-
planation or note. Her marriage has been loveless, de-
meaning, and has included one marital rape. She rents a
squalid basement apartment and begins her independent
life, supported by pension checks and whatever odd
treasures she stumbles upon in her "finding expeditions"
as bag lady. Eva is a former teacher who once aspired
to a Ph.D. Her observations and reminiscences are sensitive, often witty.   Besides occasional telephone
check-ins with her beloved son, Eva's main human contact
takes place with another lodger, John Horvath, a displaced Hungarian, a factory worker. Despite his being
some twenty years younger, John begins to fill her life.
He drinks; he is irresponsible; but he is humorous, generous, sexually warm, intelligent, and literate (having
been well-educated in his old country). In short, he
represents everything outside the barren conventional
existence she had known as a dominated wife. TOPICS:
Gender: Women, Older Couples, Intimacy, Autonomy.

46. Bernlef, J. *Out of Mind*. Translated by Adrienne
Dixon.   Boston: Godine, 1989, 150 pp. (Originally
published as *Hersenschimmen* (Amsterdam, Querido, 1984).
    The descent into severe and irreversible
dementia--one of the most terrifying physical conditions
associated with aging--is revealed in this first-person
account. What does a person experience when dementia begins to affect his mind?   What dignity is left an individual whose mind has deteriorated to the point that
he no longer recognizes his wife and no longer retains
the ability to function? Maarten Klein, 71, originally
from the Netherlands, lives in Gloucester, Massachu-
setts, with his wife of more than 40 years. Klein's
most vivid memories are associated with World War II.
Now in retirement, he begins to experience moments of

confusion and forgetfulness regarding simple tasks. Initially his wife and he rationalize these events as
slips of the mind or harmless miscues. But when his
mind deteriorates further, both face the reality of his
mental decline. Told from Maarten's point of view, the
experience of dementia is made personal and compelling.
He responds with horror at the inexorable decline of his
thought processes. His attempts to explain generate
haunting metaphors of the anxiety, fearfulness, and alienation felt by the sufferer. TOPICS: Older Couples,
Caregiving, Dementia, Anxiety.

47. Calisher, Hortense. *Age*. New York: Weidenfeld &
Nicolson, 1987, 121 pp.
        Gemma and Rupert, married and in their 70s, face
their old age with cautious hope and optimism. Gemma is
a retired architect, and Rupert is a poet. Both have
agreed to keep separate private journals in order to reflect upon their late years. In effect, the journal of
the one who dies first will be a gift to the surviving
spouse. Their alternating entries reveal two articulate, well-educated New Yorkers whose writing styles are
refined and rich with literary allusions. Their affection and capacity for sharing is evident in the
mutual give and take of their relationship, their
awareness of each other's nonverbal cues, their openness
and intimacy, and their concerns for each other's physical and emotional well-being. What they experience
they experience together--as a couple. Yet their individuality is expressed cogently through their separate
journal entries. In quick succession they experience
three sudden reminders of their own mortality. Rupert's
first wife, Gertrude, dies; two old friends commit suicide; and a close friend is admitted to a hospice.
Stunned by these events, Rupert and Gemma both take
stock of their lives and make plans for their future, no
matter how brief. They also decide to end their journals and share their narratives now, rather than holding
them until one has died. TOPICS: Older Couples, Creativity, Anxiety, Aspirations, Death.

48. Freeman, Judith. *Set for Life*. New York: Norton,
1991, 312 pp.
        A lonely Idaho grandfather receives a heart trans-
plant from a beloved teenage grandson, and must begin a
new life and a great bereavement at the same time. Phil
Doucet, a retired carpenter, seventyish, has enjoyed a
deep companionship with young Luke, killed in an auto
crash. Of his two adult daughters, Joyce has married
into a politically conservative family whose conservative political views he dislikes. Phil quarrels with
her as a result. He finds more consolation with Helen,

his other daughter, and with Leora, a cafe waitress and possible love interest. But the really new element in his life comes with a runaway sixteen-year-old, Louise, who has fled an abusive neo-Nazi stepfather and then fled from a truck driver she kept quarreling with. Phil takes her in temporarily but more and more permanently because Louise has nowhere else to turn. The girl is rough-edged, even hostile, but basically lost and lonely. Phil finally discovers that she can fill the void left by Luke. Though she is eventually placed in a Youth Ranch, Phil's heart has reopened to what lies ahead. Now he is "set for life." TOPICS: Economics, Parent-Child Bonds, Parent-Child Conflicts, Intergenerational, Doctor-Patient Conflicts, Serenity, Aging in place.

49. Gloag, Julian. *Only Yesterday*. New York: Henry Holt & Co, 1987, 170 pp.
     A middle-aged man's divorce leads to a renewal of bonds and insights across three generations of a family. Oliver Darley, a retired architect, and his wife May live alone in their London home, which is in disrepair. One day their son Rupert, who has left his second wife and his teaching job, turns up on their doorstep. The next day his daughter Miranda, a pre-med student, arrives for a planned visit. As the weekend unfolds, the members of this family learn to adapt to each other's needs and resolve some immediate and long-term personal crises. Although the new ideas of Rupert and Miranda often meet resistance and delay, the old couple gradually adapts to their helpful presence. Gloag captures the nuances and routines that have shaped the patterns of behavior of the old couple. Oliver is deftly portrayed as an old curmudgeon, often irascible, and frustrated with the physical losses associated with his aging. May is weary of Oliver's resistance to change, yet she remains devoted to him. TOPICS: Parent-Child Bonds, Older Couples, Grandparenting, Caregiving, Frailty, Mid-life.

50. Hemingway, Ernest. *The Old Man and the Sea*. New York: Scribner, 1952, 159 pp.
     Old age and hostile nature are the real opponents of a Cuban fisherman who pits his courage, endurance, and lifelong skill against a great marlin far out to sea. In the fisherman Santiago, Hemingway embodies a stoic outlook which has its share of poetry. Santiago feels comradeship with this great fish, with the wandering warbler bird, with the porpoises, even the stars. By the time he pulls the marlin to shore, the sharks have devoured all the fish but head and skeleton. The old man, both winner and loser, stumbles home to his shack and sleep. A softening element in Santiago's bleak old age

is the admiring affection of the young boy, Manolin, who takes almost parental care of his friend and who at the end vows to join Santiago as apprentice even though the old man's health may have broken. TOPICS: Intergenerational, Activity, Coping, Endurance, Spiritual Life.

51. Herman, Michelle. *Missing*. Columbus, Ohio: Ohio State Univ. Press, 1990, 146 pp.
    A lifetime of regrets and missed opportunities for closer family ties leaves an old woman lonely and embittered. Rivke, 89, has been a widow for two years. She is the matriarch of a large family. She has four sons and a daughter. She is happy to be a grandmother and a great-grandmother. But Rivke is not at peace with herself or with her family. She had felt rejected and unloved by her mother, and she, in turn, wasn't able to forgive her daughter Myra for her recurring bouts of anxiety and depression. She is convinced her children have made poor marriages and raised selfish and mean-spirited children. Of all her children and extended family, only her unmarried granddaughter Rachel, in her late 20s, is her favorite. Rachel is interested in the family's past, and she is Rivke's best friend and confidante. But their intergenerational bond is not sufficient to quell the fears, misgivings, and anxieties that plague Rivke's heart. Throughout her life review Rivke grieves for her husband, who anchored her life and completed her identity, and for her own grandmother, who was her mentor when Rivke was a child. Rivke is anxious about her increasing frailty, about her ability to live alone, and about her increasing remoteness from her family. TOPICS: Ethnicity, Family Conflicts, Frailty, Widowhood, Life Review.

52. Hürlimann, Thomas. *The Couple*. Translated by Edna McCown. 1989. Reprint, New York: Fromm International Pub., 1991, 135 pp. Originally published as *Das Gartenhaus* (Zurich: Ammann, 1989).
    How grief can alienate individuals from the support of others close to them is illustrated in this Swiss novel about an old couple's response to the death of their only son. The separateness of their grieving begins when Lucienne secures a granite monument for the grave. Her husband, a retired military officer, wanted a rose bush. Lucienne spends every day visiting the cemetery, grooming the grave, and cleaning the monument--for her a symbol of permanence set against the transitory nature of life. For his part, the Colonel finds a symbol that assuages his pain: he brings food each day for an emaciated wild cat which appears one day at the grave site. He channels all of his grief work toward the nurture of this animal, even though the cat

never allows him near enough to touch it. But he keeps
this activity a secret from Lucienne, and that secret
leads to a series of misunderstandings, suspicions, and
inevitably to fears on Lucienne's part that her husband
has gone mad. Gradually events from the past are revealed which provide clues for understanding the actions
of the couple. TOPICS: Older couples, Mental Health,
Alienation, Grief.

53. Ishiguro, Kazuo. *The Remains of the Day*. London:
Faber & Faber, 1989, 245 pp.
     A life review leading to a proud man's awareness
of a wasted life is the subject of this first-person account by an English butler in his 70s. Stevens has
served the aristocrat Lord Darlington from the 1920s to
the present 1950s. Now Darlington has died, and the new
owner of Darlington Hall, an American, directs Stevens
to take the Ford for a few days' relaxing tour of south-
western England. This journey, blended with Stevens'
reminiscences of his former glory under Lord Darlington,
is thus a journey into Stevens' own past. Stevens has
disciplined himself into becoming the ideal butler:
poised under pressure, uncritically loyal to Lord Darlington, robot-like in ignoring all personal claims.
What he comes to recognize is that he has served a Lord
Darlington who betrayed his country. He had also
thought to re-open ties with Miss Kenton, the former
housekeeper; he must now learn that he has lost a good
woman's love. Stevens ends his journey at seaside, his
pride broken, his heart cracking with grief, his one
faint hope that of pleasing his odd American employer.
TOPICS: Role Loss, Older Couples, Employment, Life
Review.

54. Laurence, Margaret. *The Stone Angel*. New York:
Knopf, 1964, 308 pp.
     Hagar Shipley, 90, facing a life-threatening can-
cer, reviews her life and gains some insight into how
much happiness and self-fulfillment she has lost because
of the unforgiving force of her character. Hagar lives
with her son and daughter-in-law, but there are few
bonds of affection between Hagar and her caregivers, and
their ministrations often fall short when they come up
against Hagar's abrasive character. Her life review begins with memories of growing up in a small Canadian
town. Her mother died giving birth to her, and that is
the source of the "stone angel," a monument to her
mother. Hagar married the man her father did not want
her to marry and raised two sons, one of whom could do
no wrong in her mind. Hagar is a well-individuated
character whose first-person narrative is at once honest, unyielding, and tragic. Her life review draws

readers into her most painful memory--the death of her
favorite son. Blinded by a possessive love, Hagar is
turned into "stone" by grief. TOPICS: Poverty, Gender:
Women, Parent-Child Conflicts, Caregiving, Enmity,
Doctor-Patient Conflicts, Alienation, Life Review.

55. Lawrence, Josephine. *The Web of Time*. New York:
Harcourt Brace, 1953, 304 pp.
     The retirement problems of an ordinary man are il-
lustrated by the forced retirement of Munsey Wills, 65,
a complaint-department clerk for a mail order house. In
no way is he fitted for this change. His job has been
his life. "If people want to work," he says, "seems to
me they ought to be allowed. 'Tisn't so much the
money--it's keeping busy at what you like to do." His
quiet suffering is intensified by the mistaken notion of
others that what he needs is either "Florida or a
hobby." In the following two years of painful idleness,
Munsey finds little better to do than stay out of his
wife's way and then to insist on adopting a dog. His
wife resents having to "retire" from housekeeping in
order to earn money; his daughter continues to make
selfish demands. At length Munsie finds part-time employment as a museum guard and recovers some balance of
spirit. Ultimately the novel stresses Munsey's failure
to live well and hence to age well. By using work as an
opiate, he has failed to explore the other possibilities
of life. TOPICS: Family Conflicts, Employment, Leisure,
Retirement.

56. Lessing, Doris [Jane Somers, pseud.]. *The Diary of
a Good Neighbour*. New York: Knopf, 1983, 253 pp.
     Few accounts of extreme old age can be as intense
or as carefully detailed as this "diary" of a fiftyish
woman's friendship with a 92-year-old recluse, Maudie
Fowler. Janna Somers, a glamorously successful London
editor in the 1970s, has heartlessly slid past the
deaths of husband and mother, as well as most human
claims upon her. One day she encounters Maudie in a
pharmacy and for some reason walks her home and begins
a curious, patient, caring relationship with the abrasive old woman. Through Janna one sees the incredible
filth of home and body in which needy old single persons
often live--their anger, their willful rejection of
help, their fear of losing independence. As Janna per-
sists, Maudie shows flashes of vinegary sweetness. She
blooms in telling of her bumpy life: its hardships,
pleasures, triumphs. Janna befriends other poor old
women. She sees what urban poverty is really like. She
learns what old people often want or fear. She sees why
the world ignores and dislikes the aged. When Maudie
goes to hospital to die, Janna learns how hospital

102 Annotations of Literary Works

staffs both fail and try to manage. TOPICS: Ageism,
Economics, Urban Aging, Friendship, Frailty, Doctor-
Patient Conflicts, Death.

57. Lester, Julius. *Do Lord Remember Me*.   New York:
Holt, Rinehart, & Winston, 1985, 210 pp.
     Reverend Joshua Smith, born in 1900, in fragile
health after a stroke, drafts his obituary and reviews
the events of his life. One of nine children, he grew
up in poverty in the South, experienced discrimination,
racism, and other forms of oppression, and yet devoted
his life to his family and to his ministry. He recalls
his father's despair over the deaths of all five daughters from childhood illnesses, his own estrangement from
his oldest brother, his taking on the responsibility for
his younger brothers after he is orphaned at the age of
16, his experiences as an African-American minister in
small churches throughout the South, and generational
conflicts with his two sons. Already an old man by the
time of the Civil Rights Era in the 1960s, Reverend
Smith was ignored by one of his sons and reviled by the
other as an "Uncle Tom." In time the conflicts between
his two sons and himself were partly resolved. Interactions between Reverend Smith and his wife, who have been
married 56 years, are portrayed with wit and humor.
TOPICS: Race, Parent-Child Conflicts, Older Couples,
Coping, Life Review, Religion.

58. Marshall, Paule. *Praisesong for the Widow*.   New
York: Putnam, 1983, 256 pp.
     An African-American widow discovers the most valu-
able part of herself--her identity as a descendant of
African peoples, and her resources and commitment as an
older woman who can affect the lives of future generations. In the middle of a Caribbean cruise Avey Johnson,
64, packs her bags, returns to the port on Granada, and
begins another journey, this one toward self-discovery.
In reviewing key events and relationships in her life,
Avey recalls how the pressure on her husband to be accepted by the white-dominated society cost him his emotional and physical well-being. She remembers childhood
visits to an island off the coast of South Carolina,
where her Aunt taught her about her own cultural and
spiritual roots as a descendant of slaves.   With a
remarkable 90-year-old man as her guide, Avey spends one
day on an excursion to a nearby smaller island with
"out-islanders," West Indian people who return each year
for a family reunion, celebration and cultural renewal.
Her experiences there lead to a reevaluation of her self
and a re-commitment to her race. TOPICS: Race, Multicultural, Leisure, Widowhood, Life Review, Religion.

59. McFarland, Dennis. *School for the Blind*.   Boston:
Houghton Mifflin, 1994, pp. 287.

Old people can live at many levels of consciousness: everyday awareness, daydream, reminiscence, hallu-
cination, unexpected flashback, association triggered by
mementoes. All are experienced by Francis Brimm, 73, a
former news photographer who has returned to his Florida
boyhood home to retire and, as it turns out, to die.
His career as the photographer of others has been an escape from himself which no longer works.   He keeps
"seeing" his World War II photograph of a young French
mother with head shaven for living with a German.   In
this and other flashes, he comes to understand himself
and his approaching death.   His sister Muriel, 78,
struggles past the memory of being violated in childhood
by a drunken father.   Through religion and friendship
she finds the balance missing in her life. A maverick
young woman, Deirdre, acts as servant and confidante for
both Brimms. Running quietly but ominously through the
novel is a double murder at the School for the Blind
where Muriel had served as librarian--an atrocity which
keeps troubling both Brimms.   This novel is complex,
sometimes bewildering but rich in passing insights.
TOPICS: Family bonds, Intergenerational, Caregiving, Employment, Life Review, Religion, Death.

60. Myers, Lou. *When Life Falls It Falls Upside Down*.
New York: Grove Weidenfeld, 1990, 193 pp.

The aging of an entire Yiddish community is reflected
in the narrator's account of his senile mother and her
past.   Their immigrant family had struggled in the New
York Bronx through the Twenties and the Depression.
After Pa's early death, "Ma" coped by taking in boarders
and selling dry goods and novelty jewelry.   Her sons
grew up in the rough world of street-fighting, odd jobs,
migrant labor, street entertainment--a hard, colorful,
voluble life shared by Yiddish, Italians, Irish.   This
life is seen in retrospect, sandwiched between chapters
showing Ma in her nineties in the Jewish Old Age Home.
Here is a gallery of disabilities and hallucinated fragments of the past. Death continually changes roommates.
Staff is kindly but overworked.   Paranoia infects the
residents, who fear thievery, invasion by "illegals,"
and even each other. But generosity and caring lighten
this darkness. Leon, the narrator, is an artist of humorous, sympathetic, and vivid awareness. TOPICS: Ethnicity, Dementia, Health Care, Life Review, Death.

61. Naipaul, V. S. *Mr. Stone and the Knights Companion*.
London: A. Deutsch, 1963, 159 pp.

The dark obscurity of white-collar retirement is
briefly postponed by Richard Stone, a London office

worker of no particular consequence. He comes up with
a brainstorm for using retirees to spread good will.
(These are to be known as the Knights Companion.) This
provides him with a brief burst of company celebrity.
He has also attracted the admiration of a neighboring
widow, fiftyish. They have married; the relationship
though congenial doesn't seem to deepen. Stone's high
point is reached at a company dinner party. Shortly
afterward, the company lets his idea drop, leaving Stone
stranded at the end of his modest career. Despite his
gloom, Stone finds a weary confidence that his own
serenity will return. TOPICS: Employment, Retirement.

62. O'Connor, Edwin. *I Was Dancing*. New York: Little,
Brown, 1964, 242 pp.
     A son resists his father's appealing but inaccu-
rate version of his life story and rids himself of the
old man, who has become an intruder in his son's house.
One year ago Daniel Considine, a former vaudevillian,
showed up on his son Tom's doorstep after not having
seen Tom for the last twenty years. Where has he been?
His only answer is, "I was dancing." Daniel is a master
of self-deception who dresses up the truth of his past
and ignores the fact that he left his wife when Tom was
a boy, returned only for his wife's funeral twenty years
ago, and then left his son again. Tom tries to make
peace with Daniel and restore their relationship. But
Daniel responds to his entreaties with an unrelenting
antagonism and enmity. Their clash is a reminder that
not all father-son conflicts can be resolved. This
father is a self-centered, vindictive old man who responded to family responsibilities with indifference and
neglect. TOPICS: Roles, Parent-Child Conflicts, Isolation, Deviance.

63. Owen, Howard. *Littlejohn*. New York, NY: Villard
Books, 1993, 230 pp.
     A North Carolina farmer decides to end his life
one day. At 82 Littlejohn McCain is driven by shame,
dark family secrets, and a fear of impending senility,
Littlejohn McCain, 82, a North Carolina farmer. Rather
than commit suicide, he settles on a curious plan to die
a "natural death"--by sitting all day in the hot August
sun. Most of the novel is his life review. His family
history reaches back to Civil War days. His childhood
was hard. He left school illiterate, and he only
learned to read and write when he was married at the age
of 40 and was tutored patiently and lovingly by his
wife. One event forever changed his life. When he was
sixteen he accidentally shot and killed his older
brother. Littlejohn spent his life trying to resolve
that incident. Now widowed, increasingly frail, and

suffering forgetfulness and blackouts. Littlejohn feels "wore out." Throughout he is portrayed as a humane and sensitive man, a good listener, someone who abhors racism and economic inequalities. Several sections are narrated from the points of view of his daughter Georgia and her son Justin. Littlejohn forms strong intergenerational bonds with Justin and is able to renew parent-child bonds with his daughter. The outcome of Littlejohn's plan to die is portrayed subtly and ambiguously. TOPICS: Rural Aging, Parent-Child Bonds, Grandparenting, Wisdom, Aging in Place, Life Review.

64. Pym, Barbara. *Quartet in Autumn*. New York: Harper & Row, 1977. Reprint, New York: Perennial Library, 1980, 218 pp.

A bleak vision of old age as a time of loneliness and often missed opportunities is seen in the lives of four clerical workers, all in their 60s, who work in the same London office. The four characters include one unmarried man, one widower, and two unmarried women. Although the four participate in the expected gossip and banter of people who work together, they know almost nothing about each other's personal lives. Norman is angry, dissatisfied with life. Edwin is intensely religious, an observant of the various Saints' Days in the Church calendar. Marcia is incurably private, still traumatized by her mother's death. Lettie enjoys a quiet friendship with another spinster. She looks forward to moving in with her friend after retirement. When the two women retire, they are given a modest send-off by the men and then go their separate ways. Marcia becomes reclusive, frail, and increasingly demented. Letty survives several unexpected changes of plans and emotionally charged circumstances. In the end she alone adjusts to new routines and affirms her freedom to make personal choices in her old age. TOPICS: Roles, Mental Health, Coping, Loneliness, Retirement.

65. Sackville-West, Virginia. *All Passion Spent*. Garden City, N.Y.: Doubleday Doran & Co., 1932, 294 pp.

An elderly widow recovers the real self that she has buried in a lifetime as the dutiful wife of a distinguished man. Deborah Holland, Lady Slane, lives quietly in a London suburb despite the objections of her snobbish, already elderly children who expect her to continue as a public figure. Young Deborah had wanted ardently to become a painter. But she succumbed to the conspiracy whereby a lady was expected to serve her husband, to be his extension and comfort. That husband was Lord Slane, distinguished public servant, charming but cold at heart. Now another man appears at her door--an

eccentric art collector she had met long ago in India
when both were young. He had seen through her facade,
to the wild spirit behind, and had fallen in love for
the only time in his reclusive life. Deborah awakens to
his recall; they enjoy a quiet but rich friendship before   she   dies;   her   new   freedom   passes   to   her
great-granddaughter, almost caught in the same web.
TOPICS: Gender: Women, Intimacy, Disengagement, Widowhood, Life Review, Transmission of Values.

66. Sarton, May. *As We Are Now.* New York: Norton, 1973,
133 pp.
   "I am in a concentration camp for the old, a place
where people dump their parents or relatives exactly as
though it were an ashcan." So speaks Caro Spencer, 76,
a resident of Twin Elms, a sub-standard nursing home in
the New England countryside, in this cautionary tale of
elder abuse both mental and physical. Caro is single,
fiercely independent, a former math teacher with a love
of poetry--and an uncrushable opponent of the home man-
ager Harriet Hatfield, a mean and vindictive woman who
makes this place an inferno. Caro tries to save her
sanity and her soul in struggling against it. She finds
moral support in Richard Thornhill, a sensitive minister; a fellow sufferer in Standish Flint, a bitter but
dignified farmer close to death; and affection in Anna
Close, a farmer's wife who serves as substitute attendant.   The battle is a losing one, reversed only by
Caro's climactic act of purgative rage in which she destroys Twin Elms by fire.   TOPICS: Intimacy, Elder
Abuse, Enmity, Doctor-Patient Conflicts, Deviance, Courage.

67. Schwartz, Lynn Sharon *Balancing Acts.* New York:
Harper & Row, 1981, 216 pp.
   A former trapeze artist, 74, and a precocious girl,
13, each brings the other out of a painfully confused
period into a new wholeness. Max Fried, a widow and
once an all-around circus performer, comes to Pleasure
Knolls Semi-Service Apartments for Senior Citizens. A
feisty urban Jew by background, a loner with a sharp
tongue, he shuns the usual senior recreations for
part-time work as gymnastics coach at a junior high
school. There he attracts the infatuated attention of
Alison, who despises her conventional home, fantasizes
wild adventure, and longs for the circus life once led
by Max. The novel alternates between Max's prolonged
grief over the loss of his wife, and Alison's pestering
Max in her search for the life he symbolizes. Some
mediation is provided by Max's neighbor Lettie Blumenthal, with whom he enjoys an amorous but contentious
friendship. The climax turns on Alison's running away,

Max's joining her parents to find her, then to die of an
overtaxed heart but at peace with his mourning. Alison
is also liberated, now to find a happier life with her
parents, her new baby sister, and her schoolmates.
TOPICS: Intergenerational, Rebellion, Long-term Care,
Retirement, Reminiscence, Death.

68. Spark, Muriel.   *Memento Mori*.   London: Macmillan,
1959, 245 pp.
      "Remember you must die" is the mysterious message
several old people receive from an anonymous caller in
this macabre comedy about a gallery of aged sinners. The
caller's words are the traditional religious admonish-
ment to consider last things. (The title is Latin for
that message.) Older people would presumably get their
souls in order on receiving such a specific reminder of
oncoming death. But not the characters of this novel.
The setting is London; time, the 1950s. The warned
people, who are upper middle-class intellectuals, continue to live as spitefully, haughtily, greedily, noisily, lustfully, self-absorbedly as they did in their
prime: Dame Lettie, who constantly re-makes her will in
order to dominate others; Godfrey, the exhausted but un-
daunted lecher; Mabel, lady's companion and blackmailer,
etc. Maybe the most comic is Alec, the amateur gerontologist who seeks to study old age by keeping elaborate
records of pulse and temperature. An exception is the
serious Henry Mortimer, who reasons: "Death, when it approaches, ought not to take one by surprise. It should
be part of the full expectancy of life." TOPICS: Social
Class, Sexuality, Wisdom, Deviance, Vanity, Death.

69. Stegner, Wallace. *The Spectator Bird*. Garden City,
N.Y.: Doubleday, 1976.   Reprint, New York: Penguin,
1990, 214 pp.
      Despite the anxiety and uncertainty that are the
hallmarks of the aging process, Joe Allston, 69, a retired literary agent, learns the best antidote to the
condition of old age is to find someone with whom to
share its attendant pain and alienation. Joe and his
wife Ruth retired to California to find their "safe
place," but Joe still feels vulnerable, alienated, and
alone in a dangerous world. He rages at the physical
changes of his aging body, the prospects for further
physical decline, and the ageism he perceives in society's rejection of the old. Joe's pain extends to two
events from the past that still haunt him. He feels
guilt because of the suicide of his son, an only child,
twenty years ago. He also has never resolved his feelings about a mysterious woman whom Ruth and he met on a
trip to Denmark after his son died. Joe relives that
trip by rereading a set of notebooks he wrote during the

visit. This process is cathartic for him. He confronts
some unfinished business and begins to restore his
self-confidence and self-esteem after facing ghosts from
his past. TOPICS: Stereotypes, Older Couples, Doctor-
Patient Conflicts, Mid-life, Life Review.

70. Taylor, Elizabeth. *Mrs. Palfrey at the Claremont*.
London: Chatto & Windus, 1971. Reprint, with a new
Introduction by Paul Bailey, New York: Dial, 1982, 205
pp.
        The brave boredom of being old in a retirement
hotel is described in the story of Laura Palfrey, widow
of a British Empire civil servant, who has come to the
Claremont. Here reside a few old ladies and an occasional gentleman, who will linger   until disability
pushes them on to nursing homes or geriatric wards. The
routine is deadly: inspecting the day's menus, dawdling
until dinner, knitting, watching television, shopping,
checking one's watch. These retirees variously handle
their age. Elvira rages against age with a spiteful
tongue inflicted on the others. Mrs. Post meets the
smallest incident with lugubrious timidity. Mrs. Burton
drinks. And so on. What sets Mrs. Palfrey apart is a
stoic dignity combined with the considerateness of an
old-fashioned lady. She has resolved to "soldier on,"
as her husband would have it, following three simple
rules: "Be independent; never give way to melancholy;
never touch capital." She declines one offer of marriage from a fellow resident. She develops a restrained
but deep friendship with Ludo, a hungry young writer who
helps her recover from a bad fall on the street. TOPICS:
Intergenerational, Endurance, Leisure, Retirement, Widowhood.

71. Tolstoy, Leo. *The Death of Ivan Ilyich*.   1886.
Reprint, translated by Lynn Solotaroff, New York:
Bantam, 1981, 134 pp. Also in Anthology 1, pp. 144-85.
Also widely available.
        Disability, eventually fatal, strikes a prosperous
lawyer at the height of his profession when he had expected life to go on pleasantly. This long somber story
opens with the final rites for Ivan Ilyich, a Russian in
the 1880s, with the mourners hypocritically thinking of
pleasantly resuming their own lives. Then Ivan's life
is recapitulated: upper-middle-class family, law, ele-
gant participation in society and night life, promo-
tions, transfers. Gradually he shuts off from his selfish wife. He refines his performance of duty into an
exact and cold but satisfying routine. Thus his life is
precisely formulated. A slight accident, a fall from a
ladder, transforms into something like deadly cancer,
with its pain thrusting into Ivan's life, drawing him on

to an awareness of approaching death. He finds that everyone around him, even the doctors, has reduced him to a routine just as he had reduced others. The deathbed scene, in which Ivan finally reaches the truth of his life and death, is strongly moving. TOPICS: Social Class, Older Couples, Doctor-Patient Conflicts, Vanity, Employment, Religion, Death.

72. Van Velde, Jacoba. *The Big Ward*. Translated by Ellen and Roy Hulbert. New York: Simon & Schuster, 1960, 120 pp. Originally published as *De grote zaal* (Amsterdam, E. Querido, 1953).

The fears, helplessness and despair of life in a Dutch nursing home are portrayed in the experiences of Trudi Van der Ween, 74, a stroke victim. The "big ward" is a public assistance ward where residents go to die, where there is little privacy, and where the cries of patients are heard day and night. The big ward also represents the old person's fear of the unknown, ultimately the fear of death. The events of the novel are told through alternating first person accounts by Trudi and her daughter, Helena. When Trudi is moved to the big ward, she and the other women who are patients survive because of their empathy toward each other. They listen to each other's stories, and they share their private griefs. The staff in the nursing home are portrayed as sensitive persons who are often overwhelmed by the task of caring for these old people. The physical, emotional, and financial constraints placed on Helena because of her caregiving responsibilities are well documented. TOPICS: Poverty, Culture, Gender: Women, Community, Caregiving, Long-term Care, Anxiety, Dying.

73. Wharton, William (pseudonym). *Dad*. New York: Knopf, 1981, 449 pp.

A middle-aged-son tries to see his Dad through an ultimate crisis of health, self-acceptance, and marriage, while also trying to cope with his own life and drop-out son. Called home from Paris by the mother's heart attack, John Tremont finds an equal crisis in Dad, aged 73. Dad is dominated by Mom, a bigoted insecure woman who manipulates all those around her. After an operation for bladder cancer, Dad goes through extreme stages of infantile withdrawal, recovery into the lively full-spirited man he might have been, submergence in a fantasy rustic life (long a secret dream). John's steady caregiving leads him to ask, "Why is it I had to wait so long to know my dad is a man like myself, more like me than anybody I've ever met. . . . What is it that keeps fathers and sons so far apart?" Owing largely to Mom's frantic hostility, Dad finally withdraws again and dies in a nursing home. Secondary themes are the possible recovery in old age of latent potential; the surfacing of spousal fears and hostilities; the possibilities of imaginative health care. John's first-person narrative alternates with narrative by his own son Bill, as the two drive away after Dad's final illness and try to understand each other better. TOPICS: Parent-Child Bonds, Older Couples, Caregiving, Disability, Mental Health.

74. Wilson, Angus. *Late Call*. London: Secker & Warburg, 1964, 316 pp.

In retirement a woman discovers a role for herself in her extended family, resolves the pain of an unhappy childhood, and overcomes her fears of intimacy. When Sylvia Calvert, 64, retires from managing a seaside resort hotel in England, she looks forward to taking a "late call" (sleeping late) for once. But her life will not be that easy. Sylvia and her husband move in with her widowed son, who lives in a New Town in the Midlands. Sylvia isn't happy there, for several reasons: her son an overbearing, sometimes authoritarian father; his three adult children are busy trying to find some individuality outside of their father's control; and Sylvia's husband is a petty, conniving loafer who gambles away money he borrows from family and friends. Sylvia finds that although she wants to contribute to the family life, she can't find a role that will allow her to fit in. Throughout the novel Sylvia tries to "remake herself," to adjust to her new surroundings. Finally, Sylvia finds a way to reclaim her identity and help her family overcome several crises. TOPICS: Adaptation, Gender: Women, Parent-Child Conflicts, Older Couples, Autonomy, Alienation, Retirement.

Plays

[Entries 75-90.]

75. Albee, Edward. *The Sandbox. In "The Zoo Story";
"The Death of Bessie Smith"; "The Sandbox": Three Plays,
Introduced by the Author*. New York: Coward-McCann,
1960. Also in Anthology 9, 247-56.
        An effective parable of elder abuse. This playlet
in an absurdist style shows a callous Mommy and Daddy
dumping Grandmother into a sandbox (read hospital, nursing home, hospice). She shows feeble hostility: throwing
sand at Mommy, complaining to the audience. As night
falls, Mommy and Daddy leave the stage voicing hollow
sadness. The nearby Young Man, pleasantly exercising
throughout the play, now comes forward, announces himself as the Angel of Death, and softly claims Grandmother, now gently ready. TOPIC: Ageism, Elder Abuse, Disengagement.

76. Anderson, Robert. *I Never Sang for My Father*. New
York: Dramatists Play, 1968, 69 pp. Also in Anthology
1, pp. 55-110.
        The bitter reality that generations cannot always
become reconciled to each other is illustrated in this
two-act play, which probes the fragile relationship between Gene Garrison, a widower in his early 40s, and his
father Tom. Gene has always respected his father, feared
him, even stood in awe of him. But Gene has never loved
his father, and he cannot forgive himself for not loving
him. Gene holds fast to the "image" of a loving father.
But that image repeatedly crumbles in the face of his
father's abrasive, self-centered behaviors. Tom is a
mean-spirited, selfish old man who never forgave his own
father for abandoning his family. Tom became the pro-

vider for his siblings, and he has always defined fatherhood as the source of food, shelter, and clothing--but not of love. Driven out of the house by his father, Gene is freed from his father's domination; but nothing can liberate him from the need to have experienced a father's love. TOPICS: Adaptation, Gender: Men, Parent-Child Conflicts, Caregiving.

77. Coburn, D. L.   *The Gin Game*. New York: Samuel French, 1977. Reprint, New York: Drama Bk, 1978, 73 pp.
     Here is a spectacular way not to grow old. Fonsia Dorsey, a charming new resident of a home for the aged, meets Weller Martin, a retired businessman who introduces her to gin rummy. So they begin to enjoy each other as witty, playful adults. But by a diabolical subversion of chance, she steadily wins despite the other's self-proclaimed status as expert. Weller's constant defeat draws him from patronizing compliment to eventual tantrum. Fonsia is frightened but under his pressure resumes play until she succumbs to rage herself. Sadistically each punctures the other's genteel pretenses to bring lifelong flaws to the surface. Weller seemingly was incompetent in business, deserted by family and partner, blaming everything on bad luck. Fonsia, far from a charming lady, was a prudish and vindictive woman who evicted her husband and spitefully hated her son. The play ends in climactic invective and imminent violence, with both characters drained of self-respect and hope for affection. TOPICS: Older Couples, Enmity, Long-term Care, Leisure.

78. Cooper, Susan and Hume Cronyn. *Foxfire*. New York: Samuel French, 1983, 104 pp.
     The bonds of love that exist between an old couple, the enduring qualities of rural living, the importance of "place" for an old person, and the ways in which the old renew their own lives when they respond to the needs of others are important themes in this play, inspired by Eliot Wigginton's *Foxfire* series of oral histories. Annie Nations, 80, a widow, lives alone on the farm "Stony Lonesome" in the Appalachian Mountains of Georgia. She is a strong-willed, no-nonsense woman who is devoted to her family. She converses with her husband, Hector, on a regular basis. But early in the play it becomes apparent that Hector has been dead five years. She holds onto his memory because she needs his "presence" to help her resolve her grief and assist her in dealing with the essential question of the play: will she leave Stony Lonesome? Further complications include the arrival of her son, a country western star whose marriage has ended, and a young oral historian interested in preserving Appalachian folkways. TOPICS: Rural Ag-

ing, Parent-Child Bonds, Older Couples, Humor, Aging in Place, Widowhood.

79. Cristofer, Michael. *The Shadow Box: A Drama in Two Acts*. New York: Drama Bk Spec, 1977, 102 pp.

Three older people are dying, each in a separate cottage on hospital grounds, each visited by loved ones. Together and variously they illustrate the stages which Elisabeth Kubler-Ross described whereby a dying person confronts death: denial, anger, bargaining, depression, acceptance. Joe has been a blue-collar city worker who finally built a house for his wife and son and dreamed of the farm they could never have. Brian has been a minor writer and intellectual whose promiscuous wife left him (though she now returns), and whose gay lover now attends him. Felicity, a farmer's widow, has always longed for her daughter Claire who ran away. Now in great pain, she is attended by her drab daughter Agnes. Because Felicity has never accepted Claire's death, Agnes has impersonated her sister by writing letters to sustain the illusion. An unseen Interviewer talks with these people from time to time, encouraging them to be open about their ordeal. The language of this play is often coarse as are many intimate details of their lives. What sings out especially at the end is that life is both fragile and precious. TOPICS: Parent-Child Bonds, Intimacy, Loss, Life Review, Death.

80. Gardner, Herb. *I'm Not Rappaport*. 1986. Reprint, New York: Grove, 1988, 90 pp.

Courageous friendship in hard-driven old age is shown by Nat, eightyish, a quixotic hero and inspired liar, as he tries to cope with a heartless city and help downtrodden friends. In doing so, he assumes one fictitious identity after another, inventing so many roles that one hardly knows when to believe him. The scene is Central Park in New York. An unwilling recipient of Nat's championship is his friend Midge, also eightyish, black, nearly blind, an incompetent janitor who wants only to stay inconspicuous. Nat assumes the role of tough union lawyer to stall the tenants' representative sent to fire Midge. Nat becomes police officer in the effort to rescue Midge from a thug "protector." Nat invents a love-child who will take him to Israel, away from the solicitous meddling of his daughter. He becomes a Mafia gangster trying to scare off a drug-dealer who threatens a young woman artist nearby. Although these impersonations fail, the play remains an eloquent testimony to courage and resourcefulness in old age. Nat's Act I manifesto on the old and their claims is memorable. TOPICS: Urban Aging, Friendship, Rebellion, Coping, Creativity.

81. Harwood, Ronald. *The Dresser*. New York: Grove Press, 1981, 95 pp.

The loneliness, alienation, and failed hopes experienced in old age combine with the stresses of long-term working relationships in this story of an aging Shakespearean actor, known only as "Sir," and Norman, his dresser, as they prepare for a performance of King Lear. The two are part of a ragged troupe of aging actors who perform several plays from Shakespeare each week, despite the perils of the Blitz in January, 1942. "Sir" is a pompous, impotent, pathetic old man, living on the edge of desperation. At the same time his skills as an actor enable him to become the characters he plays. What a magnificent contradiction! Sir is one part King Lear, one part Willy Loman, and one part Archie Rice, the consummate entertainer. His relationship with Norman, his dresser, is beset with complications. The two have been together for years. Norman understands the strengths and weaknesses within Sir's character. Although he often is frustrated in his roles as Sir's nursemaid, counselor, and confidant, he remains devoted to the old man. TOPICS: Older Couples, Caregiving, Activity, Creativity, Vanity, Employment.

82. McEnroe, Robert E. *The Silver Whistle*. New York: Dramatists Play, 1949, 113 pp.

How far must one surrender to the trials of old age and how far can one retain a spirit of adventure? The scene of this fantasy is a drab, depressed old people's home operated by a needy church. A new inmate arrives—Oliver Erwenter, whose strangely youthful spirit and appearance suggest that he is something of a sprite, a Pan figure, a Pied Piper. His mission, it seems, is to lead these aging souls back into the country of youth. Bit by bit he succeeds. Mr. Beebe, focused on his own funeral, is brought to feel romantic toward the coquettish Mrs. Sampler. The ill-tempered Mrs. Harmer at last joins the project of throwing a fund-raising bazaar. By the end, this sad little community has found rejuvenation and even joy. Erwenter turns out to be a young man, conducting in this visit a personal experiment to find "if there is any point in living to be seventy-seven." His answer is affirmative. TOPICS: Intergenerational, Long-term care, Creativity, Depression.

83. Miller, Arthur. *Death of a Salesman*. New York: Viking, 1949. Reprint, New York: Penguin, 1984, 139 pp.

This intense drama has become virtually the American classic on aging as an ordeal forcing together the lies and truths of the whole life. Willy Loman, 63, has spent thirty-six years as the New England agent of his New York company. He has lived by the American success

dream that insists that "being well-liked" is the
secret, that jokes and glad-handing together with some
ruthlessness will see one to the top. He has passed
this ethic on to his sons, Biff and Happy, with whom as
boys he once enjoyed comradeship. The dark truth of
Willy's life is that he never rose far. He has lied
about his failures. He has felt lonely, needing to wom-
anize on the road. Yet he has always dreamed of a
simpler, wholesome life in the open air. Now Willy is
heartlessly fired as useless. Past and present rush
concurrently through Willy's mind, which is the main
stage of action. His conflicting life-visions flash one
against the other. He quarrels violently with Biff,
whom he loved the most and who has seen the falseness of
his father's life. Yet the old father-son love revives
once more, and Willie plans a suicide that will provide
Biff with a large insurance pay-off. A graveyard scene
summarizes the conflicts in Willy's life. TOPICS:
Ageism, Parent-Child Bonds, Parent-Child Conflicts,
Suicide, Employment, Retirement, Life Review, Transmission of Values.

84. Miller, Arthur. *The Price*. New York: Viking, 1968,
116 pp.
        A life review occasioned by the sale of family
heirlooms brings two alienated brothers face to face after decades of silence. Victor Franz, a New York police-
man nervous about reaching retirement, has brought in
Solomon, a ninetyish estate appraiser, to bid on the
furniture and effects of his dead parents, once a
wealthy couple but ruined by the Depression. An unexpected participant is his brother Walter, a prestigious
surgeon who has come, it seems, to heal old wounds. He
had evidently welshed out of the family wreckage in
order to pursue a brilliant career, leaving Victor to
drop his own promising education in order to care for
the father. A second conflict surfaces between Victor
and his wife Esther, who desperately wants their life to
become adventurous not stale. The deep truths of the
family tragedy emerge as the conflicts heat up. The appraiser, Solomon, resembles his Biblical namesake in the
wisdom which he injects with Jewish humor. The various
"prices" of the title are the costs of preserving family, of achieving life goals, of finding oneself.
TOPICS: Parent-Child Conflicts, Retirement, Life Review,
Legacies.

85. Shakespeare, William. *The Tragedy of King Lear*.
1606. Reprint, Cambridge: Cambridge Univ. Press, 1992.
Edited by Jay L. Halio, 313 pp. Also widely available.
        The ordeals and triumphs of old age are illuminat-

ed by this great tragedy with a breadth and grandeur
that make it the all-time masterpiece on aging.   Old
King Lear, a once-powerful leader, "retires" from his
throne, planning to divide his kingdom among three
daughters, Goneril, Regan, and Cordelia.   This foolish
monarch bargains to allot the largest share to the
daughter who loves him most. The oldest two have no
trouble serving up the loving speeches he wants to hear.
Cordelia is too proud to sell herself and is instantly
disinherited. Lear hands over his kingdom to the other
two, making it clear that he expects to go on being
treated with all the honor due royalty. He is soon to
know better.   Goneril and Regan not only withdraw his
troublesome privileges but mistreat him to the point of
madness. Wandering through storms, Lear comes to understand the plight of other homeless wretches.   Finally
rescued by Cordelia's invading army, this wrecked old
king has learned his own weakness; he has learned compassion; he has learned to recognize Cordelia's true
love.   Although the two are destroyed by the evil sisters, their discovery of love and true worth mounts
above the holocaust of war and multiplied treachery.
TOPICS: Parent-Child Bonds, Parent-Child Conflicts,
Elder Abuse, Mental Health, Disengagement, Retirement,
Religion.

86. Simon, Neil. *Lost in Yonkers*. New York: Plume,
1991. Reprint, New York: Penguin, 1993, 120 pp.
     An old woman, hardened against a life of hurt and
loss, has inflicted her bleak and unregenerate vision of
life upon each of her children. Her oldest daughter Gert
was disabled emotionally by her mother's emphasis on
authority and discipline. Eddie was considered weak and
pathetic because he would "crack" under his mother's in-
timidation. Louie, now a small-time gangster, was considered tough because he wouldn't crack.   Only the
fourth child, Bella, escaped the old woman's oppression.
Although mildly retarded, she is forthright, loving, and
sincere. She emerges as the "leader" of the family,
the one who discovers her own power to resolve a family
crisis precipitated by Eddie and his two sons, Jay and
Arty, 15 and 13.   Widowed and in debt, Eddie asks his
mother to take his boys while he travels throughout the
South to buy and sell scrap metal for the Allied effort
in World War II.   The two boys survive a year "lost in
Yonkers"--that is, as exiles in Grandma's confining
world. Grandma is neither affectionate nor understanding of the pitfalls of adolescence. Bella escapes Grandma's oppressive world by admitting her own loneliness
and yearning for love. TOPICS: Adaptation, Parent-Child
Conflicts, Grandparenting, Isolation, Widowhood.

87. Thompson, Ernest. *On Golden Pond*. New York: Dodd, Mead, 1979, 191 pp.

Longstanding family tensions are resolved after Norman Thayer, a retired professor, and his younger wife Ethel open what may be their final season at the family summer home on Golden Pond in Maine. Described in the stage directions as "boyish and peppery," Norman is contentious with others, both playfully and sadistically. His manner conceals a fear of death, a distress over his failures of memory, and a nervousness about his fortyish daughter Chelsea. When Chelsea arrives for his eightieth birthday, she is once again the little fat girl being picked on by her dad. Father and daughter use this one great chance to reconcile. Bill Ray, the thirteen-year-old son of her future husband, forms a lovely friendship with the old man that allows Norman to enjoy a grandfatherly role; something of his younger self can emerge. Throughout, Norman's wife shows the courageous wit and understanding to help toward their day of serene farewell to Golden Pond. TOPICS: Parent-Child Conflicts, Older Couples, Anxiety.

88. Uhry, Alfred. *Driving Miss Daisy*. Lexington, NY: Theatre Comm, 1988, 51 pp.

A friendship develops painfully between a Jewish widow and the African-American driver her son has forced her to employ because of her many auto accidents. The conflict between Daisy Werthan, seventyish, and Hoke Coleburn, fiftyish, makes the play. Daisy resents being looked after. She vehemently rejects Hoke's diplomatic assistance. Bit by bit, his engaging and subtle tact wins her to tolerate his service and then, as years pass, to depend on it. Hoke, for his part, has a simple dignity that can assert itself when Daisy's arrogance goes too far. Both persons have suffered racial intolerance: Hoke all his life as a black; Daisy as a Jew in a gentile Southern culture, especially when the synagogue is bombed. She rejects this potential bond, but a kind of balance is reached after Daisy, in her nineties, has a disorienting stroke. When Hoke rallies to help, she says touchingly, "You're my best friend." At the end, Hoke visits Daisy in a nursing home and feeds her as she mumbles contentedly. At this basic level, a difficult aging has ended in harmony. TOPICS: Race, Multicultural, Ethnicity, Friendship, Disability, Humor, Leisure.

89. Vonnegut, Kurt, Jr. *Fortitude*. 1965. In *Wampeters, foma & granfallons (opinions)*. New York: Delacorte Press/Seymour Lawrence, 1974. Also in Anthology 9, pp. 48-73.

The scientists' natural ambition to prolong human life indefinitely meets a comic but healthy corrective

in this dramatized fantasy of a Dr. Frankenstein and his
rich 100-year-old patient, Sybil.   Sybil is now a mere
head, piped and wired to a laboratory of mechanical or-
gans which fulfill all her bodily functions.   Despite
Sybil's artificial sweetness (as stimulated by a laboratory console), her one spark of real life is ready for
death because, as her friend tells the ingenious doctor
who has created immortality: "I know there's a hell.
It's in there, and you're its great inventor."   It is
fitting that Dr. Frankenstein ends as another product of
his own ingenuity--as Sybil's immortal companion on his
infernal life machine. TOPICS: Doctor-Patient Conflicts,
Alienation, Death.

90. Wilder, Thornton. *The Long Christmas Dinner* 1931.
In *"The Long Christmas Dinner" and Other Plays in One
Act.* Reprint, New York: Harper & Row, 1963, pp. 1-27.
     This one-act play is a thank offering, not for old
age only, but for the whole of life and its coming and
growing and passing. It illuminates aging by showing its
optimum context in a flow of family achievement, affection, appreciation, memory. Ninety years in the life
of the Bayard family are condensed into one long Christmas dinner. As parents and relatives age, they put on
wigs of white hair and eventually move out through the
dark portal that denotes death. Children enter through
the flowery portal that denotes life, then mature, and
eventually follow their forebears. All the while, dinner conversation flows on. Topics range from frontier
days to urbanization. There is joy over births, fear of
death, remorse over lost chances, myths of days gone by,
the rebellion of youth, war, and decay. The stage emp-
ties as the last widow departs to live with her children in a new family center where the cycle presumably
will continue. TOPICS: Family Bonds, Endurance, Aging in
Place, Transmission of Values, Death.

Poems

[Entries 91-203.]

91. Angelou, Maya. "The Last Decision." In *The Complete Collected Poems of Maya Angelou*. New York: Random House, 1994.
    An old woman, troubled by the difficult adaptations required in old age and by the tiresome details of daily living, yields to her aging as if it were a terminal condition. She gives up reading, eating, listening (to her family), and finally--because "life is too busy, wearying me"--gives up living. TOPICS: Adaptation, Disengagement, Suicide.

92. Angelou, Maya. "Old Folks Laugh." In collection above.
    The poet celebrates the joy and freedom implicit in old people's laughter. Old people laugh in order to relieve the stresses of daily living, forgive the wrongs of the past, rekindle important memories, and place larger issues of suffering and death in some perspective. "When old folks laugh, they free the world." TOPICS: Coping, Humor.

93. Angelou, Maya. "On Aging." In collection above.
    An old woman (the speaker) defiantly resists being stereotyped as lonely, disabled, and dependent. Instead, she asks for empathy, understanding, and compassion. She reminds the reader that old people are independent and self-sufficient. She admits that physical changes have occurred in her old age, but she views her sense of identity as a constant in her life. She warns the reader, "Don't bring me no rocking chair." TOPICS: Stereotypes, Race, Gender: Women, Autonomy, Humor.

94. Auden, W. H. "Doggerel by a Senior Citizen" (1969). In *W. H. Auden: Collected Poems*. Edited by Edward Mendelson. New York: Random House, 1976, 2 pp. Also in Anthology 12.

The poet whimsically compares the modern world to the "good old days" before World War I in England. In rhyming couplets the narrator decries the changes wrought by progress, changes in religious practice, new sexual attitudes, and the decline of the English language. TOPICS: Roles, Alienation.

95. Auden, W. H. "Old People's Home" (1970). In collection above. Also in Anthologies 1 and 12.

On his way to visit an old friend who resides in a nursing home, the poet reflects with anger and frustration upon the hardships faced in old age. He ponders the useful roles old people played in previous generations, and he laments the plight of the present generation, destined to be abandoned and placed in institutions by families and by society. TOPICS: Stereotypes, Long-term Care, Alienation.

96. Bahe, Liz Sohappy. "Grandmother Sleeps." In *Carriers of the Dream Wheel*. Edited by Duane Niatum. New York: Harper & Row, 1975.

The handing down of skills from a Native American grandmother to her grandchild is described by the grandchild. First the grandmother is seen weaving at midday, then beading toward sundown, then sleeping day after day. The grandchild promises to take up these skills, saying, "I will wait for her to wake." The reader must decide whether the grandchild is simply carrying on until the grandmother can resume work, or whether the grandchild is continuing the role of the dead grandmother whose spirit lives. TOPICS: Roles, Ethnicity, Grandparenting.

97. Blumenthal, Michael. "Elegy for My Mother: The Days." In *The Wages of Goodness*. Columbia, Mo.: Univ. of Missouri Press, 1992, 11 pp.

Twenty-five years after his mother's death a middle-aged son reflects upon his unresolved grief and his desperate need for healing. Details of the mother's last eight days of life unfold in each section. Her death left her son emotionally shattered. He suffered "a man's hurt in a boy's body" and never found a way to resolve the pain of his grief. The purpose of the poem is to restore himself, to say goodbye to his mother, to complete the grieving process. TOPICS: Parent-Child Bonds, Grief, Reminiscence, Death.

98. Blumenthal, Michael. "The Pleasures of Old Age." In

Against Romance. New York: Viking Penguin, 1987. Also in Anthology 9.

The power of sexual desire even in extreme age is tenderly illustrated in the speaker's 99-year-old Jewish grandmother, who dreamed day and night of passionate romance. Even perhaps in her fatal fall down the stairs she still focused on "her great joy in beautiful men." TOPIC: Sexuality.

99. Blumenthal, Michael. "United Jewish Appeal." In collection above.

In this nostalgic remembrance of childhood and intergenerational ties, the poet recalls how when as a boy he deceived his blind grandmother by pretending to be someone soliciting funds for charity in order to get quarters to spend on ice cream and baseball cards. Still, each time he and a friend run off with the fruits of their trickery, the boy feels "full of the love of grandmothers." TOPICS: Ethnicity, Grandparenting.

100. Bly, Robert. "A Visit to the Old People's Home." In *What Have I Ever Lost by Dying? Collected Prose Poems*. New York: HarperCollins, 1992, 2 pp.

On visiting his parents in a nursing home a middle-aged son is left feeling ambivalent about their physical losses and anxious about his own aging and impending mortality. The son and his wife have learned that his mother has suffered a minor stroke. Unlike his wife, who provides comfort and touch for her, the son withdraws and feels strangely little sympathy for his mother. TOPICS: Parent-Child Conflicts, Anxiety.

101. Booth, Phillip. "Fallback." In *Selves: New Poems*. New York: Viking, 1990, 2 pp. Also in Anthology 9.

An old woman recalls the shared intimacies of her life with her husband and makes a declaration--aimed at caregivers--that the old are more than the sum of their broken bodies and vacant minds. The woman and her husband are residents in an intermediate care wing of a nursing home. The woman reflects upon their present circumstances: she is frail and physically dependent; he suffers from dementia and is only a pale reflection of the intellectually gifted man she married sixty-two years ago. TOPICS: Older Couples, Caregiving, Long-term Care.

102. Booth, Phillip E. "Old." In *Selves: New Poems*. New York: Viking, 1990.

The narrator reflects upon the pitfalls of the aging process, which include alienation, abandonment, and disability. But there are compensations to be found when the old attain a balance between growth and de-

cline, vulnerability and self-control. TOPICS: Stereotypes, Wisdom, Alienation.

103. Brooks, Gwendolyn.   "Jessie Mitchell's Mother"
(1960). In *Selected Poems*.   New York: Harper & Row,
1963, 2 pp.
      A desolate old African-American mother in poverty,
clinging to former joys, is watched by her adult daughter who sees in her only the death-bound wreckage. She
cruelly reflects: "Only a habit would cry if she should
die."   As the mother in turn looks, she sees the young
straight body and thinks of all the hardships that bend
and destroy poor women.   One spiteful consolation is her
memory of her own youthful loveliness.   She ends with
reviving the "dried-up triumphs" of her youth. TOPICS:
Ageism, Race, Parent-Child Conflicts, Reminiscence.

104. Brown, Sterling. "Virginia Portrait." In *Collected
Poems of Sterling A. Brown*. Selected by Michael Harper.
New York: HarperCollins, 1980, 2 pp. Also in Anthology
9.
      Spiritual resilience in old age is shown in this
portrait of an illiterate black farm widow as she sits
alone amid rural winter.   Much grief and hardship has
come to her--bereavement and lost crops--but she remains
not only undefeated but contented and grateful in memories of husband, friends, children.   She calmly envisions her coming death. TOPICS: Rural Aging, Race, Gender: Women, Disengagement, Serenity.

105. Carver, Raymond. "Happiness in Cornwall."   In *Where
Water Comes Together with Other Water*. New York: Random
House, 1985, 2 pp.   Also in Anthology 5.
      The growth of a happy new attachment after bereave-
ment is shown in this portrait of a man who has declined
rapidly since his wife's death.   His children find an
able housekeeper for him.   She becomes more than his butler and cook; she becomes his companion on dressed-up
Sunday walks.   Above all, in the evenings she reads great
poetry to which he listens with deep enjoyment.   All this
happens without gossip and with the friendly support of
the community. TOPICS: Community, Parent-Child Bonds,
Intimacy, Widowhood.

106. Ciardi, John.   "Matins." In *Echoes: Poems Left
Behind by John Ciardi*. Fayetteville, Ark.: The Univ. of
Arkansas Press, 1989.
      How   little human life is sometimes valued,
especially the life of anonymous street people who are
old--that is the subject of this poem, inspired by the
newspaper story of an old woman found frozen to death on
a park bench.   The poet questions why money could not

have been better spent to make her life more bearable.
The title reflects the poet's attitude of respect and
prayer for the old woman. TOPICS: Ageism, Economics.

107. Clifton, Lucille. "Miss Rosie" (1987). In *Good
Woman: Poems and a Memoir 1969-1980*. Brockport, N.Y.: BOA
Edns, 1987. Also in Anthologies 9 and 12.
     Miss Rosie, an aging black woman once a celebrated
beauty, is shown in wretched clothes, surrounded by the
smell of old potato peels, sunk in dementia. This woeful
sight stirs the speaker to militant commitment to "stand
up" through Miss Rosie's destruction. TOPICS: Economics,
Race, Enmity, Dementia.

108. Dumas, Henry. "Grandma's Got a Wig." In *Knees of a
Natural Man*. New York: Thunder's Mouth, 1989. Also in
Anthology 9.
     A rhythmic, light-hearted urge to hang onto one's
sexuality is voiced in the speaker's admiration of Grandma's beautifying herself with a red wig. He observes
Grandpa's perking up in interest, and promises to buy his
own sweetheart a red wig as long as she doesn't cut off
the "nappy hair" which is her African-American heritage.
TOPICS: Race, Gender: Women, Sexuality.

109. Eberhart, Richard. "Hardy Perennial" (1972). In
Collected Poems 1930-1976. New York: Oxford Univ. Press,
1976. Also in Anthology 5.
     In old age the poet desires to love every detail
of living. Youth is first described as reckless, ready
to test death by defying it. In age, death is felt as a
constant nagging threat to life. Instead of the headlong
rush of youth, the aged speaker would cherish everything
alive, would discover meaning in the slightest clues.
TOPICS: Intergenerational, Wisdom.

110. Emerson, Ralph. "Terminus" (1867). In *Poems of Ralph
Waldo Emerson*. Selected by J. Donald Adams. New York:
Crowell, 1965. Also in Anthologies 1 and 12.
     How to approach retirement is the theme of this
late poem, written when Emerson was perhaps aware of his
shrinking powers. The poem opens with the assertion that
it is time to accept aging and to "take in sail." The
poet counsels himself to accept the limitations of age
but by no means to lie idle. For a while, one can still
plan; one can choose one's agenda instead of trying to
do everything. One can rely upon the religious faith that
will bring all souls home. TOPICS: Disengagement,
Retirement, Religion.

111. Frost, Robert. "The Death of the Hired Man" (1914).
In *Complete Poems of Robert Frost*. Edited by Edward

Connery Lathem.   New York: Holt, Rinehart, & Winston.
1960, 7 pp.   Also in Anthology 12.
     The plight of the homeless rural aged, without
money, without negotiable skills, and without family, is
dramatized in the story of old Silas, a worn-out farm
laborer who has come "home" to the only couple who gave
him a sense of security and belonging.   The poem is a dialogue between the couple; they debate what to do about
the old man collapsed in the next room.   Finally, the
wife realizes the old man "has come home to die." TOPICS:
Ageism, Rural Aging, Family Bonds, Loneliness.

112. Frost, Robert.   "An Old Man's Winter Night" (1916).
In *Complete Poems of Robert Frost*.   Edited by Edward
Connery Lathem.   New York: Holt, Rinehart, & Winston.
1960.   Also in Anthologies 1, 9, and 12.
     An old man, living alone in an isolated farmhouse,
keeps at bay his anxiety, loneliness, and fear of mortality by walking noisily through the empty rooms of the
house while holding a lantern.   Images of the numbing
cold, darkness, and inevitable physical decline remind
him of his fragile existence. He is alone, an old man
against the forces of the "winter night." TOPICS: Rural
Aging, Frailty, Isolation, Death.

113. Giovanni, Nikki.   "Legacies."   In *The Women and the
Men*.   New York: William Morrow, 1975.
     The interaction of a little girl and her grandmoth-
er illustrates how generations sometimes are unable to
share certain deeply felt fears. When a grandmother calls
a little girl to come home from the playground for a
cooking lesson, the little girl refuses.   The girl's rebellion, and the grandmother's plaintive acquiescence,
mask the child's unvoiced fears of role changes and her
resistance to the burdens of maturity as well as the old
woman's fears for the safety and happiness of the younger
generation.   But neither "said what they meant." TOPICS:
Race, Grandparenting, Anxiety, Legacies.

114. Giovanni, Nikki.   "The Life I Led."   In collection
above.
     A young woman imagines herself an old woman: she
realizes her appearance in old age will include flabby
arms, darkened veins, gray hair, and liver spots.   But
she hopes these negative physical changes will be re-
deemed by her having led a life that is meaningful and
fulfilling.   How to accomplish that goal?   Love for her
grandchildren, appreciation of beauty and serenity, trust
and affection within an intimate relationship, and her
dedication "to grow old like a vintage wine." TOPICS:
Gender: Women, Autonomy, Serenity, Loss.

115. Graves, Robert. "The Great-Grandmother" (1938). In
Collected Poems 1975. London: Cassell, 1975. Also in
Anthology 12.

A woman's lifelong rebellion against the role she
has been forced to play as aristocratic lady comes out
in the confession of the great-grandmother. She has
lived a lie as gracious, charitable lady when she really
valued money, clean brass and linen, and above all, solitude. Now that she "has outlasted all man-uses," she has
contentment at last. TOPICS: Gender: Women, Grandparenting, Rebellion, Disengagement, Life Review.

116. Graves, Robert. "Nightmare of Senility" (1965). In
collection above.

The dismay felt by older people who continue to
think and feel as lovers though their physical attrac-
tiveness seems ravaged is chillingly expressed by the
speaker of this poem. The wasted appearance of his mate
is contrasted with his own youthful heart. What he asks
for is an end to the hypocrisy by which they both pretend
to a romantic fascination. The poem is a nightmare as its
title says, but an honest nightmare needing to be confronted. TOPICS: Sexuality, Disability, Alienation, Vanity.

117. Hall, Donald. "The Day I Was Older." In *Old and New
Poems.* New York: Ticknor & Fields, 1990, 2 pp.

The poet explores his adaptation to the process of
aging from several perspectives, including the daily
reading of obituaries, a recollection of a romantic encounter with the woman who became his wife, their quiet
enjoyment of a "late August afternoon" many years later,
and a special anniversary--the day when the poet began
to live a longer life than his father had lived. Other
details from the past remind the poet of the insatiable
thirst everyone has for more experiences, more life.
TOPICS: Role Reversal, Reminiscence.

118. Hall, Donald. "Elegy for Wesley Wells." In collection above, 2 pp.

The poem is a tribute to the memory of Hall's
grandfather, who represented the end of an era of New
England farmers who cultivated the land in small acreage
and eventually watched their oldest children leave for
the cities. Now that Wesley has died, the poet predicts
"the farm will come undone." But the poet recalls his
grandfather with great affection and tenderness. The
grandfather also was the subject of Hall's memoir *String
Too Short to be Saved* (20, above). TOPICS: Rural Aging,
Grandparenting, Widowhood, Legacies.

119. Hall, Donald. "The Hole." In collection above.
     A life-threatening illness precipitates an old
man's descent into terrible isolation. At first the old
man takes stock of himself and refuses to admit that the
strength and firmness of his body will fail him. But
when physical symptoms of his illness lead first to
frailty and then to disability, the shock of his mortality causes him to retreat into a private place within himself, where "he kept himself cold"--apart from his wife
and everyone else. He dies alone. TOPICS: Disease, Disengagement, Death.

120. Hall, Donald. "Ox Cart Man." In collection above.
     The poem illustrates how old people may be renewed
and sustained by continued work and regular activity.
Each October an old man fills his oxcart with produce and
products from his farm and then sells all that he has,
including the ox and the cart. Then he returns home and
repeats the annual cycle of building, raising, tanning,
shearing, and growing--all of which sustains him throughout the year. TOPICS: Rural Aging, Activity, Autonomy,
Employment, Aspirations.

121. Hardy, Thomas. "After a Journey." In *The Complete
Poems of Thomas Hardy*. Edited by James Gibson. New
York: Macmillan, 1976.
     The bittersweet pain of remembering a lost sweet-
heart after forty years is expressed by the speaker, who
is visiting their old haunts. He recovers the sense of
her young beauty; he recovers their old delights; he
longs for a repetition of that memory. TOPICS: Loss,
Reminiscence.

122. Hardy, Thomas. "Ah, Are You Digging on My Grave?"
In collection above.
     In this humorous and even comforting reminder of
how quickly we can all be forgotten, a dead woman flat-
ters herself about the reasons her grave is being vis-
ited--by her loved one? By her relatives? By her enemy
even? By her little dog? In each case the answer is comically deflating: all the supposed "visitors" are pursuing other interests without reference to her; the actual visitor and reporter is her little dog, who merely
came by to bury a bone. TOPIC: Loss.

123. Hardy, Thomas. "I Look into My Glass." In collection above. Also in Anthology 8.
     The aging speaker views his wasting face in the
mirror and feels the troubling force of passion in an
aged body. If only his heart had shrunk as well, he
might have peace of mind. TOPICS: Sexuality, Disability,
Vanity, Aspirations.

124. Harris, Peter. "My Father-in-Law's Contract."
Hiram Poetry Review 47 (Winter 1990), 2 pp. Also in
Anthology 9.
   The tender toughness of a frail Jewish father close
to death is described by his Gentile son-in-law. The old
man has been a successful investor and a fine golfer; but
he is fading fast. Now he is carefully arranging the estate he will pass on. He jokes about his "contract" to
live for two more years "with an option to renew." He
blesses his loving daughter, baby granddaughter, and the
speaker. TOPICS: Ethnicity, Legacies, Death.

125. Harrison, Tony. "Long Distance II." In *British
Poetry Since 1945*. Edited by Edward Lucie-Smith. New
York: Penguin, 1985.
   An old Englishman's grief remains pathetically
locked in denial two years after his wife's death. His
son reflects upon the idiosyncracies of his father's
daily routine: the old man surrounds himself with physical objects that remind him of her presence, and he
clears away her things only when people visit him. He
is convinced she will appear at his door one day, turn
"the rusted lock and end his grief." TOPIC: Widowerhood.

126. Henson, Lance. "Grey Woman." In *Carriers of the
Dream Wheel*. Edited by Duane Niatum. New York: Harper &
Row, 1975.
   A ninety-year-old Cheyenne woman scavenges the garbage bins while recalling the splendors of dancing in her
youth. The poem ends with her dignified death and in the
ancestral way, her finding the Great Spirit. Her own
spirit stands stubbornly at the speaker's door, presumably waiting for the poet's acknowledgment. TOPICS: Economics, Ethnicity.

127. Hughes, Langston. "Mother to Son" In *Selected
Poems*. New York: Knopf, 1926. Also in Anthology 12.
   "I'se still climbin'." So the old African American
mother tells her discouraged son. Her life has had
tacks, and splinters, and torn-up flooring, but she has
kept climbing to landings and rounding corners, even in
darkness. TOPICS: Race, Parent-Child Bonds, Transmission
of Values.

128. Jacobsen, Rolf. "Old Age" (1954). In *Night Open:
Selected Poems of Rolf Jacobsen*. Translated by Olav
Grinde. Fredonia, N.Y.: White Pine Pr, 1993.
   The poet views the old with admiration and respect
and portrays old age as a time of integration. The old
lead lives that are fragile and yet resilient, and the
end of life is characterized by resolution and affirmation. The poet uses analogies to convey the variety of

tasks and roles all people face in a long life. He concludes the old possess an evanescent quality: at the end
of life they "gradually become themselves once more."
TOPICS: Frailty, Serenity, Spiritual Life.

129. Jacobsen, Rolf. "The Old Women" (1954). In collection above. Also in Anthology 12.
      The poet implores readers to acknowledge the endur-
ing qualities of old women's lives. He portrays old
women as mysterious, leading complex lives.   He con-
trasts the fast-paced physical activity of young women
with the slow, methodical movements of women in old age,
and concludes they are worthy of respect and even admiration. TOPICS: Gender: Women, Wisdom.

130. Jarrell, Randall. "Aging" (1960). In *The Complete
Poems*. New York: Farrar, 1969.
      The aging speaker bemoans the ever-quickening pass-
ing of the hours, which stream away too fast for finding
one's true self. What is wanted is a child's serene Sunday afternoon when outside time one could "make a life."
He expresses the desire, often stronger as the days grow
fewer, to recover or discover one's true identity.
TOPICS: Wisdom, Anxiety, Aspirations.

131. Joseph, Jenny. "Warning." In *When I Am an Old Woman
I Shall Wear Purple: An Anthology of Short Stories and
Poetry*. Edited by Sandra Martz. Watsonville, Calif.:
Papier-Maché Press, 1987. Also in Anthology 12.
      Old   age   is   to   be   a   time   of   glorious
self-indulgence: such is the title of the anthology which
is also the first line of this poem. The speaker goes
on to list other wild tastes to explore, even suggesting
that now in middle age she "ought to practice a little."
TOPICS: Ageism, Gender: Women, Rebellion, Courage,
Leisure, Aspirations.

132. Kinnell, Galway. "Goodbye." In *Selected Poems*.
Boston: Houghton Mifflin, 1982, 2 pp.
      A son's reflection on his final goodbye to his dy-
ing mother becomes a meditation on the meaning of all
"goodbyes." The poet connects the loss of his mother to
a special goodbye from one of his former students many
years ago. He connects those experiences to the wide
range of emotions--love, commitment, grief, longing, and
regret--that are attached to the universal metaphor of
"goodbye." TOPICS: Parent-Child Bonds, Disengagement,
Grief.

133. Knopf, Helen. "Memories." In *Atlantic Monthly* 210
(August 1977).
      The bittersweet memories of an ancient Native Amer-

ican woman help define the enormous cultural change her
people went through. Nearly 100, she recalls with great
fondness and reverence a river in the Pacific Northwest
where salmon returned each year. Images of a cornucopia
of fish and wildlife tumble from her memory. Now she realizes those days are gone. Why? "And then one day a
white man came." Subsequently, the Indians lost their
hunting and fishing rights as well as a way of life.
TOPICS: Multicultural, Loss, Reminiscence.

134. Koch, Kenneth. "The Circus" (1975).   In *Selected
Poems, 1950-1982*. New York: Vintage Books, 1982, 4 pp.
     The poet reflects upon his emerging sense of his
own aging in this interior monologue packed with details
about his life in Paris, his friends, his lover, the com-
positional process, and references to an earlier poem,
also called "The Circus," written in 1962. Koch marks
the composition of "The Circus" (1975) as a turning point
in his life--from his youth to his middle age. Now in
middle age the poet has greater understanding of the
finiteness of time and the fragile and uncertain nature
of human life and relationships. The poem's title aptly
suggests the exhilaration, confusion, activity, and spontaneity found in life's "combination of experience and
aloneness." TOPICS: Creativity, Mid-Life.

135. Kunitz, Stanley. "The Portrait" (1971). In *The
Poems of Stanley Kunitz 1928-1978*. Boston: Little, Brown,
1979. Also in Anthology 10.
     The deep scars of a father's long-ago suicide are
still felt by the son at age 64 even though he had not
yet been born at the time. The anger felt by his mother
lasted so strongly that when her young son produced a
pastel portrait of his father, she ripped up the picture
and slapped him hard. He can feel his cheek "still
burning." TOPICS: Suicide, Grief.

136. Larkin, Philip. "Aubade." In *Collected Poems*.
Edited With an Introduction by Anthony Thwaite. New York:
Farrar, 1988, 2 pp.   Also in Anthology 5.
     The fear of death is vividly recreated in this poem
as the speaker lies awake at dawn, horrified at the
thought of extinction. Death has come a whole day closer.
It blots out all other thought. For this speaker nothing
can soften it--not remorse, nor repentance, nor courage,
nor religion, nor philosophy, nor the present return of
the bustling day. The ironic title, "Aubade," means
"dawn song." TOPIC: Anxiety, Death.

137. Larkin, Philip. "The Old Fools." In *High Windows*.
London: Faber & Faber, 1974, 2 pp.
     The poet rages at the processes of aging which lead

to serious physical and psychological decline. He decries
the desperate existence of "the old fools," those old
people in institutions who end their lives drooling, disabled, incontinent, and demented. The poem's images are
dark and foreboding. The poet tries to gain some perspective on the interior world of the demented, but he
finds little consolation in his imaginings. TOPICS: Ageism, Long-term Care, Alienation.

138. Lawrence, D. H. "Shadows" (c. 1930). In *The Complete
Poems of D. H. Lawrence*. 2 vols. Collected and Edited by
Vivian de Sola Pinto and Warren Roberts.   New York:
Viking, 1971, 2 pp.
    Faith in the afterlife is expressed in several ways
in this and other poems by Lawrence. The oblivion of
death like that of sleep may prepare the soul to re-
awaken. The disintegrations of this life may show the
shaping hand of God, who plans to send the speaker "forth
on a new morning, a new man." TOPICS: Religion, Death.

139. Levertov, Denise. "A Daughter (I)." In *Life in the
Forest*. New York: New Directions, 1978.
    A daughter is overwhelmed by anticipatory grief,
denial, self-inflicted guilt, and a desperate longing for
closure in her relationship with her mother, who is dying
at the age of 93. Frustrated that her caregiving is done
at a distance, the daughter wishes her mother could become strong and dominant in her life again. The reality
is that her mother is frail and helpless: "now mother is
child." This reversal of roles terrifies the daughter.
TOPICS: Parent-Child bonds, Caregiving, Grief.

140. Levertov, Denise. "A Daughter (II)." In collection
above.
    The poet attends her dying mother during the last
week of her mother's life and feels helplessness and
rage. The anguished daughter visits her mother in the
hospital and finds her shrunken, suffering, and nearly
comatose. She feeds her mother with a spoon and spends
days waiting on the hospital grounds. She desires a last
significant interaction—a "communion, here in limbo"—
to resolve whatever was incomplete in their relationship.
But she realizes such closure won't be achieved. TOPICS:
Caregiving, Grief, Death.

141. Levertov, Denise. "The 90th Year." In collection
above.
    The poem illustrates the bonds between mothers and
daughters from the perspective of a daughter who is herself an older adult. While visiting her mother, who is
90, a daughter affirms her mother's influence on her own
values and reflects on the serenity and self-containment

of her mother's life. At 90 her mother is unflinchingly
honest in her assessment of life's experiences and still
open to new ideas; for example, she is rereading Tolstoy's *War and Peace*. TOPICS: Parent-Child Bonds, Serenity, Transmission of values.

142. Levertov, Denise. "A Woman Alone." In collection
above, 2 pp. Also in Anthology 9.
  A woman looks forward to her old age. She envisions
her life alone as creative and fulfilling and places herself in that future beyond guilt, self-pity, fear, and
loneliness. The poet imagines new roles for herself and
characterizes herself with images of strength, wisdom,
and individuality; for example, as "an old winedrinking
woman." TOPICS: Roles, Gender: Women, Autonomy.

143. Maclay, Lise. "I Hate the Way I Look."   In *Green
Winter: Celebrations of Later Life*.   Revised edition.
New York: Henry Holt, 1990.
  Almost every aspect of old age is expressed through
the eighty-five short soliloquies in MacLay's book, each
as spoken by an older person with varied degrees of humor, compassion, apprehension, forbearance, and (especially) faith. The language is prose-like but eloquent.
In the poem above the speaker feels betrayed when looking
at her image in the mirror. She hates her physical ugliness but then reflects that this body is still her
friend. It has served her faithfully; it has forgiven
misuse. So the speaker should remember this friendship,
and hope that young people will learn to feel the same
way when their time comes. TOPICS: Ageism, Intergenerational, Disability, Humor, Vanity.

144. Maclay, Lise. "Infirmities." In collection above,
2 pp.
  The need to be "gentle with old people" is voiced by
a speaker who has observed a young mother playing tenderly with her baby in the supermarket. Why can't the
speaker (and others) follow that example in relating to
older people, in looking past their infirmities to the
unique selves within? TOPICS: Stereotypes, Frailty.

145. Maclay, Lise. "Occupational Therapy."   In collection above, 3 pp.
  The speaker prefers to recall her long loving life
with her husband rather than be distracted by the
well-meaning occupational therapist. Her memory takes her
from courtship to parenthood to final bereavement. Such
recollection is a treasure she never had time to enjoy
in her busy dutiful life. TOPICS: Older couples, Caregiving, Widowhood, Reminiscence.

146. MacLeish, Archibald. "The Old Gray Couple, I." In *New and Collected Poems 1917-1982*. Boston: Houghton Mifflin, 1985. Also in Anthology 12.

Years together have blended the identities of an old married couple. Their relationship is characterized as affectionate and comfortable. They don't need words to communicate. A look, a gesture, a touch suffices. The poet concludes, "Everything they know they know together." Only their thoughts of the other's death are considered separately. TOPICS: Older Couples, Serenity, Death.

147. MacLeish, Archibald. "The Old Gray Couple, II" (1973). In collection above, 2 pp.

The poet recreates an affectionate, bantering dialogue between lovers after their fiftieth anniversary. They recall their passionate love in their youth and propose that in old age love takes on a new perspective because of impending mortality. TOPICS: Older Couples, Anxiety, Life Review.

148. MacLeish, Archibald. "The Wild Old Wicked Man" (1968). In collection above, 2 pp.

The anguish of old men who feel "too old for love" and yet experience endless stirrings of love and passion is described by the aged speaker in this poem. All men, he thinks, are like aging Adams who still strut their pretense of sexuality. Yet he likens this endless stirring of passion to the love cry of the wood dove in the darkening thorn grove. In some way the old man's pursuit of these inextinguishable desires and passionate yearnings represents a "triumph" for old age. The poem bears comparison to Yeats' poem of the same title. (201, below). TOPICS: Alienation, Aspirations.

149. MacLeish, Archibald. "With Age Wisdom" (1962). In collection above. Also in Anthology 12.

The poet draws a comic contrast between the cynicism of the twenty-year-old, who thinks the world a "miserable place," and the insight of the sixty-year-old, who expresses a joyous wonder at life's eternal mysteries. TOPIC: Wisdom.

150. Moffat, Mary Jane. "Widow's Supper." In *In the Midst of Winter: Selections from the Literature of Mourning*. Edited by Mary Jane Moffat. New York: Random House, 1982. Reprint, New York: Vintage Books, 1992.

The loneliness of a bereaved woman is sharply conveyed in the few bleak details of this short poem. The dead husband is so present at her supper that she hears him asking for the salt. TOPICS: Alienation, Loneliness, Widowhood.

151. Mueller, Lisa. "Monet Refuses the Operation." In
Second Language. Baton Rouge, La.: Louisiana State Univ.
Press, 1986, 2 pp. Also in Anthology 9.

A well-intentioned medical intervention might damage the inner vision reached by an older person. In this
poem the great Impressionist painter Claude Monet resists his doctor's recommendation for an eye operation.
For Monet the "blurring" of eyesight has enabled him to
see how the outlines of "real" things merge into a mystic
harmony of light and form: this way of seeing has inspired his painting. How could the artist give up such
a perspective? TOPICS: Doctor-Patient Conflicts, Creativity.

152. Murray, Michele. "Poem to My Grandmother in Her
Death." In *The Great Mother and Other Poems*. London:
Sheed and Ward, 1974, 2 pp. Also in Anthology 10.

The speaker's need to value her grandmother is expressed a dozen years after the old woman's death. The
grandmother had seemed alien--silent, worn by poverty,
children, drudgery--so that the speaker had been ashamed
of her. Once the old woman had wanted a bunch of bright
dahlias and bought it without pricing, and now the
speaker understands her own wish to meet the old woman
again "over your chipped cups brimming with tea."
TOPICS: Poverty, Grandparenting.

153. Niatum, Duane. "Old Woman Awaiting the Greyhound
Bus." In *Carriers of the Dream Wheel*. Edited by Duane
Niatum. New York: Harper & Row, 1975.

The happy fulfillment of the grandmotherly role is
seen in this portrait of a Native American whose face
wrinkles into happy smiles as she waits for the bus. The
poet, whom she has invited to sit beside her, imagines
those grandchildren playing and joking. Then the grandmother subsides into rest, quietly serene. TOPICS: Ethnicity, Grandparenting, Serenity.

154. O'Hehir, Diane. "Home Free." In *Home Free*. New
York: Atheneum, 1988. Also in Anthology 12.

How does a daughter say goodbye to her
ninety-year-old father who is comatose and confined to
his bed in a nursing home? The poet finds solace against
impending loss when she recalls the Buddhist tradition
of releasing small birds at temples--a symbol of the
soul's flight from one existence to another. Now she
feels assured that her father's soul will be free someday
from its confinement in his broken-down body. TOPICS:
Grief, Religion.

155. P'An Yueh. "In Mourning for His Dead Wife" (4th
century A. D.). In *Love and the Turning Year: One Hun-*

dred More Poems from the Chinese. Edited by Kenneth Rexroth. New York: New Directions, 1970, 2 pp. Also in Anthology 10.

From across sixteen centuries and the Far East comes this old but familiar cry of grief at the loss of one's spouse. The speaker is distraught at work and seizes upon duty as a way to assuage his grief. At home he sees her shadow, reads her letters, smells her perfume, dreams of her only to wake until the autumn morning dawns misty and dripping. He hopes the time may come when he can be calm enough to pour out his grief in public. TOPICS: Loneliness, Depression, Widowerhood.

156. Pastan, Linda. "Ethics." In *PM/AM: New and Selected Poems.* New York: Norton, 1982.

How aging complicates and subdues youthful exuberance and calls into question the timelessness of art are illustrated in the poet's recollection of a college assignment--a professor asking students in an ethics class to decide between saving a Rembrandt painting or an old woman if there were a fire in a museum. Years later, the poet--now an old woman herself, stands before a Rembrandt in a museum and ponders the question anew. TOPICS: Ageism, Role Reversal, Creativity.

157. Pastan, Linda. "The Five Stages of Grief." In *The Five Stages of Grief: Poems by Linda Pastan.* New York: Norton, 1978, 2 pp. Also in Anthology 10.

Pastan charts her emotional responses to grief: anger, denial, bargaining, depression, and acceptance. But the end of the journey provides a final lesson: grief is a circular process that does not promise easy resolution of one's loss. TOPICS: Alienation, Grief.

158. Pastan, Linda. "Funerary Tower: Han Dynasty." In collection above.

The grave of a father is visited by a mother and her daughter, 40. The mother appears to have resolved her feelings of grief for her husband, but the daughter is restless and impatient at the grave. Fears of her own mortality plague her, and she hurries her mother home. TOPICS: Mid-Life, Widowhood.

159. Pastan, Linda. "My Grandmother." In collection above.

The poet recalls her Jewish grandmother, who never overcomes her bitterness at having been forced to marry someone she did not love. Although she was traumatized by this capitulation to familial expectations and a sense of duty, she was unable to resist repeating the cycle of abuse in her own generation. When one of her granddaughters decides to marry a Gentile "for love," the old woman responds as if the young woman had died. TOPICS: Ethnicity, Grandparenting.

160. Pastan, Linda. "Something About the Trees." In *The Imperfect Paradise: Poems by Linda Pastan*. New York: Norton, 1988.

A woman's recognition of her parents' aging helps her come to grips with her own impending old age. Her meditation is based upon her father's advice: "There is an age when you are most yourself." The poet confronts the impermanence of relationships and the difficulty of facing one's mortality. TOPIC: Role Reversal.

161. Pitter, Ruth. "An Old Woman Speaks of the Moon." In *Poems 1926-1966*. London: Cresset Press, 1968.

Overcome by the beauty and timelessness of the full moon, an old woman pours out her feelings to anyone who will listen. A girl in a shop turns away, but the speaker of the poem is attentive to the old woman's rhapsodizing. Each night the old woman watches the moon from her window and is comforted "in her lonely age" by its presence. The speaker is warmed by this interchange. TOPICS: Creativity, Serenity.

162. Ransom, John Crowe. "Old Man Playing with Children" (1923). In *Selected Poems*, 3rd edition, Revised and Enlarged. New York: Ecco Press, 1978.

The aging person should return to the child's naive openness to adventure and play: so claims an old man playing with his grandsons. He rejects the weary retreats of talky old age. He rejects the timid cautious materialism of middle age. It's time for him to recognize that "This life is not good but in danger and in joy." This theme leads naturally to asking what kinds of "play" the aged person should seek. TOPICS: Grandparenting, Activity, Creativity, Anxiety, Courage.

163. Robinson, Edwin Arlington. "Isaac and Archibald" (1902). In *Selected Poems of Edwin Arlington Robinson*. Edited by Morton D. Zabel. New York: Macmillan, 1965, 11 pp. Also in Anthology 1.

The special pain of old age is seeing "the best friend of your life" go down in small collapses. This is what Isaac and his friend Archibald each see in the other during a visit, as observed by the impressionable boy who has tagged along. Each man separately shares his sober sadness with the boy, also his faith that much good still remains in the last years. The boy later recalls these two friends as heroic, larger than life. TOPICS: Friendship, Frailty, Transmission of Values.

164. Rukeyser, Muriel. "In Her Burning." In *Out of*

Silence. Evanston, Ill.: Triquarterly Books, 1944, 2 pp. Also in Anthology 12.

The old woman of this poem begs for one more lover's thrill from her dear one. She seeks passion's restorative touch before she lies "among the bones." Love in old age may be fainter than love in youth, just as moonlight is fainter than sunlight--but it is love all the same. TOPIC: Sexuality.

165. Sarton, May. "August Third." In *The Silence Now: New and Uncollected Earlier Poems*. New York: Norton, 1988.

The poet contemplates her old age on the day she is older than her mother was when her mother died thirty-five years ago. She celebrates her mother's "inexhaustible flame," the strengths of character that fueled her creativity and tenacity, and she acknowledges those values her mother passed on to her. TOPICS: Parent-Child Bonds, Transmission of Values.

166. Sarton, May. "Der Abschied" [The Farewell]. In *Selected Poems of May Sarton*. Edited by Serena Sue Hilsinger and Lois Byrnes. New York: Norton, 1978, 2 pp.

The poet revisits a place that was important to her and to a former lover. Her memory of their relationship triggers a meditation on the temporary nature of all relationships, the change that is a constant in our lives, and the recurring losses that we experience as we grow older. She seeks an answer to what underlying permanence exists behind this suffering and change. TOPICS: Intimacy, Alienation, Loss.

167. Sarton, May. "Gestalt at 60." In collection above, 4 pp.

Sarton charts the patterns of the poet's existence that have contributed to the development of her self. The "gestalt" of her life review includes the house she has lived in for ten years, her experience of the seasons, the garden that helped her survive her griefs, and the solitude that on the one hand sustained her and yet also exposed her to "moments of panic." She views her old age with optimism. TOPICS: Coping, Leisure, Life Review, Religion.

168. Sarton, May. "The House of Gathering." In *Letters from Maine: New Poems*. New York: Norton, 1984.

The title characterizes old age as a time when obligations, tasks, concerns, and pressing needs undermine the fullness of life. As a means of mediating this ongoing tension, the poet suggests the image of ripening, which strikes a balance between unfulfilled needs and one's acceptance of the limits of human achievement.

Finally, the poet offers simple words of advice: "Work, love, be silent." TOPICS: Activity, Autonomy, Serenity.

169. Sarton, May. "Mourning to Do." In collection above.
The poet grieves the loss of Judy, her former lover, who was afflicted with dementia at the end of her life. But in her grieving she finds solace, release, and even happiness in recalling vivid memories of their companionship. The process of grieving is invigorating because it allows her to revisit what was memorable, comforting, and special in that relationship. TOPICS: Older Couples, Intimacy, Loss.

170. Sarton, May. "On a Winter Night." In collection above. Also in Anthology 12.
In this meditation on the meaning of one's old age, the poet considers the point at which her life has turned from youth to age, and thinks first of her old age as a time of loss. Then she sees in the firelight signs of hope: images of clarity, growth, seasoning, and regeneration. TOPICS: Creativity, Anxiety.

171. Sarton, May. "Who has spoken of the unicorn in old age?" In *Letters from Maine: New Poems*. New York: Norton, 1984.
The poet celebrates the wisdom and experience of old age in her revision of the mythological tale of the unicorn. The poet suggests that if an aging unicorn sought a perfect being, it would find it not in a young virgin, but in an old woman, who has experienced suffering, known love and joy, survived grief, and become complete. TOPICS: Gender: Women, Intimacy, Wisdom.

172. Sexton, Anne. "Courage." In *The Awful Rowing Toward God*. Boston: Houghton Mifflin, 1975, 2 pp. Also in Anthology 5.
This poem is a reminder of what courage is and can be at every stage of life from infancy to the deathbed. The "you" of the poem is the reader taking a first toddling step, enduring the teasing of playmates, confronting the horror of war, surviving a great despair, facing old age, and meeting death. For Sexton, courage comes not so much from others as from the valiant self. TOPICS: Loneliness, Courage, Death.

173. Stanford, Ann. "The Fathers." In *The Descent*. New York: Viking Penguin, 1970. Also in Anthology 10.
The powerful claims of the old and the dead upon their children are recognized by the speaker, who feels both blessed and oppressed by those who came before. The speaker, after all, is their extension, their life made manifest. Their spirits hover near, both claiming and

weeping, but the speaker pleads: "It is my night, I say--and yours for sleeping." TOPICS: Autonomy, Transmission of Values.

174. Stone, John. "He Makes a House Call." In *All This Rain*. Baton Rouge, La.: Louisiana State Univ. Press, 1980, 2 pp. Also in Anthology 9.

A heart specialist visiting a former patient sees beyond the complicated surgery by which he saved this man seven years ago. He understands that in spite of the man's garish ordinariness, the life he saved was sacred: "You bled in my hands like a saint." The doctor leaves enriched with vegetables which the man has raised and given to him. He is also enriched with the blessing conferred by his profession. TOPICS: Doctor-Patient Relationships, Career.

175. Tennyson, Alfred. "Ulysses" (1842). In *Poems*. London: Scolar Press, 1976, 2 pp. Also in Anthology 12.

Rarely has such a call been voiced for old age to keep on exploring life. The speaker is King Ulysses, a legendary hero of the Trojan War who spent nineteen years of epic adventure before reaching home in Ithaca. Now old, he is bored with kingly routine, hungry for new adventure. So he leaves the throne to his son and gathers his old sailors for still another voyage. His challenge can be heard by anyone who might press forward into the late years--in science, art, learning, producing, travel, personal relationship. TOPICS: Activity, Courage, Aspirations.

176. Thomas, Dylan. "Do Not Go Gentle into That Good Night." In *The Collected Poems of Dylan Thomas*. New York: New Directions, 1957. Also in Anthologies 1, 5, 8, and 12.

The title carries the theme: don't easily surrender to decline and death. Four illustrations follow, of persons who come to death knowing they had missed full achievement: wise persons, good persons, "wild" persons (poets?), and "grave" persons. All do resist death; so should the poet's failing father. It was for him that this magnificent poem was written. TOPICS: Rebellion, Depression, Aspirations, Death.

177. Van Doren, Mark. "Bay-Window Ballad" (1948). In *Collected and New Poems: 1924-1963*. New York: Hill & Wang, 1963.

An old man who no longer occupies the role of head of the household experiences a sad but inevitable transition. As he stands at the window of his farmhouse, watching his grandson leading a team of horses, he recalls a time seventy years ago, when he worked on the

farm as a young man. His wistful reflections are temp-
ered when he taps on the glass and his grandson "whirls
his hat" in recognition. TOPICS: Role Loss, Grandparenting, Alienation.

178. Van Doren, Mark. "Death of Old Men" (1928). In
collection above.
        What is lost when old men die? The poet describes
the wizened faces of the old as punctuated "with a grim-
ace, a grey grin" and compares the old to sturdy fence
posts rooted deep in the ground. Then he compares the
worlds of the old and the young and concludes that the
young will be transformed by experience and advancing
age. TOPICS: Ageism, Wisdom.

179. Van Doren. "The First Snow of the Year" (1960). In
collection above, 2 pp. Also in Anthology 8.
        The power of love that endures through a long re-
lationship is depicted in this brief interchange between
an old couple in their house while outside "the first
snow of the year danced on the lawn." An old man, bedridden, listens to his wife bringing him a tray of food
up the stairs. He is stirred by memories of their courting, and she, too, remembers details of those events.
Both are soothed by the sweetness of these memories, yet
realize the inevitability of their eventual separation.
TOPICS: Older Couples, Caregiving.

180. Van Doren, Mark. "Nothing But Death" (1937). In
Collected and New Poems: 1924-1963. New York: Hill &
Wang, 1963.
        A woman's vanity and inflexibility is overcome only
by her experience of mortality--the deaths of her friends
and her husband. Her children have suffered their mother's intractability and hostility for many years. Now
in old age she becomes understanding and compassionate.
TOPICS: Parent-Child Conflicts, Vanity, Widowhood.

181. Van Doren, Mark. "Old Man, Old Woman." In *Good
Morning: Last Poems*. Foreward by Richard Howard. New
York: Farrar, 1973. Also in Anthology 5.
        The unspoken, intuitive communication between a
frail old couple is the subject of this simple but eloquent poem. Each spouse is instantly and constantly
aware of pains in the other, a mutual awareness which
helps them "feel good together, their hearts equal."
TOPICS: Older Couples, Frailty, Serenity.

182. Van Doren, Mark. "Sleep, Grandmother" (1948). In
Collected and New Poems: 1924-1963. New York: Hill &
Wang, 1963.
        An old woman's reverie moments before falling

asleep is likened to a final life review before dying. Each stanza begins, "Sleep, Grandmother, sleep." The speaker reminds the woman of images from her past—all of which recall a loving family life at the turn of the century. A final image, of a figure at her door, seems to refers to a lucky suitor asking her to dance many years ago; but the image is likely the figure of death coming to take her. TOPICS: Family Bonds, Life Review, Death.

183. Van Doren, Mark. "Spirit" (1924). In collection above.

The poet celebrates the determination of an old woman who lives alone. Her daily ritual of making tea, which is her means of maintaining her physical and emotional well-being, is also symbolic of a ritual that connects her experiences to women in earlier times. TOPICS: Frailty, Coping.

184. Van Doren, Mark. "The Uncle I Was Named For" (1953). In collection above, 3 pp.

A man's last visit to his uncle's house in rural Oklahoma in 1939 provides some perspective on the uncle's qualities of character, rural values, and humble life. A bachelor until the age of 50, the old man is excited to see his nephew married and with a family. His wife and he are affectionate hosts, and when the guests leave the next day, the poem ends with an ironic reference to the uncle's impending death. TOPICS: Family Bonds, Legacies.

185. Van Doren, Mark. "We Were Not Old" (1937). In collection above, 2 pp.

The contrasting worlds of youth and age are examined in this poem about a group of young people who, while a blizzard rages outside their house, contemplate the fate of a neighbor, an old man who lives alone. They pity him, and they imagine that a better fate for him would have been an early death. Their patronizing concerns are contradicted by the old man's passionate response to life, which has helped him adapt to harsh circumstances. TOPICS: Ageism, Adaptation, Coping, Courage.

186. Van Duyn, Mona. "Letters from a Father." In *Letters from a Father and Other Poems*. New York: Atheneum, 1982, 4 pp. Also in Anthology 5.

An old man overcomes his listlessness and depression on receiving the gift of a bird feeder from his adult daughter. At first he takes so little pleasure that the feeder seems a waste. Then he notes his wife's interest in the birds, then finds his own. From a curious study of the new bird book, he progresses to amusement to caring for the birds. His health and morale improve accordingly. TOPICS: Disability, Depression, Serenity, Leisure.

187. Wagoner, David. "Into the Nameless Places." In *Broken Country: Poems*. Boston: Little, Brown, 1979.
   The confusion and desperation arising from dementia, as it is experienced by the demented person, is portrayed in the interview of an old woman in a nursing home. When she is asked a series of questions meant to orient her to reality, she fails the test. Reality seems to be "slipping away" from her. Because she is aphasic, she is unable to express her thoughts. Although she is in contact with a strange inner landscape (the nameless places"), peopled with fragments of memories, she can not convey that reality to her questioner. TOPICS: Dementia, Doctor-Patient Conflicts, Alienation.

188. Wagoner, David. "Part Song." In collection above.
   The deadening experience of life in a nursing home is portrayed when residents of a nursing home and their families gather for a pathetic Thanksgiving party. The old people are immobile, detached, waiting for death. The family members at the Thanksgiving party are caught up in their private memories of personal losses. TOPICS: Ageism, Dementia, Long-term Care, Disengagement, Alienation.

189. Walker, Alice. "Goodnight, Willie Lee, I'll See You in the Morning." In *Goodnight, Willie Lee, I'll See You in the Morning*. New York: Delacorte Press, 1979. Also in Anthology 10.
   Forgiveness at death is expressed by the speaker's mother, who looks down at her husband's dead face to utter the words of the title. This civil and heartfelt speech, spoken without tears or smiles, means pardon for everything, a pardon which to the speaker underscores the promise of reunion after death. TOPICS: Race, Widowhood, Religion.

190. Wheelock, John. "Dear Men and Women." In *Dear Men and Women: New Poems*. New York: Scribner, 1966, 2 pp. Also in Anthology 10.
   The old speaker thinks of the dear men and women who have died before, then thinks of the meaning of death. He knows that death is the cutting-off of future joys; it underscores "the heartbreak at the heart of things." But if these dear people are lost in death, in his loving remembrance they are all his forever. The poem moves clearly and serenely, drawing on nature imagery to mark the passage of life. TOPICS: Serenity, Spiritual Life, Transmission of Values, Death.

191. Wheelock, John. "Song on Reaching Seventy" (1956). In *The Gardener and Other Poems*. New York: Scribner, 1961, 3 pp. Also in Anthology 5.

The preciousness of life as it can appear to an older person is celebrated in this poem. Just as a thrush may lift up its heart against the night, so may the speaker as he looks into the greater night of death. Every detail of nature is now seen in piercing beauty and longing; so is every tender memory. The poem ends with a prayer for just a little more of this joy. TOPICS: Wisdom, Spiritual Life, Death.

192. Whitman, Walt. "Song at Sunset." In *Leaves of Grass*. 1860. Reprint, Edited with an Introduction by Jerome Loving. New York: Oxford Univ. Press, 1990, 3 pp.

The beauty of day's end and implicitly of life's end is celebrated here, as Whitman's *Leaves of Grass* celebrated American life in all its variety. Stanza after stanza utters a great joy in all that life brings, including death. Though death approaches the poet still sings "unmitigated adoration." TOPIC: Spiritual Life.

193. Williams, William Carlos. "Dedication for a Plot of Ground" (1917). In *The Collected Poems of William Carlos Williams*. 2 vols. Edited by Christopher MacGowan. New York: New Directions, 1988, 2 pp.

Celebrating the life and legacy of his grandmother, the poet lists the adversities she overcame in a long and difficult life: emigration from England, widowhood, a second marriage, surrogate mother to two of her grandsons (including the poet). The "plot of ground" is her house and land in West Haven, Connecticut. The old woman also is the subject of "The Last Words of My English Grandmother" (see below). TOPICS: Widowhood, Legacies.

194. Williams, William Carlos. "The Last Words of My English Grandmother" (1939). In collection above, 2 pp. Also in Anthology 12.

A feisty, unregenerate old woman is moved noisily from her untidy lodgings to an ambulance, where she utters her final words of tired wisdom. Before she dies, she hurls several pithy barbs at her caregivers. An earlier version of the poem, written in 1924, adds insights on intergenerational relationships. TOPICS: Rebellion, Autonomy, Wisdom, Anxiety, Death.

195. Williams, William Carlos. "To a Poor Old Woman" (1935). In *The Collected Poems of William Carlos Williams*. 2 vols. Edited by Christopher MacGowan. New York: New Directions, 1988.

The poem celebrates an old woman's capacity for finding comfort and serenity in one of life's small

pleasures--enjoying food. The old woman stands alone on
a street corner and savors the sweet taste of plums. All
of the woman's senses are concentrated in her act of eating the plums. The poet repeats, "They taste good to
her." TOPICS: Ageism, Economics, Serenity.

196. Williams, William Carlos. "To Waken an Old Lady"
(1921). In collection above.
     The poet likens the small joys of old age to those
of small birds which in midwinter struggle against the
harsh elements and find contentment in a field of broken
seed husks. Impending mortality, personified by "a dark
wind," does not deter the activity and determination of
the birds. TOPICS: Activity, Coping.

197. Williams, William Carlos. "Tract" (1917). In collection above, 2 pp.
     The pretension, hypocrisy, and sham which surround
funeral customs are targeted in this sarcastic and rauc-
ous tirade. The poet strips away all vestiges of pomp
and formality, advises mourners to remain open to the experience of the ritual, and challenges them, "Or do you
think you can shut grief in?" TOPICS: Humor, Grief,
Death.

198. Williams, William Carlos. "The Widow's Lament in
Springtime" (1921). In collection above. Also in Anthology 10.
     A widow voices the piercing sorrow of losing a
long-time spouse at a time when the world is bursting
into flower. The widow feels incapacitated by her grief
and subsequent depression. She despairs at the show of
spring flowers and colors. TOPICS: Depression, Widowhood.

199. Yeats, William Butler. "A Prayer for Old Age"
(1935). In *W. B. Yeats: The Poems*. Edited by Richard J.
Finnegan. New York: Macmillan, 1983.
     Yeats emphasizes his longstanding desire to recover
the powers of imagination and creativity against the on-
slaught of time and age in this poem. He decries the nar-
rowness of intellectual thought and prays for a song that
"thinks in a marrow-bone." He ends with a fervent cry
for a response to life that will redeem his soul. TOPICS:
Creativity, Wisdom.

200. Yeats, William Butler.   "Sailing to Byzantium"
(1927). In collection above, 2 pp. Also in Anthologies
5, 8, and 12.
     The poem features one of the most eloquent expres-
sions of Yeats' often-felt dismay and rage at how society demeans the old. He writes metaphorically of an old
man as "a tattered coat upon a stick." Then the aged

speaker rejects the sensual world of the young and embraces the city of Byzantium, an ancient symbol of the
timeless and everlasting nature of art. TOPICS: Roles,
Creativity, Alienation.

201. Yeats, William Butler.   "The Wild Old Wicked Man"
(1938). In *W. B. Yeats: The Poems*. Edited by Richard J.
Finnegan.   New York: Macmillan, 1983.

In this exuberant celebration of sexuality in aging, two voices are heard--those of a wild old man and
a pious woman.   Their dialogue has the flavor and cryp-
tic refrain of an old ballad.   The old man begs the woman
to give him love because he is still "mad about women"
and can pierce their hearts with the words and wit denied
to younger men.   The poem bears comparison to a poem by
the same title, written by Archibald MacLeish (148,
above).   TOPICS: Sexuality, Creativity, Alienation.

202. Yeats, William Butler.   "The Wild Swans at Coole"
(1919).   In collection above.   Also in Anthology 12.

In this haunting vision of the streaming away of
youth into old age, the poet explores one way in which
timeless beauty compensates for the changes effected by
time and circumstance.   Standing by the water at Coole
on a still October day, the narrator looks out upon a
flock of swans and notes the nineteen years that have
passed since he first saw these swans appear.   Saddened
by the thought of how much has changed in that time, he
realizes that there is something eternal and mysterious
in what the swans represent. TOPICS: Wisdom, Mid-Life.

203. Zuckerman, Marilyn.   "After Sixty." In *Ourselves,
Growing Older: Women, Aging with Knowledge and Power*,
edited by Paula Doress-Worters. New York: Simon & Schuster, 1987, 2 pp.   Also in Anthology 5.

How much life can still open for a woman approaching sixty!   The speaker of this poem refuses to believe
that old age is a dull and limited country from where her
voice will never be heard again.   Now that she has passed
the great compulsions of passion, children, marriage, she
is ready "to throw everything away and begin again"--to
become an activist for peace, for womanhood, for all
causes needing woman's wisdom. TOPICS: Gender: Women,
Wisdom, Leisure, Retirement.

Stories

[Entries 204-358.]

204. Adams, Alice. "The Girl Across the Room" (1976). In *The New Yorker*. N. p. Also in Anthology 5 and Anthology 11, pp. 248-60.

The wife, Yvonne, examines her long marriage to Matthew, as the two sit after dinner on the California coast. How close had she come to losing him long ago, when a beautiful young Susanna had fallen in love with him? But Yvonne had quietly held her own; the affair evaporated and rightly, for Matthew would not have lasted very well with the girl. Yvonne also thinks wryly of their sex life, which ceased after her cancer in her late fifties; was sex really that important in old age? She thinks too of their reducing their exposure to harsh climate and long trips. Finally she wonders which one will survive the other, and concludes that since Matthew is deeply dependent on her, it must be herself. Their social background is upper-middle-class intellectual. TOPICS: Older couples, Sexuality, Coping, Leisure, Life review.

205. Adams, Alice. "Ocracoke Island." In *After You've Gone*. New York: Fawcett Crest, 1989, pp. 113-126.

A retired professor whose younger wife has left him spends a painful day visiting old ties in New York. Duncan Elliott, a distinguished scholar, has had to endure the humiliation of his wife's highly publicized running off to an island resort with a celebrated young poet. He mulls over the difference between jealousy in an older person and in a younger person. He overexposes his agony in meetings with a suave but shallow former student, a pretentious old colleague, and a sensible for-

mer wife.   Despite her assurances that his wife Cathy
will eventually return, Duncan ends in a tormented, enraged, sleepless night in his hotel room as he imagines
that resort island, a place of glamorous youth from
which, as an older man, he feels forever barred. TOPICS:
Ageism, Older Couples, Intimacy, Isolation, Loss.

206. Adler, Warren. "The Angel of Mercy." In *The Sunset
Gang*. New York: Viking, 1977. Also in Anthology 4, pp.
174-92.
      An old man's private investigation of a mysterious
old woman's activities in a retirement village provides
insights into how old people deal with the ever present
reality of death and suggests on a metaphorical level the
spirituality that lies at the heart of caregiving. Yetta
Klugerman is known as the "angel of mercy" to the residents of Sunset Village, a retirement complex in Florida. Although she regularly visits people who are convalescing at home, no one knows much about her personal
life or background until one of the recipients of her
care decides to solve the mystery. He becomes obsessed
with the idea that this old woman is not a human being
at all--but a ministering angel who has the power to heal
people. TOPICS: Neighbors, Caregiving, Religion, Transmission of Values.

207. Aucamp, Hennie. "A Bridal Bed for Tant Nonnie." In
House Visits: A Collection of Short Stories. Selected
and Translated by Ian Ferguson. Cape Town, South Africa:
Tafelberg, 1983, pp. 38-44.
      A young man recalls a special fondness for an aunt
who inspired him with her passion and zeal for life. He
returns home and finds her living with his parents. The
last time he saw her he was a schoolboy and Tant Nonnie
was in her 50s; now she is 70 and "the prey of rheuma-
tism." Her nephew loves to talk to her, and he is curious about the men she loved and lost. Nonnie hints at
some of her liaisons but never reveals any details. Then
one day the nephew sees the old woman bristle when a
guest mentions someone's name; later, the nephew learns
from his mother that this man left Nonnie after she had
his child. The nephew realizes she never overcame the
humiliation felt in this loss. A few weeks later Nonnie
dies. The nephew promises to prepare her grave as a
"bridal bed," lined with fragrant herbs and leaves to
honor her memory. TOPICS: Gender: Women, Family Bonds,
Transmission of Values, Dying.

208. Aucamp, Hennie. "Soup for the Sick." In collection
above. Also in Anthology 7, pp. 3-12.
      An interracial bond between an elderly white woman
in South Africa and her "colored" servant-woman puzzles

the twelve-year-old narrator who has proudly brought a
gift of partridge soup. No one knows much about the past
of either Tant Rensie or her servant Sofie, but gossips
wonder about their apparently intimate relationship. To
his surprise the boy finds the two with Sofie's hands
folded over Tant Rensie's; and then Tant Rensie insists
that all three eat the soup together--a breach of apart-
heid etiquette. He is moved. Later, after Sofie dies,
Tant Rensie wants her servant buried in the white cemetery, a request disallowed by the town council. But she
visits Sofie's grave whenever her own health allows; and
her will directs that she be laid to rest next to Sofie.
TOPICS: Multicultural, Older Couples.

209. Auchincloss, Louis. "The Cathedral Builder." In
Second Chance: Tales of Two Generations. Boston:
Houghton Mifflin, 1970, pp. 19-42.
    The way in which lofty goals and aspirations may
define characteristics of an indomitable human spirit is
illustrated in an old man's lifelong dream to complete
a gothic cathedral in New York City. St. Matthew's Cathedral (based on the Cathedral of St. John the Divine) was
an aging edifice in a deteriorating 1960s neighborhood.
But to John Lancaster, 89, it was to be "the most beautiful church in the world." Lancaster shares his vision
with Jerry, a young clerk who works for him in an ac-
counting firm: he will finish the cathedral by spending
the twenty million dollars he has accumulated in the past
sixty-five years. But delays and rising costs force modi-
fications. Eventually John realizes even his fortune is
insufficient; the cathedral will remain unfinished. He
dies shortly after terminating the project. But Jerry
remains inspired by Lancaster's aspirations toward the
unattainable. TOPICS: Poverty, Intergenerational, Aspirations, Religion, Legacies.

210. Auchincloss, Louis. "The Double Gap." In collection above, pp. 144-71.
    An irreconcilable conflict between two genera-
tions--a "double gap" of values--emerges in this dispute,
carried on by letters in the 1960s, over whether or not
a grandson will join his grandfather's prestigious law
firm in Manhattan. "Albert Ellsworth, 77, corresponds
with his grandson, Philip Kyles, 22, who has just graduated from law school. The old man reveals his rebellion
against his own father, who neglected the family, and the
redemption he found in a hero and surrogate father in Mr.
Carter, his boss at the firm. Philip is a rebel, too.
He resents the way his grandfather sided with Philip's
mother--against his father--in all disputes: "I faced not
one but two older generations, solidly united." Philip
also learned that Carter was a Machiavellian who de-

stroyed others to attain his goals. By contrast Philip
views the law as an avenue of serving the disadvantaged.
Neither man yields to the other, and the old man ends the
correspondence with an invective. TOPICS: Gender: Men,
Parent-Child Conflicts, Intergenerational, Employment.

211. Auchincloss, Louis. "Suttee." In collection above,
pp. 219-41. Also in Anthology 4, pp. 327-45.
    The extent to which an older woman's identity is
dependent upon her husband's status, and the consequences
of fearing the risks of intimacy in old age are illustrated in the experiences of Agnes Lynn, widowed at the
age of 67. Her husband was senior partner in a law firm.
After his death, Agnes finds herself set adrift from the
firm and isolated. Another partner, a man of 51, proposes friendship and a business alliance. She is restored to her former place in a variety of social functions, but then discovers, to her dismay, that he wants
to marry her. Agnes flees from his proposal and embraces
the image of the eternally grieving wife: her final capitulation is reminiscent of the Hindu "suttee," the ritual in which Hindu wives hurled themselves on their husbands' funeral pyres to affirm their fidelity. TOPICS:
Roles, Gender: Women, Intimacy, Isolation, Widowhood.

212. Bausch, Richard. "Evening." In *Rare and Endangered
Species: A Novella and Stories*. Boston: Houghton Mifflin, 1994, pp. 83-98.
    An unaccountable depression nags at William Wal-
lingham as he finishes a painting chore in early evening.
This "misery" had started on his seventy-fourth birthday,
when he realized that he had lived beyond his father's
age. After a gust of awful gloom, the feeling passed but
has seeped back between the good days. He knows of no
cause, no remedy. On the surface his long marriage with
Cat goes smoothly with minor bickering. She has told him
to get himself busy: hence his painting. Now his daughter Susan visits, angry with a divorced husband.   He
plays fitfully with his grandchild Elaine. The suspicion
that the women in his family talk about him ends his
evening with deep loneliness, which he covers with false
cheer. TOPICS: Alienation, Depression, Retirement.

213. Bausch, Richard. "Letter to the Lady of the House."
In *The Fireman's Wife and Other Stories*. New York: Simon
& Schuster, 1990. Reprint, New York: Norton, 1991. Also
in Anthology 11, pp. 287-300.
    How do lifetime marriages turn sour in old age?
On the midnight eve of his seventieth birthday, the
narrator tries writing a letter to his wife, now sleeping
after another "long, silent evening" following a stupid
argument--this time over whether he should use pepper on

his potatoes. He tries to sum up months of thinking
about it all, an effort which leads to his recalling a
boyhood visit to his newly married cousin Louise. That
marriage, which to the boy had seemed so idyllic, later
dissolved in hatred and death. Now the old man thinks
that that ruined marriage must still have been worth that
wonderful first loveliness. He ends by expressing the
same conviction to his wife, his "dear adversary."
TOPICS: Older Couples, Intimacy, Alienation.

214. Bausch, Richard. "Rare and Endangered Species."
In *Rare and Endangered Species: A Novella and Stories*.
Boston: Houghton Mifflin, 1994, pp. 155-257.
    The radiating anguish begun by the unexplainable
suicide of a sixtyish woman is followed through the lives
of her husband, children, and friends. Andrea Brewer
calmly lunches with two friends, then registers at a
motel and takes a lethal dose of pills. What brought her
to it? True, she had a love affair many years ago.
Recently she and her husband have sold their beloved
Virginia farm to move into smaller quarters--but that
seems the only present stress. Her family begins to
recall instances when Andrea had drifted off into
solitude. But her death remains a mystery whose pain
angers her husband Harry; it enters the marriage of her
son James and his wife, her pregnant daughter Maizie and
her husband. It affects her friend Pauline who is
dealing with a wild daughter. It draws Maizie into a
close friendship with an older man, a friendship which
threatens his marriage. This pain seems to converge upon
Maizie's agony in the hospital delivery room. Her agony
gives way to the general joy at her successful giving
birth, an affirmation of life amid grief and self-doubts.
TOPICS: Family bonds, Older couples, Alienation, Suicide,
Widowhood.

215. Bausch, Richard. "What Feels Like the World." In
Spirits and Other Stories. New York: Simon & Schuster,
1987. Also in Anthology 5, pp. 205-19.
    A widower caring for an orphaned granddaughter
tries to support her in a childhood ordeal. Brenda, a
fifth grader, has put herself under an almost morbid discipline to lose weight and to leap over the vaulting
horse in a gymnastics exhibition at school. She is
afraid she can't do it, nor does the story at its end
tell whether she can. The core of the story is the
little girl's struggle and the grandfather's sensitive
but restrained companionship. In the background are the
mother's divorce and recent death; the difficult bond between her and the grandfather; the grandfather's indigna-
tion at the unrealistic expectations which adults can lay

on children; and the grandfather's not knowing what to
do with retirement. TOPICS: Grandparenting, Retirement.

216. Baxter, Charles. "Fenstad's Mother." In *The Best
American Short Stories 1989*. Edited by Margaret Atwood.
Boston: Houghton Mifflin. Also in Anthology 5, pp. 139-
51.

A mother's eagerness for life and the adult son's efforts to help are intensified by their contrast: the
mother being a lifelong radical and her good-hearted son
Fenstad being quite conventional. He takes her to the
evening class which he teaches; she captivates the students while criticizing his traditional values. He takes
her to a restaurant, where she tries to give her coat to
a beggar and scolds him for substituting cash. She comes
out to a skating rink to watch her son as he skates with
his girl friend. After her bronchitis which follows,
Fenstad finds his mother being visited by a student
friend she has made, sharing jazz tapes with her. Over
her happiness Fenstad prays nightly in thanksgiving,
"even though he knew she would disapprove." TOPICS:
Parent-Child Bonds, Employment.

217. Baxter, Charles. "Horace and Margaret's Fifty Second." In *Harmony of the World*. Columbia, Mo.: Univ. of
Missouri, 1984, pp. 44-58.

A woman's descent into dementia, portrayed from her
point of view, is illustrated in this story of a couple
whose relationship, after fifty-two years of marriage,
remains painful and unfulfilled. Margaret has placed her
husband Horace in a nursing home, ostensibly because he
was losing his memory. Early in the story it becomes apparent that Margaret--much more so than Horace--is
experiencing symptoms of advancing dementia. She is
losing her grasp of reality, including the identities of
family members, her comprehension of simple household
tasks, and other memories. Her words become tangled and
her perceptions muddled. Margaret's visit with Horace re-
opens old emotional wounds, and Margaret retreats from
any attempts at resolution. TOPICS: Older Couples, Dementia, Anxiety, Aging in Place.

218. Bentley, Phyllis. "Mother and Daughter." In *Kith
and Kin: Nine Tales of Family Life*. London: Victor Gol-
lancz, 1960. Also in *Family: Stories from the Interior*.
Edited by Geri Giebel Chavis. Saint Paul, Minn.: Graywolf, 1987, pp. 66-92.

Parent-child tensions can resurface with each generation, especially when the older generation lacks insight. Dorothy Bitt, English, of college age in the
1920s, enjoys her crowd, all inflamed with the radicalism
of the post-war decade. Although she worships her kindly

father, she furiously resists her hard-hearted, critical, intolerant mother, who in return resents the current visit of the grandmother. Dorothy escapes into marriage with an incipient playboy. The second part of the story shows middle-aged Dorothy saddled with an irresponsible husband, trying to deal with her rebellious daughter Carol. The conflict repeats many of the motifs of her own youth. Only at the end does Dorothy hit upon a compassionate understanding of "the eternal strife of the generations"--an insight useful to parents of any age. TOPICS: Parent-Child Conflicts, Mid-Life.

219. Berriault, Gina. "The Bystander." In *The Infinite Passion of Expectation: Twenty-Five Stories*. San Francisco: North Point Press, 1982, pp. 29-37.
      The aged wreckage stored up in public institutions is hauntingly shown as a son goes to visit his aging father, whose violent breakdown has landed him in a psychiatric hospital. The son is vividly aware of the alienation of the patients. The small talk is ghastly. In a final awareness, the son sees his father in other male patients: "He was the parent who breaks down under the eyes of his child, the parent in the last years when all the circumstances of his life have got him trussed and dying, while the child stands and watches the end of the struggle and then walks away to catch a streetcar." TOPICS: Economics, Parent-Child Bonds, Doctor-Patient Conflicts.

220. Berriault, Gina. "The Diary of K. W." In collection above, pp. 135-51.
      Many lonely old people live in impoverished solitude, but few are as eloquent as K. W., an elderly loser who keeps a strangely engaging diary over several weeks as she starves physically and spiritually. K. W. has been fired as cafeteria substitute helper at a grammar school because she couldn't bear feeding the children who would only grow up in misery. From her rambling thoughts, one learns that K. W. had been a high school valedictorian; she had once been married; she has read philosophy; she has painted; she has worked most of her life on her feet. She fantasizes about loving a young man who has moved upstairs. The brief final entry by this fearful, pessimistic, but tender and loving woman is headed "The Last Day." TOPICS: Economics, Loneliness, Aspirations, Death.

221. Berriault, Gina. "Nocturne." In collection above, pp. 224-32.
      Empathy for the difficulties of helpless aging is here shown with rare insight. Eulalia, a dependent old woman and would-be hanger-on of the Rand family, is seen through the eyes of another dependent, the young daugh-

ter-in-law Val, whose husband has deserted her and her
two children. Eulalia is a gossipy, grasping, senile,
ugly woman who makes Val uncomfortable "in the presence
of a hunger that buzzed like a huge bee." But on exam-
ining her own life, Val sees in Eulalia "the end result
of Val herself." Though instructed by her mother-in-law
not to give Eulalia food, Val when left alone invites the
old woman to supper. TOPICS: Intergenerational, Dementia.

222. Berry, Wendell. "Are You All Right?" (1991). In
Fidelity: Five Stories. New York: Pantheon Bks, 1992,
pp. 191-200.
      Two middle-aged men learn a lesson about the
vitality and independence of old age. The story is told
from the point of view of Andy, who with his neighbor
Elton sets out in the middle of the night to check on the
safety of Art and Mart Rowanberry after a flood cuts the
old men off from human contact for four days. Before
long Andy and Elton have imagined the worst. Elton's
concern is rooted in his special relationship with the
brothers. They were like family to him when he was a
young man. After a long and arduous trek across high
ground, they come upon the house in darkness. Their
calls are answered by Art's voice--a long-rising
"Yeeeaaah?"--a triumphant assurance of the brother's
safety, self-confidence, and security. Andy reflects
upon the irony of this image of two old people riding out
the flood--because a year later Elton died, and his old
friend Art survived Elton by a dozen years. TOPICS: Ageism, Gender: Men, Friendship, Intergenerational, Coping,
Aging in Place.

223. Borges, Jorge Luis. "The Immortals." In *The Aleph
and Other Stories, 1933-1969, Together With Commentaries
and an Autobiographical Essay*. Edited and Translated by
Norman Thomas di Giovanni in Collaboration with the Author. New York: Dutton, 1970. Also in Anthology 7, pp.
205-10.
      The folly of extending the human life span beyond
any real quality of life is revealed in this dry brief
fantasy. A Doctor Narbondo has engineered perpetual existence for four human heads. Each is supported by a
"body" which is none other than an electric prosthesis.
"The rest," so the Doctor boasts, "is Formica, steel,
plastics. Respiration, alimentation, generation, mobil-
ity--elimination itself!--belongs to the past." Unfortu-
nately the capacity for speech has not yet been designed
for these heads. When the Doctor invites him to sign up
for immortality, the narrator flees in panic, assumes
disguise, and changes his name. TOPIC: Health Care.

224. Brecht, Bertolt. "The Unseemly Old Lady." In *Short*

Stories 1921-1946.   Edited by John Willett and Ralph
Mannheim.   London: Methuen, 1983. Also in Anthology 5,
pp. 268-72.
    A widow builds a new life quite distinct from her
former life as wife and mother. Her grandson, the narrator, tells how his German grandmother dropped old ties
and habits and relished her newfound independence. She
took on new tastes which somewhat shocked her conservative children: movies, congenial hobnobbing at the disreputable cobbler's shop, meals at the inn, hired carriage, racetrack, befriending a "half-wit" young woman.
As the sympathetic narrator sums it up: "She had savored
to the full the long years of servitude and the short
years of freedom and consumed the bread of life to the
last crumb." TOPICS: Adaptation, Gender: Women, Parent-
Child Conflicts, Autonomy, Leisure, Widowhood.

225. Brooks, Gwendolyn.   "Death of a Grandmother." In
Maud Martha. New York: Harper & Brothers, 1953, pp. 11-
15.
    The repulsive last hours of an old woman are wit-
nessed by the granddaughter. Maud Martha sees Grandmother
as a "semi-corpse": ugly, repellent, capable only of responding to questions with "Hawh." Yet in the isolation
of death, this ordinary woman was about to enter the most
interesting door of all. So she "towered, triumphed over
them, while they stood there asking the stupid questions
people ask the sick. . . . " The callous irritability of
an overworked hospital staff is voiced by the nurse who
bitterly refuses to fetch a bedpan for another patient.
Maud returns home to learn that the grandmother has
died--an announcement that brings back to Maud the loving, doting Gramma of her childhood. TOPICS: Race,
Grandparenting, Dementia, Health Care, Death.

226. Brown, Mary Ward. "The Amaryllis." In *Tongues of
Flame*. New York: E. P. Dutton, 1986. Also in Anthology
5, pp. 104-16.
    In this story a widower rediscovers the beauty of
life through a single unexpected gift. Judge James Man-
derville, a widower, has received from his daughter an
amaryllis bulb which has now produced a magnificent first
bloom. For the lonely judge, this flower so wonderfully
sums up the possible loveliness of life that he spends
the whole day inviting and entertaining friends, colleagues, business people to share in celebration of this
rare plant. Incidentally he learns to appreciate these
people more fully. Even his memory of his dead wife is
sharpened by his taking a new look at her notebooks. Although the amaryllis fades, he is assured that it will
grow and bloom again. TOPICS: Community, Creativity, Serenity, Leisure, Widowerhood.

227. Canin, Ethan. "Emperor of the Air." In *Emperor of the Air*. Boston: Houghton Mifflin, 1988. Also in Anthology 9, pp. 297-307.

A quarrel between an old man and his neighbor is resolved when the old man gains insight into the depth of his neighbor's affection for his son. The old man, a retired high-school teacher of biology and astronomy, has lived all his life in this home next to a magnificent old elm, now fatally infested with insects. His new neighbor, an aggressive man, wants to cut down the elm to save his own elms. After resisting in vain, the old man plots to infect his neighbor's trees with the same insects and thus to nullify his neighbor's demands. On the night of the intended crime, he hears his neighbor outside, star-gazing with his son, and assigning some of the stars—wrongly—poetic names like "Emperor of the Air." This glimpse of fatherly imagination restores the old man to his sanity and wholeness. TOPICS: Neighbors, Enmity, Deviance.

228. Canin, Ethan. "We Are Nighttime Travelers." In *Emperor of the Air*. Boston: Houghton Mifflin, 1988. Also in Anthologies 9 and 11; and in Anthology 12, pp. 235-247.

The growing gap between husband and wife has left Frank Manlius a frightfully lonely man, with his wife equally so in her parts of the home which he built a half-century ago. Diabetic, dim-visioned, and lame, Frank spreads his time over reading poetry and visiting the aquarium and the coffee shop. Alone in the kitchen at night, he makes stabs at writing his own and others' poetry. His wife Francine begins to fancy that a strange man appears nightly at her window, leaving scraps of poetry on the sill. The story ends with a leap of new awareness, each of the other. TOPICS: Older Couples, Intimacy, Retirement.

229. Carver, Raymond. "After the Denim." *In What We Talk about When We Talk about Love*. New York: Knopf, 1981. Also in Anthology 4, pp. 290-99.

How a narrow-valued older person can be threatened by unconventional youngsters is shown in James Parker, a retired accountant who attends a Bingo game with his wife Edith. Their usual parking space and their usual seats are taken by a young couple in denims: the man wearing ponytail and earring. Parker and Edith live a narrow life in which, as a substitute for his former drinking, he knits. Regularity is important so that he resents the intrusion of these hippie kids, especially when he sees that the man is cheating (and winning). The evening ends with Edith reporting serious health symptoms; they will have to see a doctor. Alone and ter-

rified, James wishes those young people could learn what
life really had in store for them "after the denim." He
grimly and bravely returns to his knitting. TOPICS: Intergenerational, Disease, Alienation.

230. Cather, Willa. "Neighbor Rosicky" (1928).   In
Obscure Destinies. New York: Knopf, 1932, pp. 3-71.
     Old farmer Anton Rosicky risks his life in generous
assistance to the daughter-in-law he loves. Originally
a tailor, Anton had worked in New York until he sickened
of city life and moved West with his wife Mary. As farmers they have been industrious but never anxious.   They
enjoy each other and their five sons. They are hospita-
ble and good neighbors.   They can be said to be aging
beautifully. The action begins with Anton's doctor warning him of a bad heart. A main concern is his beloved
Polly, his son Rudolph's American wife, a woman who finds
farm life hard. He wins her affection by kindness; then,
in a fatal act of paternal love, he overtaxes his heart
by plowing up thistles on her farm. Anton's reminiscences not only explain the present action but show the values of life review. TOPICS: Rural Aging, Ethnicity, Family Bonds, Older Couples, Life Review.

231. Cather, Willa. "Old Mrs. Harris" (1931). In collection above, pp. 75-190.
     Old Mrs. Harris, though failing in health, con-
trives for her granddaughter Vickie to attend university
despite the indigence of the family. The time is early
1900s. The Templeton family have settled in a Colorado
town in migration from the feudal culture of Tennessee
to this bustling Western democracy where they do not
thrive. The mother has been a spoiled darling. The father has fine manners but little business sense; he has
tied up the family fund in investment. Young Vickie is
bright; she wins a scholarship but can't afford the full
expense. Mrs. Harris with humble courage asks and gets
help from a neighbor who has encouraged young Vickie.
Mrs. Harris quietly dies, thankful for her life and family.   The story ends with an eloquent appeal for the
young to notice such qualities. TOPICS: Role Loss, Neighbors, Grandparenting, Mentoring, Transmission of Values.

232. Chekhov, Anton (1860-1904). "Grief." In *The Stories
of Anton Chekhov*. Edited by Robert Linscott. New York:
Modern Library, 1932. Also in Anthology 10, pp. 24-29.
     Grief with no one to share it can be double grief,
as with this simple old Russian coachman. On a snowy
night, Iona Potapov tries to tell his passengers that his
son died that week. An officer replies perfunctorily
while bawling at him to hurry. Three drunken young men
ignore Iona's sad news, actually beating him to hurry on.

Stopping at an inn, he tries to confide in a young man
who is too sleepy drunk to respond. Bursting with un-
shared sorrow, Iona finds his way to the stable, where
he unburdens himself to, of all creatures, his little
horse. TOPICS: Poverty, Parent-Child Bonds, Grief.

233. Chekhov, Anton. "Old Age." In *The Stories of Anton
Chekhov.* Edited by Robert Linscott. New York: Modern
Library, 1932. Also in Anthology 1, pp. 256-59.
   How grief for an unhappy past can overtake an older
person is shown as a prosperous Russian architect,
Uzelkov, revisits his native town, the scene of his
wretched marriage and divorce. He is amazed how much the
town has changed, not to mention the lawyer who had nego-
tiated the divorce. Once a cunning, thoroughly predatory
attorney, Shapkin has become a gray-haired shrunken old
man. As he accompanies Uzelkov to the cemetery, he
shamelessly reveals how much he had cheated Uzelkov and
his temperamental wife, how he had witnessed and even
shared in her moral deterioration which ended in death.
Shaken with sorrow, Uzelkov returns to his wife's grave
and tries barrenly to weep. TOPICS: Older Couples, Widowhood.

234. Collier, Eugenia. "Marigolds." *Negro Digest* 18
(November 1969). Also in Anthology 6, pp. 133-41.
   The persecution of an old black woman by thought-
less children is told by the teenage girl who led the
harassment. Old Miss Lottie, the poorest of the poor in
a Depression black quarter, has raised beautiful marigolds as her one resistance to a grinding life. Lizabeth
and other children throw stones at the marigolds to spite
Miss Lottie, whom they see as a witch-woman. That night
Lizabeth overhears her parents--the father in shame and
despair over unemployment, the mother becoming the source
of family strength. In rebellion against the hopelessness
of life, Lizabeth runs over at dawn to rip out Miss
Lottie's flower bed. When Miss Lottie appears to witness
the destruction of her only treasure, Lizabeth wakes to
compassion and the end of innocence. TOPICS: Poverty,
Race, Gender: Women, Older Couples, Alienation, Leisure.

235. Coon, Betty. "Daisies." In *Women and Aging: An
Anthology by Women.* Corvallis, Oreg: Calyx Bks, 1986,
pp. 74-78.
   To retain her independence, this old Italian woman
shows remarkable obstinacy in resisting manipulation by
her children. Maria Pavese is nearly blind. She wants
to be free of her old house in its run-down neighborhood.
But she stiffens under the importunate urging to move out
that comes from her daughter-in-law Gina, her flashy son
Max, the hungry real estate lady, and the family priest.

Actually the house tires Maria, as does the memory of her
husband who "worked on this place the way some people
climb a mountain," constantly repainting, redecorating,
raising a glut of tomatoes. One thing she cares for: the
daisies that bloom in the back yard. After she has in-
sulted children, realtor, and priest into leaving her
parlor, Maria sits dreaming of all the gladiolas, tulips,
narcissus, and mums she is going to plant. TOPICS: Gender: Women, Parent-Child Conflicts, Autonomy, Creativity,
Leisure, Aging in Place.

236. Cooper, Bernard. "Picking Plums: Fathers and Sons
and Their Lovers" (1992). In *Harper's* (August 1992).
Also in Anthology 12, pp. 120-128.
    An unconventional father and his gay son learn to
be open with each other. The father, injured by falling
from a plum tree, has lived a depressing life as divorce
lawyer, prone to tantrums, widowed after a hard marriage.
He then lived with a neurotic African-American woman from
whom he has now separated. The son has admired the father's courage in undertaking such a controversial union,
even though it hasn't lasted. When his father on being
taken home from the hospital, presses for equal openness,
the son is able to confess his homosexual love. This
candor brings them together. TOPICS: Multicultural,
Parent-Child Bonds, Sexuality.

237. Dodd, Susan. "Bifocals." In *Hell-Bent Men and
Their Cities*. New York: Penguin Books, 1990, pp. 29-50.
    A long friendship between two grandfathers, one
Irish, the other Jewish, comes to its somber end. When
Phil O'Dowd, 77, meets Jake Nelkin for one of their regular lunches, he is depressed because he hates his new
bifocal glasses and because he has overheard his adult
children speaking of his rapid decline. As young men,
the two had worked hard to establish their businesses:
Phil as mortuary director, Jake as florist who often
served the mortuary. Now they still kid around like
horny youths; but a magic memory comes up of how the two
had danced ecstatically at Jake's silver wedding
anniversary. On Jake's sudden death overnight, Phil
prepares his old friend for Jewish burial and sits beside
him as the melody tries to return. TOPICS: Urban Aging,
Ethnicity, Friendship, Loss, Death.

238. Dodd, Susan. "Nightlife." In collection above, pp.
163-174.
    A father-daughter relationship, always ambivalent,
intensifies as the daughter visits her old parent in the
hospital. Caroline Dundy, 35, a divorced Vermont artist, has flown to the Southwest to tend Lucius, seventyish. She finds him not terminal but "mortally worn

out"--ornery, abrasive, repelling all her tenderness. But at the father's condominium where she is staying, she meets a lovely old woman who speaks sweetly of Lucius as "dashing," thus triggering Caroline's memories of college graduation and her father's almost-romantic squiring her to the dinner dance. Then she begins to receive midnight telephone calls from Lucius, affectionate, generous, solicitous. She thus finds herself between two images of her father--at night, the beloved, caring parent from whom she could never free herself, and by day, the curmudgeon who makes freedom possible. TOPIC: Parent-Child Bonds.

239. Dodd, Susan. "Sinatra." In collection above, pp. 1-11.
   The communications of a failing old person can be contradictory and indirect, as Sharon discovers on responding to her octogenarian father's plea for help. Mike's terrified call, she learns, was prompted by an episode of getting lost. Now she finds him feisty, preoccupied with diet but ready to visit a retirement village. They are welcomed by an old friend of Mike's and proudly shown the recreation room. Suddenly a phonograph scratches out a ballad sung by Frank Sinatra, and one of the old men invites Sharon to dance. She smilingly accepts. On leaving with Mike, Sharon asks pleasantly whether the dancing "wasn't something." Mike snaps back his dislike of Sinatra, "that bum"--but is clearly expressing his contempt for the retirement home and its cheerfulness about human decline. TOPICS: Ageism, Parent-Child Bonds, Long-term care, Anxiety, Leisure.

240. Dodd, Susan. "Subversive Coffee." In collection above, pp. 213-224.
   The dilemma of choosing between radical treatment or benign resignation for a cancer-ridden octogenarian is argued by Zvi, a young Jewish doctor, and Alcie, the patient's thirtyish daughter. Nathan, the father, has been failing for two years and a hospital patient for months. Should radiation be tried? When that fails, should chemotherapy be tried? Alcie, who has lived passively through daughterhood and previous marriage, wants Nathan to die in peace without further medical intrusion. Zvi, youthful, pleasantly arrogant, and warm-hearted enough to become her lover, wants to keep fighting. As doctor he says, "We must care greatly." A vivid interchange deals with the role of God in human suffering. Whether the treatment succeeds is not shown. TOPICS: Ethnicity, Parent-Child Bonds, Disease, Doctor-Patient Conflicts.

241. Dokey, Richard. "The Autumn of Henry Simpson"

(1978). In *August Heat: Stories by Richard Dokey*. Chicago: Story Press, 1982, pp. 51-64.

The aching loneliness of a widowed old age is deeply felt by Henry Simpson. His empty days are marked by melancholy and guilt, as he wonders how his life could have been better and what it all could have meant. A major disruption occurs when his over-solicitous daughter tricks him into visiting the Mid-Valley Retirement Home she plans for him to enter. Seldom has such a facility been seen in more repellent light than this Home as it strikes upon the horrified consciousness of Henry. He runs from the building in panic. Sitting alone later in the park, he comes at last to a kind of peace over his own mortality. TOPICS: Parent-Child Conflicts, Long-term Care, Wisdom, Widowhood.

242. Dorner, Marjorie. "Before the Forgetting." In *Winter Roads, Summer Fields: Stories by Marjorie Dorner*. Minneapolis, Minn.: Milkweed Editions, 1992, pp. 186-99.

An old woman, 94, whose advancing dementia threatens to overcome her, reviews her life and recalls a perfect moment of intimacy and freedom, symbolic of the fullness of her life. When the old woman thinks about the time before dementia, she refers to it as "before the forgetting." One day her memory leads her back to the time before her marriage, when her father responded to her future husband's request for her hand by setting him to a task worthy of the Biblical Jacob. Eventually, she settles on the memory of a day when her husband and she were haying on the farm before the children were born. The intimacy they shared that day is etched on her memory. TOPICS: Dementia, Anxiety, Reminiscence.

243. Dorner, Marjorie. "Tree House." In collection above, pp. 171-85.

A 54-year-old farmer survives his retirement crisis with the assistance and advice of an old woman who responds to his needs with sympathy and friendship. Jim Mueller has turned the management of his farm over to his son and moved into town with his wife. Now retirement looms before him, a foreign and forbidding prospect. He spends time musing under a massive tree on a corner of his former property, and one day decides to build a large tree house for his three grandchildren. While he is contemplating the project, Celie Lanzer, 70, one of his neighbors, stops by to chat. Mueller never has talked to the old woman before, but in subsequent visits the two converse easily and forge a happy partnership. Celie helps Matt design the tree house and decorate it. The project complete, they part company. Both have found fulfillment through their shared experience. The characters are featured in separate stories (Jim at age 12

and Celie at 15) earlier in the collection.   TOPICS:
Roles, Friendship, Creativity, Leisure, Retirement, Legacies.

244. Dreiser, Theodore. (1912).   "The Lost Phoebe." In
The Best Short Stories of Theodore Dreiser.   Edited by
Howard Fast.   Chicago: Elephant Paperbacks, 1989.   Also
in Anthology 1, pp. 344-55.
     Bereavement stretches from grief to denial to in-
sanity for Henry Reifsneider, a simple old farmer of another time.   He and his wife Phoebe have lived half a
century in the same isolated house--a comfortable life
flavored with minor friction, homely banter, and steady
mutual support.   Months after Phoebe's death, this lost
and lonely widower sees her image in the moonlight, so
real as to evoke his calling to her.   The image repeatedly appears until Henry strikes out in the countryside to
find her.   He becomes a nomad, taking his few belongings
from county to county until one moonlit night near the
edge of a cliff, he sees Phoebe moving before him, now
young and sweet, drawing a youthful spirit into his worn
body, drawing him into his fatal and joyful fall. TOPICS:
Rural Aging, Older Couples, Dementia, Loneliness, Aspirations, Widowerhood.

245. Ekström, Margareta.   "The King Is Threatened"   In
Death's Midwives. Translated by Eva Claeson.   With a Preface by Nadine Gordimer. Princeton, N.J.: Ontario Review
Press, 1985.   Also in Anthology 11, pp. 227-47.
     An evolving friendship leads to sex between two
eightyish residents in an English retirement home.
Charles has been placed in Waybridge Manor by his weary
wife Christabel.   There he meets an old friend, Maud, a
lively woman whose considerate attentions make him feel
"younger, healthier, and even more manly" despite his
wheelchair.   What a contrast to the "small meannesses"
by which Christabel diminished him at home! Charles and
Maud continue their warm friendship over several sep-
arations to visit their homes. In particular they enjoy
chess (hence the title of the story).   On one visit, the
prying Christabel opens Maud's door to find the two making love.   Her anger and shock are met by Maud's defense
that they are all old, what can be the harm?   TOPICS:
Older Couples, Intimacy, Long-term Care.

246. Ferber, Edna.   "Old Lady Mandle" (1920).   In *One
Basket: Thirty-One Short Stories*.   New York: Simon &
Schuster, 1947, pp. 145-61.
     An old woman, pampered and spoiled by her
middle-aged son, learns that sometimes the older generation must yield to the hopes and dreams of the younger
generation. Old Lady Mandle lives in an exclusive Chi-

cago neighborhood with her son Hugo. Her husband, who
speculated wildly and lost all their savings in the economic depression of 1893, had died the following year.
Thanks to Hugo's hard work and business acumen, Ma Mandle
enjoys a prosperous, comfortable, sheltered life. But
when Hugo marries suddenly, Ma Mandle is dethroned as the
center of Hugo's universe. For several years she complains about all details of her daughter-in-law's management of the household. Finally, she realizes the
depth of the couple's commitment toward each other and
decides to adapt to the changed circumstances in the
household. TOPICS: Adaptation, Parent-Child Bonds, Vanity.

247. Ferber, Edna. "Old Man Minick" (1922). In collection above. Also in Anthology 1, pp. 20-34.
    Old Man Minick, a retired Chicago businessman in the
1920s, finds his way through widowerhood and toleration
by adult children. He has enjoyed a marriage of forty-odd
years in which each partner has learned to skirt past
small differences to nourish each other. On Ma Minick's
death, he is taken in by his son and daughter-in-law to
share their small apartment. As considerate as they are
at first, he learns gradually that he has become a burden, a bore, an obstacle to their own life plans. He is
perfunctorily tolerated as an old geezer. Finally he
discovers a circle of old men who flourish on lively debate in Washington Park. They also relish their independence as residents of nearby Grant Home. Happily he
enters the Home. TOPICS: Housing, Parent-Child Conflicts,
Caregiving, Elder Abuse, Autonomy, Loneliness.

248. Fisher, M. F. K.   "The Reunion."   In *Sister Age*.
New York: Knopf, 1983, pp. 142-48.
    A startling reminder to "seize the day" and live
now is provided in this fantasy or parable about an old
man whose life has *literally* passed him by. Having aged
while dawdling over his unfinished doctoral thesis, Professor Lucien Revenant plans a little party for "five
dear people he had neglected as they all grew older and
more preoccupied by their own dwindling parties." It
turns out that all are dead, including the Professor,
whose funeral was held that morning. (The name "Revenant"
means one who returns after death.) TOPIC: Death.

249. Forster, E. M. "The Road from Colonus" (1911). In
The Collected Tales of E. M. Forster. New York: Knopf,
1948, pp. 125-43.
    The personal expansion that can await the questing
spirit in old age is suggested by this powerful fantasy.
Mr. Lucas, dreading a trivial old age, has a mystic experience while on a tour of fabled Greece, a country he

had always wanted to explore. Wandering along a road, he
sees a lovely spring of water and rests beside it. Suddenly an awareness invades him, a sense of beauty in all
things. But his touring party overtakes him and overcomes
his passionate desire to stop at the inn near this mir-
aculous spring. They bear him back to London and the
trivial fussy life he had dreaded. Colonus was the site
of the sacred grove where the legendary Oedipus came to
die and meet his gods; from there Mr. Lucas, so to speak,
took the sad road back. TOPICS: Wisdom, Leisure, Retirement, Religion.

250. Frame, Janet. "The Bath." In *You Are Now Entering
the Human Heart*. Wellington, New Zealand: Victoria Univ.
Press, 1983. Reprint, London: Women's Pr, 1984.
   How long can a frail elderly person Remain independent? This question is asked implicitly in a frightening
account of a New Zealand widow trying to take a bath.
Mrs. Harraway, in planning to visit her husband's grave
the next day, prepares for the bath which she physically
can not manage more than weekly. Carefully she arranges
the towel, the nightclothes to change into, the chair to
aid in her escape from the tub. She descends into the
tub as one might descend a cliff. Only after a fearful
and heroic struggle does she finally climb out after the
bath itself. Following a peaceful visit to the grave, she
returns to her "world narrowing and growing darker"--and
to the waiting tub. TOPICS: Frailty, Autonomy, Courage,
Aging in Place, Widowhood.

251. Frame, Janet. "Winter Garden." In collection
above, pp. 188-92.
   An old man learns that dying is inextricably linked
to the process of living. Mr. Paget's wife has been in
a coma for two months. He visits her in the hospital
daily, talks to her, touches her, kisses her goodbye.
But she remains unresponsive, and any queries about her
condition elicit the same response from staff: "no
change." One day, when he brings a flower from his garden
into her room, he notices that her hair has been cut and
her nails trimmed. He has a revelation: she is alive;
her bodily growth continues. Only in death would the processes of living cease. Now he can relate to her as a
living being, not as an inert body connected to wires and
tubes in a hospital bed. After her death in the autumn,
he lavishes his attention on his garden--even on winter
days. Now the garden is alive in ways he never under-
stood before. TOPICS: Disability, Long-term Care, Anxiety, Leisure, Widowerhood.

252. Freeman, Mary Wilkins. "A Mistaken Charity." In

"A Humble Romance" and Other Stories. 1887. Reprint, New York: Garrett Press, 1969, pp. 234-49.

Two aged sisters rebel against the "mistaken chari-ty" of those who would deprive them of independence for their own good. The setting is New England in the last century; the issue--of institutionalizing the elderly--is contemporary. Harriet Shattuck, stubborn and proud, and her sister Charlotte, blind and a bit simple, eke out a living in a ruined cottage. They raise a few crops and take gifts from neighbors. A vigorously philanthropic townswoman benignly conspires with a well-to-do widow and the minister to install the sisters in an Old Ladies' Home, which turns out to be unendurably proper and stuffy. The sisters run away and return to their home, proud and happy though the means of their survival will stead-ily diminish. TOPICS: Community, Family Bonds, Long-term Care, Autonomy, Endurance.

253. Freeman, Mary Wilkins. "Two Old Lovers." In collec-tion above, pp. 25-36.

The painful consequences of delaying the declara-tion of one's feelings for another person are illustrated in the story of an old couple in nineteenth-century New England. Everyone regards Maria Brewster, 60, and David Emmons, 62, as "sweethearts." Maria lives alone with her widowed mother. Every Sunday evening for fifteen years David has called on her. But he never has proposed mar-riage. Maria loves David, but she accepts his unusual reticence. As the years pass they remain sweethearts and see each other more frequently. Maria often cleans house and cooks for David. One night he stops at her door af-ter a visit and asks her to forgive him for his unortho-dox "courting." Even now he cannot bring himself to pro-pose. She forgives him on the spot, but grieves quietly later. The next day she is called to his house--an emergency--to find him on his deathbed, at last ready to propose. TOPICS: Older couples, Intimacy, Loneliness.

254. Gallant, Mavis. "His Mother." In *From the Fifteenth District, a Novella and Eight Other Stories*. New York: Random House, 1979. Also in Anthology 7, pp. 167-80.

When adult children live far away without maintain-ing family bonds, the emotional cost to devoted parents can be consuming. The central character is a mother in a Budapest colony of displaced persons, whose son, never having shown much love or vitality, has moved to Scotland and never come back except through dutiful letters. She vies with the other mothers, who score points according to where their children had gone, and the number of let-ters and gifts received. She comes to take boarders, whose own lives show similar displacements. Her rooms be-come an untidy slum. She begins to dream of persons from

her past. Finally, she writes her son. She describes the
city and its small attractions and assures him she is
still alive, still a lady, and still the grateful bene-
ficiary of his small gifts. TOPICS: Multicultural, Gender: Women, Parent-Child Conflicts, Coping, Loneliness.

255. Gurganus, Allan. "Blessed Assurance: A Moral Tale."
In *White People*. New York: Ivy Books, 1990, pp. 232-305.
    An old African-American woman becomes an unlikely
mentor to a white teenager, teaching him to respect the
hard lives of black people and to honor the individuality
and life-affirming strengths of old people. The narrator, now in late middle age (59), recalls selling funeral insurance to poor black people in North Carolina in
1949. He recounts his weekly visits to what first seemed
to him anonymous clients. Many of them had paid premiums
for more than forty years, and they knew that two missed
premiums voided all policies. Then he meets Vesta Lotte
Battle, nearly blind, 94. She is self-assured, tolerant,
forgiving, and wise. She possesses a goodness and spirituality that overwhelms the young man. When she gets
behind in her payments, he covers them for months before
finally turning her in. His reminiscence is triggered by
his need to resolve guilt and pain over betraying the old
woman. TOPICS: Rural Aging, Multicultural, Intergenerational, Wisdom, Life Review, Religion.

256. Gurganus, Allan. "A Hog Loves Its Life: Something
About My Grandfather." In collection above, pp. 167-217.
    A grandson's affectionate, yet bittersweet remem-
brance of his grandfather illustrates how the younger
generation may be forced to adapt to changed circumstances in an intergenerational relationship. Set in
small-town North Carolina in the 1950s, this story is
part fiction and part memoir. The narrator recalls his
boyhood, when he was 10 and loved to listen to Grandpa
Grafton, known as "Grand," tell long-winded stories about
the past. One of Grand's favorites is the tale of
"Lancaster's mule," meant to teach virtues of obedience,
good behavior, and common sense. The boy's identity,
character,   and   values   are   forged   by   this
intergenerational bond. But years later, after his
wife's death, Grand suffers prolonged grieving and then
advancing dementia. He becomes the town oddity, "one
very old and cruelly healthy senile man." The narrator,
then a young man, recounts several awkward and painful
encounters with the old man. TOPICS: Grandparenting,
Dementia, Creativity, Leisure, Life Re-view, Legacies.

257. Gurganus, Allan. "It Had Wings." In collection
above, pp. 162-66.
    The strength, compassion, and resourcefulness which

can restore an old person is revealed in this whimsical
fantasy about a widow who finds an angel lying uncon-
scious in her back yard. The old woman, who lives alone,
hurries outside to minister to what is evidently a young
angel, its wings ruffled but intact. When she touches
the angel, her aches and pains are healed, at least temporarily. After she helps the angel to drink some warm
milk from a mug, the angel flies away. No one else has
seen this encounter. The old woman feels rejuvenated,
her self-esteem restored. Her encounter sparks a lesson:
"I'm not just somebody alone in a house." TOPICS: Ageism, Activity, Autonomy.

258. Hardy, Thomas. *Old Lady Chundle: A Short Story* (c.
1880-90). New York: Crosby Gaige, 1929, 27 pp.
     The risks of attending to the needs of older people
without an accompanying sense of compassion and sincerity
of purpose are illustrated in this tale of a young Ang-
lican curate in nineteenth-century England. After befriending reclusive Old Lady Chundle, he learns she never
attends church because she is hard of hearing. To ac-
commodate her disability, he provides a special hearing
tube rigged from the pulpit to the pew. But his plan
backfires, and in a comic scene he is practically overcome by her malodorous breath transmitted through the apparatus. Now he avoids Mrs. Chundle, especially when he
learns she could now "hear beautiful!" and is enthusi-
astic about attending church every Sunday. When he makes
a long-delayed visit to her house, neighbors are there
to tell him Mrs. Chundle died hours earlier. She had
praised the young curate, saying, "I've found a real
friend at last," and had willed him all of her humble
furnishings. He is devastated by this turn of events.
TOPICS: Stereotypes, Intergenerational, Disability, Religion.

259. Hemingway, Ernest. "A Clean, Well-Lighted Place"
(1938). In *The Short Stories of Ernest Hemingway*. 1938.
Reprint, New York: Scribner, 1966. Also in Anthology 9,
pp. 16-19.
     For solitary old men without hope, the clean,
well-lighted place of a late-hours tavern is the one consolation available in this bleak story. A deaf octogenarian widower sits drinking one brandy after another as
on other nights. Though he has money, in his quiet desperation he has tried to commit suicide. The waiters
finally turn him out; he departs with dignity. The elderly waiter sympathetic to him reflects upon the hopelessness of life; he imagines a nihilistic Lord's Prayer;
he thinks how important is the little comfort which is
left: a clean, well-lighted place. He goes to his room

for a night of insomnia. TOPICS: Disease, Loneliness, Spiritual Life.

260. Hemingway, Ernest. "Old Man at the Bridge." In collection above, pp.78-80.

How simple dignity and responsibility can be maintained in the face of certain extinction is shown in this old man caught in a battle area of the Spanish Civil War. He had been left behind to mind the animals, but has now been warned by the military to clear out. Having got as far as this bridge, the old man is too exhausted to walk farther even though the enemy is closing in; still, he shows a touching anxiety for the goats and the cat he had to leave behind. TOPICS: Roles, Frailty, Isolation.

261. Higgins, Joanna. "The Courtship of Widow Sobcek." In *The Best American Short Stories, 1982*. Edited by John Gardner and Shannon Ravenal. Boston: Houghton Mifflin. Also in Anthology 11, pp. 48-73.

The awakening of love in an old widower does not easily happen in the Polish working-class culture of John Jielewicz. He lives in a world of chores and hardships, with only a fading memory of his long dead wife. He is too proud to accept help from his adult daughter, too independent and hot-tempered to accept his priest's instruction to consider God's love. When John carries his lace curtains to the Widow Sobcek for washing, he has a sudden vision of her as someone younger, like his lost Masha. Although he doesn't recognize this little miracle as a sign of divine grace, John gravitates unconsciously to the homely hospitality of the widow despite the alarm of his daughter. One day John falls on the ice and is hospitalized. When the widow fails to make her customary visit, he breaks out of the hospital and finds her collapsed in her home. In joy, John takes over washing the curtains she had promised for Easter. TOPICS: Ethnicity, Parent-Child Conflicts, Older Couples, Religion.

262. Highsmith, Patricia. "The Cries of Love." London: McIntosh & Otis, 1968. Also in Anthology 2, pp. 339-44.

Two old sisters live in malignant symbiosis at a retirement hotel where they alternate in playing spiteful tricks upon each other. Whether nightmare or black comedy, this tale exemplifies the painful orbit into which older couples can find themselves locked. Hattie rises at night and takes scissors to mutilate her sister Alice's fine new sweater. In the morning Alice sobs at the desecration while Hattie doubles over in glee. Alice returns to speaking terms while considering revenge, which she takes at night by cutting off Hattie's braid at its base. Thus the grief and glee are reversed. Hattie moves to another room, but in a few days returns to make peace; they really can't live apart. So life resumes, with Hattie quietly planning a new atrocity come Christmas. TOPICS: Family Bonds, Family Conflicts, Older Couples, Deviance.

263. Humphrey, William. "The Hardys." In *The Collected Stories of William Humphrey*. New York: Delacorte Press, 1985, pp. 1-15.

The lifelong gap that sometimes exists between spouses in a long marriage is illustrated in the Hardys, who review their life together and anxiously prepare for the auction of their farm. They are forced to sell because their eight sons (three from Mr. Hardy's first marriage) have chosen not to farm. The couple engage in separate life reviews which uncover the lack of companionship and affection in their marriage. Prominent in Mr. Hardy's memories are those of his first wife, who died in childbirth. His love for her remains in the foreground even in old age. He married a second time out of necessity--to find someone who could raise his children. Mrs. Hardy's memories linger on her years of childbearing--evidence of her commitment to Mr. Hardy--and her frustration that she was unable to replace Mr. Hardy's first wife in his affections. TOPICS: Older Couples, Anxiety, Loss, Life Review.

264. Humphrey, William. "September Song." In *September Song*. Boston: Houghton Mifflin, 1990. Also in Anthology 11, pp. 19-37.

Virginia Tyler, 76, has the chance to divorce a dull husband in order to marry the lover with whom she had had an exciting adulterous romance many years before. That lover, John Warner, had also been married but with Virginia had enjoyed years of secret trysts until his wife had found them out. The affair has long been dropped until just now, when John telephones that his wife died; he is free. Virginia's husband Toby is bookish, unexcitable; he is hard of hearing, with the mannerisms which can irritate in a boring union. But he accepts her wish for a divorce. Her children approve. Then Virginia, out of pity, guilt, and a sense that time has stranded her, sees that she cannot leave this helpless, decent man, though little remains for her except their last gray years together. TOPICS: Older Couples, Intimacy, Disengagement.

265. Jacobsen, Josephine. "Jack Frost." In *The Substance of Things Hoped For*. Edited by John B. Breslin. New York: Doubleday, 1987. Also in Anthology 5, pp. 124-34.

Determined to live alone in her isolated New Hampshire cottage in spite of advanced age and approaching winter, Mrs. Travis enjoys the last blooming days of her

beloved flower garden. Two visitors tactfully suggest
that she move into the village for the cold days ahead.
Mrs. Travis refuses as she has done before. Then her
radio announces an early cold snap with frost expected.
Frantically the old woman harvests her flowers in whatever containers she can find. She brings them indoors but
then recalls one especially lovely begonia. Exhausted,
she sallies out into the chill moonlight but falls badly.
Barely able to crawl back, she suffers what may well be
a fatal heart attack. But she is surrounded by the glorious flowers she loves. TOPICS: Rural Aging, Frailty, Autonomy, Leisure.

266. Jhabvala, Ruth Prawer. "The Man with the Dog." In
Out of India: Selected Stories. New York: William Morrow, 1986. Also in Anthology 7, pp. 45-56, and Anthology
11, pp. 199-226.
    A revolution in personality comes to a widowed
grandmother in India. She tells of her conventional earlier life as affluent, beautiful, and characterizes herself as "one who faithfully fulfills all her duties in
life." A consuming change occurs after her husband dies
and her children scatter. She meets an earlier admirer,
a cultivated but indigent Dutchman. When she lets him
take quarters in her spacious house, they become occasional lovers but they differ in many ways, especially
over his dog which she detests. They quarrel more and
more violently until, at her son's request, she asks the
Dutchman to leave. But he is needy; he has become the
center of her life; she cannot give up "the great happiness I find in that old man." TOPICS: Multicultural,
Older Couples, Widowhood.

267. Jhabvala, Ruth Prawer. (1986). "Miss Sahib." In
A *Stronger Climate*. London: John Murray. Also in *Love
and Loss: Stories of the Heart*. Edited by Georgina Hammick. Boston: Faber & Faber, 1992, pp. 1-23.
    Old age may bring a special loneliness to a single
person exiled in an alien culture. Miss Tuhy, sixtyish,
has lovingly taught school in India and remained there
after the British rule. Now unemployed and on a small
pension, she lives in a squalid tenement, still loving
India and in particular little Sharmila, lively daughter
of the landlady. Gradually this tenement world seems to
become noisier, dirtier, more sensual. Sharmila becomes
a fat blowsy matron, self-preoccupied and vain, so coarse
as to disgust Miss Tuhy at a flamboyant funeral which is
in tawdry contrast to the decorous, comforting funerals
back in England. Bitterness floods Miss Tuhy's gentle
heart. But she no longer has the fare home. TOPICS:
Multicultural, Intergenerational, Alienation.

268. Jie, Zhang. "An Unfinished Record." In *Love Must Not Be Forgotten*. Translated by Grace Yang. San Francisco: China Bks, 1986. Also in Anthology 7, pp. 72-86.

Displacement from a long-lived-in home can release a torrent of reminiscence both tender and sad. Here the unnamed scholar is taking leave of the shabby room where he has spent a career writing works on Chinese history. Besides a disreputable cat, he has had almost no companionship. He has lived dust-dry, a bore to others and himself. Now the hospital has called him in for an operation and--as he sees it--probable death. One glowing memory opens up: a lovely young woman who long ago had lighted the office "as if there had been another window in the room." The young scholar fell hard in love, only to be invited to her wedding. The old scholar still thinks of her in gratitude but regrets the incompleteness of his own life. TOPICS: Loneliness, Employment, Life Review.

269. Johnson, Josephine. "Old Harry." In *Winter Orchard and Other Stories*. New York: Simon & Schuster, 1935, pp. 85-103.

Two lonely old men find companionship and solace in a world that seems to isolate, abandon, and even discard the old. For ten years Pagsbrey, a retired professor, has spent his days in a museum where Old Harry is a guard. Old Harry is a source of companionship for Pagsbrey and his link to the real world. He listens enthusiastically to Pagsbrey's rambling discourses and shares the details of his own household life. Their relationship ends abruptly when Old Harry, in despair because of failing health and the pressure of family obligations, ends his own life. Pagsbrey's days spent in the museum now are empty and unfulfilling. He seeks solace by imagining that Old Harry's struggle to survive symbolizes human suffering. TOPICS: Poverty, Gender: Men, Friendship, Loneliness, Suicide, Retirement.

270. Jolley, Elizabeth. "A Hedge of Rosemary." In *Stories: Five-Acre Virgin and The Travelling Entertainer*. 1984. Reprint, New York: Penguin, 1988, pp. 92-99.

An Australian widower finds respite from feelings of loneliness and alienation by revisiting his former home each evening. The old man lives with his son and daughter-in-law. Both treat him civilly, but he doesn't feel welcome in their home. Three years earlier, when he was suffering from pneumonia, they had brought him to their home and later sold his house. But so far the house has been spared demolition. As the old man goes about his daily routine, people ignore him. No one in the family knows where he goes every night, and no one asks. During his visits to his former home, he sits at a table by candlelight, smokes a pipe, and tries not to think too much about either the past or the future. A fragrant hedge of rosemary marks the boundary of his back yard. TOPICS: Parent-Child Conflicts, Alienation, Aging in Place.

271. Jolley, Elizabeth. "Mr. Parker's Valentine." In collection above, pp. 208-19.

An old man's unwanted presence as neighbor leads to feelings of resentment, hostility, and rage that end in tragedy. Pearson and Eleanor Page, recently moved from England to Australia, have found the perfect house. There is one complication: Old Mr. Parker has lived for years in a small shed at the back of the property. They allow the old man to remain because "he has no other home." Soon the old man becomes a nuisance to Pearson, who resents the many intrusions into his routine. But Eleanor enjoys the old man's company, and she feels compassion for him when he shows the couple an old valentine he received anonymously some fifty years ago. She even cares for him one night when he has a fever. Jealous of her attention, her husband directs his frustration at the old man and causes his accidental death. TOPICS: Ageism, Neighbors, Intergenerational.

272. Jolley, Elizabeth. "A New World." In collection above, pp. 220-28.

A dreary and regimented existence in an Australian nursing home is made bearable for an old widower by recalling happier days. "Number fourteen," as Fred Nash is called by the number of his bed, escapes his surroundings by reviewing his life. He recalls his hard childhood, happy marriage, and move to Western Australia, where his wife and he let holiday cottages to vacationers. As he aged, he loved to rise early in the morning and feel the newness of creation. Then busy highways and new subdivisions changed the landscape. Fred's wife died, and Fred moved to the institution. At the end of the story Fred, concerned that his neighbor has been restless the last few nights, performs a simple act of kindness to alleviate the old man's anxiety. Then Fred steps back "into the edge of his dream." TOPICS: Long-term Care, Coping, Loneliness.

273. Jolley, Elizabeth. "Pear Tree Dance." In *Woman in a Lampshade*. New York: Penguin, 1982. Also in Anthology 7, pp. 144-53.

The passion to realize a small but long-held dream is discovered by a hard-bitten cleaning woman in Australia. Because she is so full of community gossip which she spreads at every house she serves, she is nicknamed "Newspaper" or "Weekly." She has come from a poor,

pinched background; she has never owned anything sub-
stantial except for an old car. Underneath her loquacious
gossip she dreams of actually owning a piece of land.
She combs the real estate ads. She studies pamphlets on
fruit-growing. She saves every penny she can from the
pittance she earns. The story culminates in her purchasing a distant five acres and taking possession. In her
joy she plants a sapling pear tree and dances around it.
TOPICS: Employment, Aspirations.

274. Kalpakian, Laura. "A Christmas Cordial." In
Winter's Tales: New Series: 4, edited by Robin Baird
Smith. New York: St. Martin's Press, 1988, pp. 187-236.
     How the fantasies of middle age may persist into
old age is portrayed in the story of a 75-year-old spinster, who lives alone in a large house in London. Since
1946 Louisa has worked as a clerk for the Explorer's
Club, an institution with some renown in the nineteenth
century but now sadly diminished in stature. Louisa grew
up feeling a terror of spinsterhood. So when she was in
her 30s and still not married, she began to invent
stories about a former lover who was killed at Dunkirk.
She embellished the stories over the years and has come
to believe her own fantasy. The title refers to a cordial
which she brews every Christmas and distributes to her
close circle of acquaintances. TOPICS: Mental Health,
Coping, Loneliness, Employment, Aging in place.

275. King, Francis. "The Tradesman" (1988). In collection above, pp. 11-22.
     An old woman calmly and deliberately spends her
last day putting her affairs in order before choosing to
end her life by means of active euthanasia. Mrs. Masterson is widowed and lives with her spinster niece, who
is recovering in the hospital after an operation. Mrs.
Masterson herself is convalescing from a long illness.
She is unusually active and energetic, and she spends her
morning tidying up and completing long-delayed tasks:
writing letters, clearing out bills and papers. She has
two visitors, a Meals-on-Wheels service provider and a
young hairdresser. She enjoys their company, and she
gives each a special gift as a token of her affection.
Then she is alone. She awaits the arrival of a "tradesman." When he arrives, the two interact cordially but
professionally as he assists her with her own suicide.
TOPICS: Services, Doctor-Patient Conflicts, Disengagement, Suicide, Serenity.

276. Knight, Wallace E. "The Resurrection Man." In
Atlantic 233 (1974). Also in Anthology 4, pp. 365-77.
     An old man's failed suicide attempt teaches him a
lesson about the unpredictability of nature and the risks

of trying to ignore his own thirst for life. Alva Mason,
a widower, lives in retirement in southern Indiana. He
is a man of the earth who has always valued his independence. When he thinks he may be dying from cancer, he
begins to feel loneliness, anxiety, and despair. He
spends more than a year working out an elaborate and ingenious suicide. But when Alva is ready to act on his
plan, he is saved by the same persistence and creativity
he employed to prepare for his death. Instead of taking
his life, he begins to concentrate on living it. TOPICS:
Rural Aging, Activity, Anxiety, Isolation, Suicide, Aging
in Place.

277. Koger, Lisa. "Ollie's Gate." In *Farlanburg Stories*.
New York: Norton, 1990, pp. 100-129.
        An intergenerational relationship with an old
neighbor woman brings a girl companionship, acceptance,
and affection. Ollie, the old woman, has the reputation
of having failed her family and the values of her Southern culture because she had an illegitimate child when
she was 18. The story follows the relationship of the
narrator and the old woman, Ollie, from the time the narrator was a girl of eight to the time she graduated from
college and moved north. The girl loved being with Ollie
because the old woman told interesting stories, talked
frankly about sexuality and intimacy, and respected her
individuality. The title refers to the symbolic "gate"
Ollie had locked herself behind. Late in life, after the
girl has moved north, Ollie is able to walk through that
gate and recover a measure of freedom. TOPICS: Rural Aging, Gender: Women, Family Conflicts, Intergenerational,
Transmission of values.

278. Labozzetta, Marisa. "Making the Wine." In *When I
Am an Old Woman I Shall Wear Purple: An Anthology of
Short Stories and Poetry*. Edited by Sandra Martz. Watsonville, Calif.: Papier-Maché Press, 1987, pp. 104-111.
        Dementia is vividly realized through the disordered
consciousness of an Italian woman as she tries to think
of her husband Angelo. She--or "Boss" as Angelo calls
her--recalls their early days near Rome, the country
place they earned in America, the raising of children.
It becomes apparent that Boss is living all this dis-
connectedly in the past. She has had a disabling attack
while making wine. Now she spills food, she has a stove
accident, she fails to recognize her son-in-law. One finally realizes that Angelo is long dead, a discovery all
the more poignant as the monologue ends with Boss asking
Angelo to come to her that night. TOPICS: Culture, Dementia, Widowhood, Life Review.

279. Lessing, Doris.   "Casualty." In *The Real Thing:*

Studies and Sketches. New York: Harper Perennial, 1992, pp. 72-78.

A peevish old woman in a wheelchair pollutes the atmosphere of a hospital emergency reception room with loud complaints and malicious comment. Through the pain, noise, and indefinite waiting of such a place, her bitter voice rises: "They don't care at all." But she protests indignantly at having her "broken shoulder" examined. With surly condescension she accepts a cup of tea from her elderly niece, noting that it's not worth drinking. She falls silent when a serious and probably fatal casualty is carried in from an accidental fall, but regains her ornery spirits by gleefully crowing that she herself has made it to eighty-five and has a lot more to come. TOPICS: Enmity, Doctor-Patient Conflicts.

280. Lessing, Doris. (1957). "Flight." In *The Habit of Loving*. New York: Crowell, 1957. Also in *Love and Loss: Stories of the Heart*. Edited by Georgina Hammick. Boston: Faber & Faber, 1992, pp. 24-29.

A lonely grandfather finally lets go of his possessiveness toward his last unmarried granddaughter. He scolds her for falling in love with the postmaster's son whom she will shortly marry. Similarly he has resented the marriages of his other granddaughters as well as that of his own daughter, even though all matches have turned out well. His other possessiveness centers on his dovecote. Knowing at last that he can't keep what he loves, he releases his birds as a symbolic act of relinquishment. His granddaughter, understanding the act, watches with tears in her eyes. TOPICS: Grandparenting, Disengagement, Courage.

281. Lessing, Doris. "The Pit." In *The Real Thing: Studies and Sketches*. New York: HarperCollins, 1992, pp. 138-168.

The chance to win back the husband who had left her long ago comes to Sarah, fiftyish, now a self-sufficient grandmother. James visits her to plead that he again needs her, that he wants her to go away with him. He has had four children with Rose, his second wife; but she has taken on a lover, and he wants to recover the clean-cut easy relationship he and Sarah had enjoyed in their ten-year marriage. Left alone, Sarah considers the other wife--Rose, a siren, a predatory female who has found security by drawing the world (men especially) into her orbit. She would do the same with Sarah. Rose is a dangerous "pit." Sarah telephones a friend in Norway to expect her and leaves just as the telephone (from Rose?) begins ringing. TOPICS: Gender: Women, Coping, Courage.

282. Lessing, Doris. "Womb Ward." In *The New Yorker*,

7 December 1987. Also in Anthology 5, pp. 180-86.
      The healing power which one woman can offer another
is illustrated, as a strong 70-year-old woman is able to
comfort and subdue a hysterical middle-aged wife in a
London gynecological ward. Mildred Grant, the wife, has
never been separated from her husband in twenty-five
years of marriage. She cries uncontrollably as he brings
his visit to an end. Even after lights-out her weeping
continues to disturb the ward until Miss Cook takes over.
Never married but conscious of what she may have missed,
Miss Cook combines a broad sense of humor with a toughness of fiber. She both comforts and scolds Mildred, finally taking the wretched woman in her arms--"probably the
first time in years she had had her arms around another
person." Peace descends upon the darkened ward. TOPICS:
Gender: Women, Humor.

283. MacDonald, D. R.   "Of One Kind." In *Eyestone:
Stories by D. R. MacDonald*. Wainscott, N.Y.: Pushcart
Press, pp. 165-87.
      The frustrated passion of a 70-year-old man for
a blind widow is featured in this story. Red Donald
worked for years as a handyman for a couple from the city
who summered each year in a cabin in Nova Scotia. Now
the widow has decided to live in the cabin all year, surrounded by memories of her former life. Red Donald has
long been attracted to Mrs. MacKay. One evening, when he
finds an excuse to stay for conversation, their interaction leads to some innocent flirting between the two.
Then it crystallizes into an open declaration by Red
Donald, which she rejects, being content with her solitary life. They come from different worlds and different
values. Just being old and alone is not enough to make
them "of one kind." TOPICS: Social Class, Sexuality, Disengagement, Loneliness, Aspirations.

284. MacDonald, D. R.   "Poplars." In collection above,
pp. 87-106.
      A young man's affection, determination, and care-
giving skills are directed to his uncle, who is recovering from a stroke. Their visit to the uncle's farm in
Nova Scotia stimulates some important childhood memories
on the nephew's part and reveals the indomitable will and
courage of his uncle. TOPICS: Caregiving, Disability,
Coping, Courage, Transmission of values.

285. MacDonald, D. R. "Work." In collection above, pp.
65-86.
      The deep feeling and intense loyalty that can de-
velop in male friendships is revealed in the final separation of two old fellow laborers. Jack, disabled and
suffering episodes of dementia, plans to move to a senior

citizen's home with his wife. His friend Little Norman
joins him for an evening of drinking and reminiscing
under the baleful eyes of the friend's wife, who resents
their camaraderie. Frustrated that his friend has given
up, and unable to articulate his feelings directly,
Little Norman vents his emotions in a solitary rage.
TOPICS: Role Loss, Gender: Men, Friendship, Loneliness.

286. Malamud, Bernard. "In Retirement" (1973). In collection above. Also in Anthology 4, pp. 162-73.
    The stirrings of erotic desire prompt a lonely old
doctor to take a possibly disastrous risk. Simon Morris,
a widower with few friends, leads a depressive routine
of studying Greek and walking around lower New York. One
morning after a boldly attractive young woman passes him
in the apartment lobby, he discovers a letter she had
dropped, lying on the floor. He cannot keep himself from
reading it--a father's exhortation that this woman,
Evelyn, abandon her loose sex life. Morris fantasizes
about making love with Evelyn. He thinks how little an
age difference should count between a young woman and an
elderly but still virile man. So he writes a dignified
letter inviting her to make his acquaintance--only to
witness her sharing the letter with her male companion,
then tearing it to shreds. TOPICS: Urban Aging, Sexuality, Loneliness, Leisure, Aspirations, Widowerhood.

287. Malamud, Bernard. "The Jewbird" (1963).   In *The
Stories of Bernard Malamud*. New York: Farrar, 1983, pp.
144-154.
    An old black bird who speaks in Yiddish idiom and
takes the name of Schwartz flaps into the Cohens' apartment and becomes a disputed member of the family, much
like an intrusive grandfather. In this way Schwartz symbolizes the victim of elder abuse, since the father dislikes the bird (who smells and has eccentric eating
tastes). Schwartz also demonstrates the supportive role
of a grandfather in his listening to the boy Maury
practice the violin and in tutoring him toward better
grades. The wife Edie attempts a conciliatory role between the two. Cohen climaxes his persecution of the
"A-number-one troublemaker" by heaving Schwartz into the
winter night and death. The story is troubling but also
witty, in the verbal sparring of Schwartz and Cohen.
TOPICS: Ageism, Ethnicity, Grandparenting, Elder Abuse,
Humor.

288. Malamud, Bernard. "The Mourners" (1958). In collection above, pp. 26-34.
    An old man who has lived a bad life is the center
of this story laid in the slums of New York's East Side.
Kessler, a retired egg inspector living on Social Se-

curity, long ago deserted his wife and children. A nasty, bad-tempered character, he has lived alone in an untidy flat on the fifth floor, shunned by the other tenants as a dirty old man. Kessler quarrels so bitterly with the janitor that the landlord, Gruber, orders him to vacate. Kessler refuses. An eviction battle ensues. In the final scene, Gruber comes to make a final appeal and finds Kessler on the floor mourning his wasted life. Gruber, suffering from his own mistreatment of the old man, joins him as fellow mourner. TOPICS: Urban Aging, Enmity, Alienation, Religion.

289. Mann, Thomas. "Death in Venice" (1913). In *"Death in Venice" and Seven Other Stories*. Translated and with an Introduction by David Luke. London: Secker & Warburg, 1990, pp. 197-267.
What can happen in the old age of a disciplined person who has always suppressed the passionate needs of life? In this long, troubling story, an aging novelist yields to the sensual drives that he has ignored over a lifetime of creative purpose. Gustave Aschenbach, celebrated as the artistic voice of his age, is prompted by a strange intuition to come to the great resort city, Venice, for a needed rest. Here he notices a lovely Polish lad, divine in beauty, a living symbol of Eros, god of love. Though never a word is exchanged, Aschenbach slips into an infatuation quite out of keeping with his serious disposition. He follows the boy, he beautifies his own aging head, he ignores the cholera plague which has infiltrated the city--and dies still with the boy's image before him. TOPICS: Intimacy, Disease, Death.

290. Mansfield, Katherine. "Life of Ma Parker." In *The Short Stories of Katherine Mansfield*. New York: Knopf, 1964, pp. 484-90. Also in *Love and Loss: Stories of the Heart*. Edited by Georgina Hammick. Boston: Faber & Faber, 1992. pp. 135-141.
A lifetime of enduring one misery after another reaches an unendurable point with Ma Parker, an old cleaning woman who has just lost her grandson. At sixteen, Ma Parker had come to London, where she suffered under slave-like employment until she married. Her husband died, as did seven of her thirteen children; five had long been out of touch. Little Lennie, fragile but affectionate child of the thirteenth, had become her one delight in old age but has just died. Not once has Ma Parker given way to tears until now, when she rushes out into the rainy streets looking for a private place to have her cry out. There is no such place. The pain of Ma Parker's life is contrasted with the finicky condescensions of the "literary gentleman" she cleans for. TOPICS: Alienation, Depression, Grief.

291. Marshall, Paule. "Barbados." In *Soul Clap Hands and Sing*. New York: Atheneum, 1961. Reprint, Washington, D.C.: Howard Univ. Press, 1988, pp. 3-28.

The humanly paralyzing effect of racism appears in the cold isolation of Mr. Watford, 70, returned to his native Barbados to start a commercial coconut grove with his American savings. Though he lives like a decorous gentleman, he cannot overcome the subservient muteness he always felt toward whites. Nor can he feel identity with the black Barbadians he deals with. Pressed to accept a native girl as housekeeper, he first rejects her, then comes to feel a desire "to share a little of himself"--in short, to love her. It is too late. She cruelly rejects him: "You ain't people, Mr. Watford, you ain't people." He is left in despair, a person without love, without country or culture. TOPICS: Role Loss, Race, Multicultural, Community, Sexuality, Aspirations.

292. Masters, Olga. "You'll Like it There." In *The Home Girls*. London: Queensland Press, 1982. Reprint, New York: Norton, 1990, pp. 175-82.

Issues of elder abuse and neglect are raised in this story about an old Australian woman who faces the prospects of living in a nursing home after being shuttled back and forth between the homes of two other sons. After living with one son and his family for six months and finding herself neglected through their lack of care, the old woman moves in with a second son. There she experiences emotional and physical abuse at the hands of her daughter-in-law. The old woman finds an outlet for her stifled emotional life in her rapport with her granddaughter, who is in elementary school. But this respite is temporary; now her son and his wife begin to pressure her to move to a nursing home. TOPICS: Services, Intergenerational, Elder abuse, Autonomy, Anxiety, Aging in Place.

293. Matthews, Jack. "The Eternal Mortgage" (1979). In *Dubious Persuasion: Short Stories by Jack Matthews*. Baltimore: Johns Hopkins Univ. Press, 1981, pp. 90-98.

The pressure in old age to come to terms with one's failures is illustrated in this story of an old man's remorse. The narrator, a dealer in second-hand books, tells how this strange old man, looking "a little wrong," came to his trailer searching for copies of a certain pornographic photo-book published decades ago. The man buys it and asks to be told of any other copies that turn up. He confesses that he had posed for this sordid book. He has lived in agonizing fear of the divine judgment that awaits him. His one hope is to live long enough to buy the last existent copy. Years later, the book-dealer comes across another copy. When he learns that the old man is dead, he burns the copy. TOPICS: Alienation, Deviance, Life Review, Religion.

294. Matthews, Jack. "First the Legs and Last the Heart" (1973). In collection above, pp. 22-31.

A middle-aged son's ability to empathize with his confused parent, who has wandered off among strangers, helps to resolve an awkward and possibly harmful crisis. When the son finds his old Dad in a wrecked telephone booth keeping a senseless watch over rush-hour traffic, he tries a battery of approaches, from pointing out rationally that the booth is a useless place to stay, to urging emotionally that he himself has got to get home. Dad remains perfectly satisfied where he is. What finally works is a leap of empathy, as the son supports his father against an unfeeling public, saying: "Hang on, Dad! Stay in there, old Buddy!" At hearing so much expected of him, Dad replies that he really isn't as young as he used to be; would his son take over now? TOPICS: Parent-Child Bonds, Dementia.

295. Matthews, Jack. "Storyhood As We Know It."   In *"Storyhood As We Know It" and Other Tales*. Baltimore: The Johns Hopkins Univ. Press, 1993, pp. 187-203.

The courage and eloquence of the old when confronted with threats to cherished institutions is illustrated in a rich old widow who confronts a speaker at a country club function because he had written an article dismissing the family as outmoded and obsolete. Disregarded initially by the speaker as a harmless old drunk, she demonstrates that she is a worthy adversary and carries the day. She accuses him of being reckless in his advancement of his propositions. She defends the "family" as being the source of "storyhood as we know it"--the wellspring of gossip, grudges, customs, traditions, shared joys and pains--all of which richly define the family as institution. Other members of the club warm to her defense. TOPICS: Ageism, Roles, Family Bonds, Rebellion.

296. McGuane, Thomas. "Family." In *The New Yorker*, 69 (January 1994): 66-69.

An old rancher's surge of memories on his deathbed marks his effort to meet death. The passing of one culture into another colors Bill's reminiscing to his visiting son, Clay. On the land where Clay now runs a seedy used car lot, his father and forebears worked a ranch in the old heroic days, one adventure of which the father relates to his impatient son. Still, as the son reflects, "It made a kind of sense, his trying to shape the days of his life, as if they could be put in an ammunition tin when he was gone." TOPICS: Parent-Child Bonds, Family Bonds, Life Review.

297. Menaker, Daniel. *The Old Left: Stories by Daniel Menaker*. New York: Penguin, 1988, 132 pp.

This collection of eight interrelated stories ex- amines the responsibilities, burdens, and rewards of caregiving in its depiction of the ongoing relationship between Dave Leonard and his eccentric uncle Sol, a for- mer radical and member of the "old left." Uncle Sol, a cantankerous, independent, and tough-minded man, is 86 when Dave brings his wife Elizabeth to visit him at his farmhouse in the Berkshires. Now in his late 30s, Dave teaches journalism at Columbia University. He recalls spending summers as a child and teenager at Sol's farm- house. In many respects Sol was a surrogate father to him. Each story reveals the progress of the caregiving relationship over a six-year period. As Sol ages, Dave with help from Elizabeth takes on caregiving responsibil- ities for his uncle. Elizabeth helps further the bonding between Dave and his uncle at a time when Dave is feeling the stress of caregiving. Through his commitment to the caregiving relationship, Dave resolves some longstanding concerns about his identity and his relationship with Uncle Sol. TOPICS: Family Bonds, Caregiving, Doctor- Patient Conflicts, Mentoring, Legacies.

298. Miller, Sue. "Appropriate Affect." In *Inventing the Abbots and Other Stories*. New York: HarperCollins, 1989. Also in Anthology 9, pp. 271-80.

The suffering and hardship beneath an older woman's stereotyped role as affectionate matriarch come up to the surface in this story. Grandma Franny has "loved" every- body from husband to children and grandchildren. She has remembered all family relationships and birthdays. And everyone has "loved" her. Then Grandma suffers a stroke. From her fractured consciousness during convalescence some ugly truths emerge which she utters to the shock of her family: her husband's insensitivity as partner, lover, and adulterer; his children's messiness as kids and greed as adults. As health returns and her scabrous outbursts recede, Grandma and family return to their charade of happy togetherness. TOPICS: Gender: Women, Family Conflicts, Disability, Alienation.

299. Minot, Stephen. "Small Point Bridge." In *Cross- ings: Stories by Stephen Minot*. Urbana, Ill.: Univ. of Illinois Press, 1975, pp. 13-23.

An arrogant, self-assured widower in his 70s learns that he does not have dominion over the natural world. He also learns that time is running out for him in old age, and that a meaningful human relationship--even at

this stage of life--can serve as an adequate buffer
against the tides that control his life. Isaac Bates
made his fortune by operating a cannery. Isaac's neighbor, Seth, a maintenance man, has lived on Small Point,
owned by Isaac, for nineteen years and never paid rent.
If he occupies the land one more day, he will own it outright. Isaac visits Seth to take care of this "small
point." But forces in the natural world prevail to place
their dispute in a new light. TOPICS: Economics, Rural
Aging, Gender: Men, Coping.

300. Minot, Stephen.   "The Tide and Isaac Bates." In
collection above, pp. 39-51.
      An old man's repressed feelings of loss and grief
lead to a gradual unraveling of his self-control, his
faith in himself, and his relationship with his daughter. Isaac Bates' wife lies dying of cancer in a local
hospital, and Isaac has just wrecked his boat in a fierce
New England storm because he was careless. He and his
18-year-old daughter Cory barely survive the wreck. When
the two return to the house, Isaac's grief begins to play
tricks on him. Confused by memories of a youthful sexual
encounter, he transfers his feelings of loneliness and
separation to his daughter. The atmosphere of the house
becomes charged with sexual tension. Events in this story
occur two years before the events in "Small Point
Bridge." TOPICS: Rural Aging, Intimacy, Anxiety, Isolation, Grief.

301. Mori, Toshio. "The Man with Bulging Pockets." In *The
Chauvinist and Other Stories*.   Los Angeles: Univ. of
California, 1979. Also in Anthology 7, pp. 21-26.
      The aggressive rivalry between old persons is shown
here as emblematic of the splits which continually divide
all humanity. The setting is Tanforan Assembly Center,
an internment camp for Japanese-Americans in World War
II. "Grandpa," the kindly man "with bulging pockets," has
long befriended the children of this Japanese-American
community by distributing sweets and affectionate conversation. Then a former friend of his identified as The
Old Man seeks to win the children with his own gifts--not
to share the generous role but plainly to monopolize the
grandfatherly role. "Grandpa" responds with forbearance
but is deeply sad that he and The Old Man, like all humanity, cannot belong to "one big circle" where no ill
feelings and furtive deeds need enter. TOPICS: Ethnicity,
Enmity, Intergenerational, Transmission of Values.

302. Mungoshi, Charles. "The Setting Sun and the Rolling
World" (1972). In *The Setting Sun and the Rolling World*.
London: William Heinemann, 1987.   Also in Anthology 7,
pp. 13-18.

The universal struggle of a new generation to seek
its identity separate from the old is featured in this
tale of a young Zimbabwean who decides to leave home.
Old Musoni and his last-born son, Nhamo, stand on the
edge of a stony field to say their goodbyes. The father
is afraid to let go of his child; the son is impatient
to begin a new life. When the old man looks ahead, he
sees deprivation and ruination for his son; when the
young man looks ahead, he sees expansiveness, freedom,
promise. Old Musoni fears that his son's leaving will be-
tray the values of respecting the family and the land.
But the son repudiates those values and reminds him that
the family is breaking up and the land is useless. The
young man realizes, "The psychological ties were now
broken, only the biological tied him to his father."
TOPICS: Culture, Anxiety, Loss.

303. Mungoshi, Charles. "Who Will Stop the Dark? (1980)."
In *The Setting Sun and the Rolling World: Selected Stories by Charles Mungoshi*. London: Heinemann, 1987, pp.
7-27.
A grandfather becomes a surrogate father, teacher,
mentor, and companion to his grandson in this African
story of a boy's painful adaptation to the changed circumstances in his household. When Zakeo's father is
paralyzed in an accident, his mother becomes the head of
the household. Zakeo's father spends his days weaving
baskets--a woman's occupation in the Zimbabwean culture.
Neither he nor his wife speaks to the boy about this crisis in their family. Confused and alienated, the boy
spends time with Sekuru, who listens to the boy's dreams
and teaches him about the individual's relationship to
the natural world. Eventually Sekuru realizes there is
a limit to what he can provide for the boy. Zakeo must
adapt to the new dynamics within his household. TOPICS:
Culture, Grandparenting, Transmission of Values.

304. Munro, Alice. "Mrs. Cross and Mrs. Kidd." In *The
Moons of Jupiter*. New York: Knopf, 1983, pp. 160-80.
A lifelong friendship between two women, residents
in a nursing-home gallery of decrepit people, saves one
from a humiliating rejection. Mrs. Cross, educated and
a lover of science, is an atypical opposite of her
friend. Mrs. Kidd is an extrovert who befriends other
patients, particularly Jack, an inarticulate stroke victim. Her imaginative attentions are eventually spurned
by Jack, who comes to prefer the dim attractions of
Charlotte, younger but silly. His final tantrum almost
crushes Mrs. Kidd, except for the tenderness shown by her
old friend Mrs. Cross, who sees her safely to her room
at the cost of her own exhaustion. Care is taken to explain the two women's contrasting pasts: their schoolgirl

personalities, their parents, their educations, their families. TOPICS: Gender: Women, Friendship, Long-term Care.

305. Norris, Leslie.   "My Uncle's Story."   In *Atlantic* 246 (1980): 55-61.

How misfortune can break a person's spirit and ruin the prospects for a fulfilling old age is the lesson of this Welsh story of a young man's memories of his uncle, a vibrant mischief-maker who joined the Army at 16, fought in France, and then returned home to work in the mines. When the mines shut down in the Depression, the uncle left home. The boy imagines the adventures his uncle must be having as he walks the "Great North Road" across England. Years later, when the uncle returns, his nephew is shocked to find that this supposed adventurer is now an old man who sits silently and forlornly in the corner of the room. A final encounter with the uncle leaves the boy overwhelmed by the tragedy of the uncle's hard life on the road. TOPICS: Ageism, Intergenerational, Frailty, Disengagement.

306. O'Brien, Edna. "Christmas Roses."   In *A Fanatic Heart*. New York: Farrar, 1984. Also in Anthology 11, pp. 3-18.

A late love may require more courage than one can muster. Miss Hawking, a former cabaret dancer with international engagements, has retired to a London flat and a hobby of raising flowers. She keeps herself fit, so immaculately groomed and dressed that she could pass for forty. One day she finds a young man sleeping overnight in her garden, a theater student just arrived from Africa, a beautiful youth with manners and charm to match. Their friendship roots and grows to the point that she invites the young man to move in. In preparing a welcome supper, she flutters about as happy as a bride. Morning brings panic and memories of unhappy loves in other days. She bolts from London leaving a note for him never to come again. TOPICS: Intimacy, Activity, Disengagement, Coping, Creativity.

307. O'Connor, Flannery. "The Artificial Nigger" (1955). In *The Collected Works*. New York: Library of America, 1988, pp. 249-70.

The love-hate relationship between a grandfather and grandson is developed as they visit a big city where both are strangers. Mr. Head, a rural widower, fondly believes that age has qualified him as a suitable guide for the young. Nelson, the orphaned grandson who lives with him, "was never satisfied until he had given an impudent answer." So the two battle each other until the boy accidentally knocks down an old woman and attracts a crowd of bystanders. Mr. Head is so frightened and ashamed that he denies knowing his grandson. This terrible act imposes a horrid silence between them until the old man, afraid for his very soul, manages to joke about an "artificial nigger," a plaster figure. The boy is relieved; the grandfather feels God's forgiveness. TOPICS: Grandparenting, Aspirations, Religion.

308. O'Connor, Flannery "A Late Encounter with the Enemy" (1953). In collection above, pp. 134-44.

The folly of prizing immortality is hilariously enacted in this tale of Civil War veteran "General" Tennessee Flintlock Sash, aged 104, a vain and thoroughly addled star of parades and stage appearances. Probably once a foot soldier, the "General" has reached extreme old age as little more than a picturesque doll. "The past and the future were the same thing to him, one forgotten and the other not remembered." Now his sixtyish granddaughter Sally wants him to attend her belated graduation from college. There he makes his final appearance and, as corpse, his final exit. TOPICS: Dementia, Vanity.

309. O'Connor, Frank. "Requiem" (1957). In *Collected Stories*. Introduction by Ronald Ellman. New York: Knopf, 1981. Also in Anthology 10, pp. 163-71.

A sixtyish Irish widow who wants Mass said for her dead poodle presents Father Fogarty with an awkward crisis. First supposing her to have lost her husband, the Father learns that the husband was fifteen years gone. "Timmy," her poodle, had been such a comrade to the widow that she thinks of it as a person with a soul and mourns it as one. Although he cannot grant the poor woman's wish, their conflict and reconciliation convey provocative convictions about spiritual values. TOPICS: Older couples, Loss, Religion.

310. Olsen, Tillie. "Tell Me a Riddle." In *Tell Me a Riddle*. New York: Dell, 1961. Reprint, New York: Dial, 1976, pp. 72-125. Also in Anthology 11, pp. 301-58.

Lifelong conflicts surface at last as Eva, a bitter, passionate old Jewish woman dying of cancer, reflects on a life as wife and mother whose vitality has been squeezed out by the demands of children, husband, poverty. Her husband wants to move to an old folks' home to be with lodge friends. Eva rebels against his masculine self-centeredness. She craves solitude: "Never again to be forced to move to the rhythms of others." Growing in sympathy, her husband takes her to their children's homes, and finally to Los Angeles, where she is wonderfully ministered to by her granddaughter Jeannie, a nurse. She relives her turbulent life from childhood in Russia, her youthful utopianism, prison, young love, her

village and its music, which she hears on her deathbed.
TOPICS: Ethnicity, Gender: Women, Grandparenting, Life
Review, Death.

311. Osborn, Carolyn. "Man Dancing." In *Fields of Memory*.
Bryan, Tex.: Shearer Pub, 1984. Also in Anthology 5, pp.
252-64.
     A lonely widower finds many ways of reconnecting
with life. Professor Theo Isaacs, retired and fusty,
meets a friendly widow who invites him to move into her
spacious home. The invitation prompts him to spruce up
by purchasing a new wardrobe, after which he dances a
little jig. He accepts the new chance and notifies his
children that he is selling the old home. The new perspective takes on color the following Saturday, when he
does light duty at the art museum. Here the day's main
event is an art competition happily won by the picture
of a man dancing (a parallel to Isaac's little jig). A
secondary theme in this story of renewed life is the role
of friendships--Isaac's museum co-worker; the Mexican lad
fascinated by art; the African-American caretaker.
TOPICS: Older Couples, Retirement, Widowerhood.

312. Parise, Goffredo. "Beauty" (1982). In *Abecedary*.
Translated by James Marcus. Marlboro, Vt.: The Marlboro
Press, 1990, pp. 61-66.
     Beauty is expressed in the simple routines of an
"old country laborer," a peasant who finds odd jobs in
the Italian countryside. The old man spends most of his
days in the fields, mowing, clearing grass, spreading
hay, digging roots, cutting branches. He is shy, illiterate, has few clothes, is polite to strangers, loves
to smoke, and spends most of his days outside the house.
He is married and has a large family. But the old man
is devoted to his life outdoors; he is sympathetic to the
environment and to the ecology of the countryside.
"Almost no social event interested him." He has thought
about death, but does not dwell on it. Instead, he continues to plan new projects. His story is a character
study of a dignified, austere old age. TOPICS: Rural Aging, Gender: Men, Activity, Autonomy, Employment.

313. Parise, Goffredo. "Fear." In *Solitudes: Short Stories*. Translated by Isabel Quigly. London: Dent, 1984,
pp. 125-28.
     One of the greatest fears of an old person, that
of being the victim of an assault, is played out by the
experiences of a widow, 70, who survives a confrontation
with two thugs by drawing upon her strong will and resourcefulness. One night in Venice, Italy, while walking
home and thinking of a winter cruise she may take, she
is accosted by two boys who try to rob her. When one of

the boys threatens her life, she has a moment to imagine
her death in the swirling waters under the bridge she was
crossing. She admits her fear, yet responds defiantly,
"Kill me, then." When the boy repeats his threat, and
then strikes her, she maintains her resolve and doesn't
back down. The boys run off, and gradually her fear
leaves her. TOPICS: Coping, Courage, Death.

314. Parise, Goffredo. "Memory." In collection above,
pp. 144-48.
        Feelings of disappointment, sadness and loss per-
vade an old man's chance meeting with his former gay
lover. When this old poet arrives in Milan from Rome,
he learns that his former lover, Bertino, now works as
a hotel porter. Bertino was "one of a gang of boys" the
poet had surrounded himself with twenty years ago. The
poet remembers his fascination for the young Bertino and
is drawn to visit him. But he is struck with sadness
that the man who was once his lover is now a heavy-set
man with a "pale, emaciated head" who has become a dutiful, dull, and responsible husband and father. Bertino
never mentions their relationship, although he does ask
if the poet recalls a poem he once wrote in Bertino's
honor. They part after this brief reunion. TOPICS: Culture, Gender: Men, Intimacy, Loss.

315. Porter, Katherine Anne. "The Jilting of Granny
Weatherall" (1930). In *Flowering Judas and Other Stories*.
New York: Harcourt, Brace, 1935. Also in Anthology 5, and
Anthology 9, pp. 74-81.
        How an early crisis can disturb the ending of life
is shown as the long-buried memory of a terrible jilting
pushes up into the hallucinating consciousness of Ellen
Weatherall on her deathbed at nearly eighty years.
Richer memories also crowd in: of husband, children,
home-keeping, farm work, tending sick animals and bed-
bound neighbors. She is proud of the life she has made
since that awful day of abandonment, but dies with her
final moment still in that shadow. TOPICS: Family Bonds,
Dementia, Life Review, Death.

316. Porter, Katherine Anne. "The Last Leaf." *In The
Leaning Tower and Other Stories*. New York: Harcourt,
Brace, 1934. Also Anthology 5, pp. 291-94.
        Although set a century ago, this brief portrait of
an aging African-American woman may suggest a serene independence which has its relevance today. "Nannie," a
freed slave and pure Bantu, has toiled her whole life for
an unnamed white family. Now in extreme old age, she
leaves the family household as an expression of earned
independence, to live in a nearby abandoned cabin. Her
former husband, her grandchildren, her white family visit

her with gifts--the white family in particular realizing at last how much she had kept the house going. She accepts visits and gifts but without great caring, wanting only to "pass my last days in peace." TOPICS: Multicultural, Disengagement, Retirement.

317. Porter, Katherine Anne. "The Old Order." In *The Leaning Tower and Other Stories*. New York: Harcourt, Brace, 1934, pp. 33-56.

The relationship between two women from different worlds evolves into a lifelong multicultural friendship based on equality and acceptance of differences. Sophia Jane was a descendant of Daniel Boone, a spoiled daughter of slave-owning parents who appropriated Nanny, a child of newly-purchased slaves, as her "little monkey." Old Nanny became the latter's property when Sophia married and was nursemaid for several of Sophia's children. After Sophia's husband died in the Civil War, she moved to Texas with her eleven children and scraped together a living for her family with the help of Nanny and other former slaves. The two have spent the past fifty years growing old together. Now they are like an old couple, inseparable, tolerant of each other's faults. TOPICS: Roles, Multicultural, Older Couples.

318. Powers, J. F. "The Old Man: A Love Story." In *Prince of Darkness and Other Stories*. Garden City, N.Y.: Doubleday, 1947, pp. 197-214.

An old man, unemployed, fearful, and desperate, learns firsthand the debilitating effects of ageism when he lands a temporary job in a company's shipping department. Charley Newman has worked in offices for many years, but now he faces hard times in the post-World-War-II economy. He looks for any job, no matter how menial. Nervous and easily intimidated by authority, Charley strives to make a good impression. But in the afternoon he overhears his supervisor refer to him as "an old bird" who belongs in "the old people's home." Now he knows the full indignity of what it means to be old. Numbed and dispirited, he returns home to describe the day to his wife who seems to understand his need to be listened to and pampered. TOPICS: Ageism, Role Loss, Older couples, Employment, Aspirations.

319. Pritchett, V. S. "A Trip to the Seaside." In *A Careless Widow & Other Stories*. London: Chatto & Windus, 1989, pp. 69-88.

A 65-year-old English widower's vanity, insensitivity, and lack of insight into passion and relationships are revealed when he is repudiated by a woman he intends to marry. Mr. Andrews visits, unannounced, a former secretary, now middle-aged, who left his company

five years earlier after a quarrel and now lives in a
seaside resort. But his hopes of marrying her are dashed
when she announces she married a recently divorced man
a year ago. Then she reminds him why she left the company: she had waited for years for Mr. Andrews to leave
his wife and marry her. When he seemed incapable of making the break, she quit her job and found another man.
Humiliated by her replay of events, Mr. Andrews departs.
TOPICS: Intimacy, Vanity, Widowerhood.

320. Ricci, Julio. "The Concert." In *Falling Through
the Cracks: Stories of Julio Ricci*. Fredonia, N.Y.:
White Pine, 1989. Also in Anthology 7, pp. 217-27.
      Under the pressure of ageism, the older people in
this fantasy tale survive by voicing a mindless optimism
rather than admit their difficulties and assert their
real worth. The narrator is one of hundreds of needy
oldsters who receive starvation wages for the laughter
they crank out whenever a noted comedian gives a concert.
No one has any sense of humor--not the harsh director,
not the visiting comedians (whose routines are mechanical), and certainly not the geriatric audience which
laughs uproariously out of fear of being fired. At the
climactic "concert," one old man takes center stage to
give a supreme and transcendent performance which rises
above the hypocrisy of the rest. TOPICS: Ageism, Humor.

321. Rosner, Anne. "Prize Tomatoes" (1981). In *Best
American Short Stories, 1982*. Edited by John Gardner and
Shannon Ravenel. Boston: Houghton Mifflin, pp. 260-86.
      The rebellion of an aged widower against an
over-protective daughter leads to his dedication to new
interests. Walter Brinkman's daughter Barbara and her
family have moved in to keep a close eye on him after his
attempted suicide over his wife's death. They begrudge
and hamper his new interests in ham radio and then in
seed catalogs. What they miss to the point of cruelty is
that Walter has grown into a different person from the
dynamic businessman they knew and want to recover. Walter
manages a successful revolt, in part through his new
friendship with a black man also misunderstood by his
children, in part through gardening. At the end, he
breaks away to get to a fair where he finds that his
tomatoes (and he) have won the blue ribbon. TOPICS:
Friendship, Parent-Child Conflicts, Leisure, Aspirations,
Retirement, Widowerhood.

322. Sayles, John.   "At the Anarchists' Convention."
In *Atlantic* 243 (1979). Also in Anthology 4, pp. 230-41.
      The excitement of old adventure brings together and
renews a memorable gallery of old activists who have
never forgotten the exuberance of their days of protest.

The "Anarchists' Convention" is the annual reunion in New York City of a group of anarchists who were active in the 20s and 30s. In old age these characters continue to defy authority, to hold old grudges and longstanding feuds, and to resist any regimentation of thought or action. They have maintained old friendships and not lost touch with their social and political agendas. Set against the pain of their losses and the memories of oppression that haunt them is the renewal that occurs every time they are confronted with oppression. The comic ending of the story shows the anarchists united again against a common foe. TOPICS: Stereotypes, Ethnicity, Community, Rebellion, Humor, Courage.

323. Sayles, John. "Dillinger in Hollywood." *Triquarterly Magazine* 48 (Spring 1980). Also in Anthology 9, pp. 336-46.
.   The routines and sufferings of old age are seen under the wild humor and institutional slang in this account by an attendant at a geriatric hospital for movie folk.   Among the iridescent wreckage of second- and third-rate Hollywood characters, the central one is Casey, a former studio driver who now claims to be John Dillinger--the real gangster, not the "double" actually shot down long ago. Beyond the comedy of Casey, one sees the quixotic courage shown by such eccentrics (and how many others) in facing their own extinction.   TOPICS: Frailty, Long-term Care, Courage.

324. Scofield, Sandra. "Loving Leo." In *Women and Aging: An Anthology by Women*.   Edited by Jo Alexander and others.   Corvallis, Oreg: Calyx Bks, 1986, pp. 68-73.
        Whether or not to enter a late marriage is debated by Greta Boll, a tough but poetic widow. She has had a hard life in hard jobs with many disappointments; yet she has good memories of her husband and grandparents; she loves to harvest the sweet-scented apricots from her back yard. Leo Clark, a nearly blind old man, has courted her for months. He is tender, confident, a good provider. He will share his interests and learn hers. Something in Greta responds: "something wild, young, long ago given up for dead." But she can't quite give up her old life and her contented privacy. The story ends ambiguously with Greta quietly enjoying the taste of her apricots. TOPICS: Social Class, Intimacy, Aging in Place.

325. Singer, Isaac Bashevis. "The Hotel." In *Death of Methuselah and Other Stories*. New York: Farrar, 1988. Also in Anthology 5, pp. 165-74.
   When retirement is unbearable for a lifelong busy person, reentry into the career may prove a real option, as it does for Israel Danziger, a Jewish businessman now

floundering in Miami Beach idleness. His favorite foods are ruled out, the women are fat and selfish, there's nothing sensible to do with his money. "What [he] was living through now was not mere boredom; it was panic." So he takes a bus to a familiar cafeteria, where he strikes up a chat with another stranded businessman. His new friend has learned of a hotel for sale, it seems, which if properly managed could make a profit. Both prepare to visit the property and to plunge back into the business world which had formed their whole lives. The characters think and speak in dry Yiddish humor. TOPICS: Ethnicity, Loneliness, Employment, Retirement.

326. Singer, Isaac Bashevis. "Old Love" (1975). In *The Collected Stories of Isaac Bashevis Singer*. Translated by Saul Bellow and others. New York: Farrar, 1982, pp. 421-33.

The possibilities and impossibilities of love in the late years are explored in Harry Bendiner, 82, rich, three times a widower. He is living a lonely, apprehensive life in Miami Beach when he meets his new neighbor, Ethel Brokeles. Ethel is younger and physically attractive. She had loved an older husband and has always liked older men. She and Harry share a Polish Jewish culture. They have both thrived financially. Both feel a call to new life. On her husband's death she had fallen mentally ill; now Harry can fill the void. On this very day the two engage to marry, and at once the new life fades. Ethel suddenly looks aged; her suicide that night means that she has answered her husband's call from the grave. Left once more alone, Harry conceives the adventurous idea of finding Ethel's daughter and becoming a father to her. TOPICS: Ethnicity, Intimacy, Disengagement, Suicide, Aspirations.

327. Stegner, Wallace. "The Double Corner." *In Collected Stories of Wallace Stegner*. New York: Penguin, 1990, pp. 159-78.

A young couple learns that viewing a demented old person as necessarily frail, vulnerable, and helpless may ignore the real danger that person poses to her caregivers. Tom and Janet, who live on a farm in California with their two boys, reluctantly agree to take in Tom's mother after several members of the family have given up on caring for her. Tom views his mother's dementia as irreversible and advocates committing her to an institution. But Janet believes Grandma is a helpless old woman whose strangeness and fearfulness will be restored by their patient and nurturing care. For months she ignores evidence of the old woman's violent tendencies. Janet awakens to the horror of their predicament as caregivers only when she encounters Grandma, malevolence darkening

her face, spying on her sleeping children. TOPICS:
Ageism, Rural Aging, Parent-Child Conflicts, Caregiving,
Dementia.

328. Steinbeck, John. "The Leader of the People." Chap.
IV of *The Red Pony*. (1937). In *The Short Novels of John
Steinbeck*. London: Heinemann, 1953, pp. 143-53.
     The difficulty of telling the young about one's
life achievements is discovered by an old pioneer.
Grandfather was once "leader of the people" who had led
a wagon-train in frontier days--a classic exploit in the
American westward movement. Over and over he tells of
the Indians, the hunger, the drought, until he has bored
many listeners, especially his son-in-law Carl Tiflin,
whose family he has come to visit. Carl complains bitterly to the family just as Grandfather enters the room.
Carl's anguished apology hardly softens the awful moment.
Jody, the old man's grandson, had actually been excited
by these stories. He joins Grandfather on the porch.
The old pioneer expresses grief that he can't really
communicate that great adventure; he laments that "westering has died out of the people." TOPICS: Parent-Child
Conflicts, Grandparenting, Leisure, Loss, Reminiscence,
Transmission of Values.

329. Stern, Richard. "Arrangements at the Gulf" (1964).
In *Noble Rot: Stories, 1949-1988*. New York, Grove Press,
1989, pp. 252-58.
     A rich widower, lonely and alienated because of the
patronizing and selfish attentions of his large family,
finds love and commitment in a longstanding friendship.
Mr. Lomax, 86, in failing health, spends every winter in
Florida. Before his departure this year, he told his
family, "I'm going to die in Florida." Appalled by his
family's show of sentiment, he flees their clutches and
looks forward to renewing his friendship with Henry Glanville, a lifelong bachelor, who also winters in Florida.
When he is reunited with his old friend, he tells
Glanville what he said to his family. Granville is
sympathetic, but speechless. Then Lomax asks a favor:
"I'd like to die when you're around, Herbert." He ex-
plains that their friendship is special: "Old friends are
true family." Glanville promises to be with Lomax when
he dies. TOPICS: Friendship, Disengagement, Alienation,
Anxiety, Death.

330. Stern, Richard. "Dr. Cahn's Visit." In *Packages:
Stories by Richard Stern*. New York: Coward, McCann &
Geoghegan, 1980, pp. 145-51. Also in Anthology 9, and
Anthology 12, pp. 90-94.
     The interaction between a son and his parents il-
lustrates how one's neat expectations of old age and

illness can be overturned by unpredictable events and the
idiosyncracies of character. Dr. Cahn, 91, suffers from
the advanced stages of Alzheimer's Disease. His wife,
80, near death from cancer, is a patient at the hospital
in which Dr. Cahn practiced throughout his career. Inspired by his mother's courage and defiance despite the
suffering inflicted upon her by her cancer, the son arranges a last visit between his parents, even though no
one believes the old man will recognize his wife. For
a few moments lucidity returns to Dr. Cahn, and his wife
and he seem to interact meaningfully. Then Dr. Cahn
lapses into dementia, and the moment passes. TOPICS:
Parent-Child Bonds, Older Couples, Dementia, Doctor-
Patient Conflicts, Endurance.

331. Stern, Richard. "Packages." In *Packages: Stories
by Richard Stern*. New York: Coward, McCann & Geoghegan,
1980, pp. 49-59.

After his mother's death a middle-aged son
struggles to resolve a lifetime of conflicts felt between
his mother and himself. He achieves closure when he
forgives her for having been a slave to duty and
practicality while neglecting creativity and spontaneity.
The plot and characters of this story are a continuation
of those in "Dr. Cahn's Visit" (see above). Dr. Cahn's
advancing dementia complicates the family's grieving
after the mother dies. After Dr. Cahn dies, the son reviews his mother's pampered life as a doctor's wife, recalls her courage in the face of life-threatening cancer,
and realizes that the appropriate and "practical" way to
say goodbye to his mother is to allow the "package"
(which contains the urn with his mother's ashes) to be
picked up in the garbage. TOPICS: Parent-Child Conflicts,
Caregiving, Dementia, Legacies.

332. Swift, Jonathan. (1726). [The Immortal
Struldbruggs]. Part III, Chap. 10 of *Gulliver's Travels,
and Other Writings*. Edited by Louis A. Landa. London:
Oxford Univ. Press, 1976, pp. 167-73. Also widely
available.

The folly of wanting to live forever is brilliantly
demonstrated in this section of Swift's great satiric
fantasy. Merely staying alive isn't the same as living
well; death in extreme old age is a release not a doom.
Captain Lemuel Gulliver travels to strange countries in
which human faults appear in exaggeration. He learns of
certain freaks, the Struldbruggs, who never die. Gulliver
enthusiastically describes what he himself would seek if
immortal: wealth, knowledge, influence. After laughing,
his hosts describe the actual condition of the
Struldbruggs. They keep on aging with increasing disability; they become more peevish, covetous, morose, vain,

talkative, envious—and so short of memory that they can
not read from one end of a sentence to the other. Their
best luck would be to sink into dementia where they no
longer know their own misery. TOPICS: Disability, Dementia, Disengagement, Death.

333. Taylor, Peter.   "Porte-Cochere" (1949).   In *The
Widows of Thornton*. New York: Harcourt, 1954.   Also in
Anthology 9, pp. 184-191.
     The stresses of a morbid family pattern—the toxic
blends of rage and affection, of doting and demanding,
of rebellion and surrender—are shown in Old Ben Brantley
and his adult children. Ben, 76 and nearly blind, is a
despotic father whose children have come to celebrate his
birthday. His favorite is his son Clifford, whose affection he aches for. But he quarrels violently with
Clifford over a trifle. We learn that Ben had been
cruelly beaten by his father, an abuse which he has
translated into the subtler and more oppressive tyranny
of snooping on his children and expecting them to coddle
him.   What should have been a patriarchal celebration
ends with Old Ben reverting to his own father's rage as
he whips the chairs in his locked study, calling them by
his children's names. TOPICS: Parent-Child Conflicts,
Transmission of Values.

334. Thomas, Annabel. "Ashur and Evir." In *The Phototro-
pic Woman*. Iowa City, Iowa: Univ. of Iowa Press, 1981,
pp. 65-75.
     How to balance security and adventure in old age
is the theme of this affectionate conflict between
brother and sister. Ashur, a dairy farmer, is selling
the farm and investing his share of the proceeds into
permanent care at a retirement home. He has taken a
fierce pride in farming, but a fire that had nearly destroyed their home has scarred him with an anxious temperament. His older sister Evir, by contrast, is happy
in that most insecure of occupations, giving piano lessons. She will not invest her share in the home. At her
last students' recital, Evir is seen radiant in the
music-making she loves best. She happily decides to rent
a room in town and continue giving lessons to the students whose lives she has touched. TOPICS: Poverty,
Creativity, Anxiety, Courage, Retirement.

335. Trevor, William. "Attracta" (1978). In *William
Trevor: The Collected Stories*. New York: Penguin, 1992,
pp. 675-90.
     The heroism possible for old age is demonstrated
by Attracta, an aging Protestant schoolteacher, who
learns of the atrocious murder of a former student at the
hands of terrorists. She herself had lost her parents by

a mistaken ambush (intended for British soldiers), but grew up receiving affectionate, expiatory attention from the man and housekeeper who had laid the plot. She now tries to explain to her pupils what such atrocities mean, how the criminals may become decent, how God still has mercy. The pupils, who are merely confused, report the talk to their parents. They in turn complain to the archdeacon, who decides that retirement time has come for Attracta. Misunderstood and unappreciated, she accepts without loss of faith. TOPICS: Endurance, Retirement, Transmission of Values.

336. Trevor, William. "Broken Homes" (1978). In collection above, pp. 522-35.
     The appalling damage that insensitive "charity" can inflict on the helpless old is experienced by Mrs. Malby, an 87-year-old London widow being "helped" against her will. She lives contentedly in a sunlit apartment but fears that senility may one day force her to give up independence. This contentment is fractured one day when a teacher comes from a nearby school to inform Mrs. Malby that her kitchen is to be decorated by the students free of charge "to foster a deeper understanding between the generations." A nightmare ensues, as the students slosh paint on walls and carpet, smoke cigarettes, turn up the radio, have sex in her bedroom. The rape of Mrs. Malby's little world is complete. TOPICS: Services, Intergenerational, Elder Abuse, Autonomy, Anxiety, Aging in Place.

337. Trevor, William. "The General's Day" (1967). In collection above, pp. 30-45.
     An aged rake wastes the day in seeking pleasure one more time. General Suffolk has served England famously as leader in two great wars. He has also freely womanized and drunk. Now at 78 his hot temper, wandering hands, and easy boredom have lost him several retirement employments; he lives in a modest cottage with a predatory housekeeper. On this day he sets out aching for companionship and fun. But he is fobbed off by a young male acquaintance; then by a former drinking companion; then by a lady he tries to pick up in a restaurant; then by a fellow bus-rider--all this punctuated with his increasingly drunken chatter. General Suffolk ends his day stumbling home. "My God Almighty," sobs the General, "I could live for twenty years." TOPICS: Roles, Sexuality, Disease, Alienation, Leisure, Retirement.

338. Updike, David. "Indian Summer." In *Out on the Marsh: Stories by David Updike*. Boston: David Godine, 1988. Reprint, New York: New American Library, 1989, pp. 71-79.
     A young man learns how much resolution and even

courage may be required of an old person who faces ever
increasing demands of the natural and social environ-
ments.   When he visits his grandmother on the family
farm, the young man marvels at her self-control and eq-
uanimity. Widowed several years earlier, she has maintained the farm by herself, and she has surrounded herself with a variety of animals. But now she is experiencing symptoms of physical decline, is wary of the coming winter season, and is fearful of impending changes.
How long can she hold on? What will happen to the farm
when she dies? Her grandson respects the hard choices
she is forced to make in order to survive. TOPICS: Rural
Aging, Grandparenting, Coping, Endurance, Aging in Place.

339. Vivante, Arturo. "The Bell" (1973). In *The Tales
of Arturo Vivante*. Selected and with an Introduction by
Mary Kinzie. Riverdale-on-Hudson, N.Y.: The Sheep Meadow
Press, 1990, pp. 100-110.
     The pain felt by the unappreciated caregiver is il-
lustrated in this story of a middle-aged son who tries
to minister to his dying father. Bedridden and sometimes
slipping into dementia, the old man, 82, rings for his
son at all hours.   But the son is frustrated that his
caregiving seems to count for nothing. His father tol-
erates his attentiveness but is unresponsive and remote.
After the father survives several crises, the son overcomes his hostility, comes to admire his father's strong
will and acceptance of death, and resigns himself to the
distance between them. When the son takes a job in America, an old cook returns to join the maid in the months
before his father dies. The son concedes, "They were far
better company, those two old women." TOPICS: Parent-
Child Conflicts, Caregiving, Dementia, Doctor-Patient
Conflicts, Dying.

340. Vivante, Arturo. "A Gallery of Women" (1978).   In
collection above, pp. 93-99.
     An old man's anxieties and discomfort during the
last months of his life are relieved by his son's
ingenuity as a caregiver. The bedridden old man, widowed
six years earlier, fears the "abyss of death." Despite
his son's attempts to provide solace and comfort, his
father is unresponsive. The son's novel idea: "What he
wanted was the company of women." Initially the son invites some of his women friends to the father's house.
Soon he retains a young manicurist, then a hairdresser,
to visit the old man weekly.   This unusual "therapy"
works wonders. The women "brought an air of freshness
into the room." The old man becomes more alert and engaged; he reads poems to the women; they enjoy his humor
and sweetness and are enchanted by the old man's attention.   The women continue to visit his father as he

nears death. TOPICS: Services, Gender: Men, Caregiving, Leisure.

341. Vivante, Arturo. (1965). "Last Rites." In collection above, pp. 89-92.   Also in Anthology 5, pp. 344-48.
The painful death of a brave woman and her perfectly fitting last rites are the subject of this brief narrative. After being subjected to heroic surgeries and medicines, she learns that she has terminal cancer--this being told to her by a doctor son who believes in the right of the patient to know. She bravely tries to control the pain but dies suddenly. Her last rites would seem bare, for she was not a religious person. But the procession winds through the countryside she loved, glorious in spring bloom. Her vault is sealed by a skillful mason she had known and admired. The grave is bordered by travertine hand-worked by a gentle stonecutter she had known. So although she could not control her illness, her last rites were just as she might have directed. TOPICS: Community, Disease, Doctor-Patient Conflicts, Spiritual Life, Death.

342. Vivante, Arturo. "The Orchard" (1968).   In *The Tales of Arturo Vivante*. Selected and with an Introduction by Mary Kinzie. Riverdale-on-Hudson, N.Y.: The Sheep Meadow Press, 1990, pp. 35-42.
Perseverance and a lifelong dedication to an avocation is illustrated in an old man's devotion to growing an orchard of peaches in an area of Northern Italy where vineyards and olive groves predominate. A philosopher and novice to agriculture, he is 43 when he plants the orchard in the 1930s. After a few promising years early frosts devastate the orchard; and after the family spends World War II in England, they return to find the orchard in ruins. Now 56 the father reads new agricultural pamphlets and moves the orchard to higher ground. Everyone speaks against his plans. But he perseveres and the trees bear fruit despite frosts in the valleys. His son sums up the old man's later years: "The orchard fills his needs. Year after year, he watches the trees blossom in the spring, the girls gathering the peaches in the summer." TOPICS: Poverty, Activity, Serenity, Leisure, Aspirations.

343. Vivante, Arturo.   "The Soft Core (1972)".   In collection above, pp. 70-79. Also in Anthology 4, pp. 270-82.
The limits that must be placed on some of the rewards of caregiving are illustrated in the ambivalent relationship between a middle-aged son and his 80-year-old father, who is recuperating from a stroke. The father has always been self-centered and insensitive to his

son's needs. His son survives this hurtful relationship by constructing in his mind an image of the old man as an ideal father figure, someone who is sweet and worthy of admiration. When the old man experiences another stroke, the son works patiently to help his father recover from his mental confusion. He uncovers, temporarily, his father's "soft core," an affectionate and loving self which the old man has buried over the years with selfish preoccupations and an unyielding temperament. TOPICS: Parent-Child Conflicts, Caregiving, Dementia.

344. Vonnegut, Kurt, Jr. "Tomorrow and Tomorrow and Tomorrow" (1953). In *Welcome to the Monkey House: A Collection of Short Works by Kurt Vonnegut, Jr.* New York: Delacorte, 1968. Reprint, New York: Dell Books, 1988, pp. 293-308.

The possible miseries of a future gerontocratic society are warned against in this ghoulish little fantasy. By 2158 the life span has extended indefinitely. Thanks to medical science and to a wonder drug called "anti-gerasone," Em and Lou Schwarz, the main characters, are 112 years old and 93, respectively. But life has remained at least as drab as our own plastic culture has made it. Overpopulation is crushing. Overcrowding is rife. Income is drained off for defense and old-age pensions. The oldest Schwarz is Lou's grandfather, 172, who rules the roost because he is oldest. He tyrannizes over all the others until Lou and Em decide that Gramp will never leave if not helped along a little. The rest of the story deals with "helping Gramps along a little," with an outcome that will make most readers glad to be living in our own time. TOPICS: Economics, Grandparenting, Doctor-Patient Conflicts, Death.

345. Walker, Alice. "To Hell With Dying." In *Love and Trouble: Stories of Black Women.* New York: HarBraceJ, 1973. Also in Anthology 4, and Anthology 12, pp. 279-84.

A deep intergenerational affection is felt between an old black widower and the neighboring children. The narrator tells of her girlhood, how Mr. Sweet in spite of frequent drunkenness had a special charm for the kids who played with him. Barred by his blackness from other callings, he had turned to fishing, haphazard farming, brewing his own liquor, and playing sweet sad wonderful songs on his guitar. When he fell sick, the narrator's father would bring his children to Mr. Sweet's bed, saying, "To hell with dying. These children want Mr. Sweet!" Their affection would actually revive him. The narrator, now adult, tells of meeting him once again at his real deathbed. TOPICS: Race, Intergenerational, Disease, Creativity.

346. Walker, Alice. "The Welcome Table." In *Love and Trouble: Stories of Black Women*. New York: HarBraceJ, 1973, pp. 81-87.

An old black woman is expelled from a white church in Georgia. Ancient, dazed, nearly blind, she somehow seems an archetypal figure of her race as she enters. She ignores two polite invitations to leave, whereupon the ladies are determined to protect "God, mother, earth, church." They forcibly usher her into the winter morning. Outside, the sad old woman sees Jesus striding down the highway. When he says "Follow me," she does so joyfully. She is later found dead on the road. TOPICS: Race, Frailty, Religion, Death.

347. Weaver, Will. "From the Landing." In *A Gravestone Made of Wheat: Stories*. St. Paul, Minn.: Graywolf, 1989, pp. 125-35.

The guilt which can be felt on restricting the activities of an older adult is shown when an old man suffers the indignity and humiliation of having his driving privileges taken away. The story begins when two cousins were boys and their grandfather took them fishing. His erratic driving leads to a minor accident, and one of the boys tells the truth about the old man's driving habits to his father, who compels the old man to give up his keys. Years later the cousins, now adults with families of their own, spend an evening fishing. Suddenly the talk turns to their grandfather, and one cousin admits that for years he felt he had betrayed the old man, who "shriveled up and died" after that fateful day. The two men comfort one another, and their unfolding camaraderie leads to a sharing of their deepest hopes and fears. TOPICS: Rural aging, Grandparenting, Frailty, Mid-Life.

348. Weaver, Will. "A Gravestone Made of Wheat." In collection above, pp. 13-30.

The values of aging in place and family bonds are given special intensity in this tale of an old Norwegian farmer who keeps a promise he made to his wife and buries her on the farm, despite the warning from the sheriff that such burials are illegal. His wife, a German immigrant, came to Northern Minnesota to marry him when she was 18. Frustrated by authorities because of the anti-German sentiment after World War I, the two never obtained a marriage license. But they lived together forty-five years, considered themselves "married," and raised a family. With his children's help, the old man buries his wife in the middle of an eighty-acre field. Now the mother will have a "gravestone made of wheat" when next year's crop flourishes. TOPICS: Rural aging, Parent-Child Bonds, Rebellion, Aging in place, Life Review.

349. Welty, Eudora.   (1941). "Old Mr. Marblehall."   In
The Collected Stories of Eudora Welty.   New York:
HarBraceJ, 1980, pp. 91-97.
     Boredom may lead an older person into fantastic es-
capes, as with Mr. Marblehall, a lifelong bachelor who
marries lovelessly at sixty and also begins a double life
of bigamy.   Mr. Marblehall's people have lived for generations in the conservative town of Natchez, Missis-
sippi. He is a perfectly decorous gentleman, always cold,
always careful, every hair in place. Neither of his two
wives is attractive, nor does he show them much af-
fection--except that by each he has had a small imp-like
son.   His one evident excitement is reading "Terror
Tales" and similar pulp magazines. For the rest, he is
totally a non-person to the townsfolk. His hope, at 66,
is that his double life will be found out one day, with
a scandalous explosion which will somehow validate his
tedious life. TOPICS: Roles, Older Couples, Alienation,
Aspirations.

350. Welty, Eudora. "A Visit of Charity." In collection
above.   Also in Anthology 9, pp. 331-35.
     The contradictions, alienation, and desperation of
old age are the fruits of an unforgettable encounter between a young campfire girl and two old women in a
nursing home.   The girl arrives one day at the Old
Ladies' Home to visit one of the residents and earn
"three points" as part of her campfire service.   Her
visit is a traumatic one; nothing in her experience has
prepared her for it. Instead of finding a passive, sweet
old woman who sits calmly in her rocking chair and reads
her Bible, the girl encounters two aged crones who argue
heatedly, share some of their deepest secrets and fears,
and probably confirm every negative stereotype the young
girl has of old age. TOPICS: Ageism, Intergenerational,
Alienation.

351. Welty, Eudora.   "A Worn Path." In *The Collected
Stories of Eudora Welty*. New York: Harcourt Brace
Jovanovich, 1980. Also in Anthology 9, pp. 9-15.
     An old black woman's strength of character and
purity of heart is more than a match for a hostile world.
Phoenix Jackson walks for miles along the Old Natchez
Trace into the city of Natchez in order to pick up some
more medicine for her young grandson, who swallowed lye
three years ago. She overcomes all obstacles in her path
in order to carry out her mission. The author portrays
her in heroic terms as a woman of indomitable will and
spirit. When she arrives at the clinic, it becomes apparent that her grandson may, in fact, no longer be
alive. Perhaps the purpose of the old woman's journey
is to remain engaged with the challenges and rhythms of

a life dedicated to love and caregiving. TOPICS: Poverty, Race, Gender: Women, Activity, Endurance, Serenity.

352. Wharton, Edith. "After Holbein" (1930). In *The Stories of Edith Wharton*. Selected and Introduced by Anita Brookner. New York: Carroll & Graf, 1990. Also in *Love and Loss: Stories of the Heart*. Edited by Georgina Hammick. Boston: Faber & Faber, 1992, pp. 74-95.

Two demented old crocks relive an evening in New York's high society--showing that in old age one can become a caricature of lifelong shortcomings. Anson Warley has smothered his timid real self in a career as much sought-after dinner guest. On this wintry evening he determines to dine out despite his increasing frailty and his valet's warnings. He forgets where he was invited but ends up at the door of Evalina Jaspar. She has smothered any real self in a career as leading hostess. She is now so addled that she fancies she is giving a dinner tonight. So she greets Anson and the two sit down to a "dinner" hastily improvised by the servants: mashed potatoes, fruit, mineral water (served as premium wines). Pleased with his guestly performance, Anson steps out into the night and collapses. The tone is both comic and horrifying. TOPICS: Social class, Frailty, Dementia, Reminiscence.

353. Wideman, John Edgar. "Presents" (1988). In *Fever: Twelve Stories*. New York: Henry Holt, 1989, pp. 97-105.

An old African-American man recalls a special moment between his grandmother and himself on a Christmas Eve when he was seven years old and offered to sing his "Big Mama" a song. The old woman, moved as if by a premonition, pulled an old guitar out from under her bed, told him to "squeeze" music out of it, and then prophesied that he would have a hard life. That night the old woman died in her sleep. The old man has "preached" this story many times because his story is of a life filled with love and pain, joys and regrets, just as Big Mama had prophesied. He misses the old woman and sums up his life by referring to the day she gave him that guitar: "Something born that day and something died." TOPICS: Race, Grandparenting, Creativity, Reminiscence, Legacies.

354. Winslow, Thyra Samter. "Grandma." In *Picture Frames*. New York: Knopf, 1923. Also In Anthology 1, pp. 35-49.

A spectrum of mishandling old people is shown as Grandma, a widow of seventy-three, rotates through three roles as resident grandparent in the homes of her children. The first family though affectionate loads her with household drudgery. The second, rich and upper-class, is civil to her but leaves her care to servants. The third, a family of malcontents, criticizes her as well as one another. Grandma bears all, covering up her real feelings but looking forward to the intervals of traveling from one home to another. On those journeys she enjoys her playing "the old lady she sometimes dreamed she was." She distributes small attentions among fellow passengers, and describes to them her ideal life as a sweet, happy picture-book Grandma. TOPICS: Role Loss, Parent-Child Conflicts, Elder Abuse, Aging in Place.

355. Wiser, William. "The Man Who Wrote Letters to Presidents." In *Ballads, Blues and Swan Songs*. New York: Atheneum, 1982, pp. 36-47.
The older person as lifelong loser is the center of this darkly comic episode. Paul Green, hotel salad chief, is accosted at the bar by an old drifter who proceeds to bore and then frighten him with the account of his long warfare against the "system." For decades this old fellow has written to U. S. presidents demanding benefits, warning against catastrophe, protesting job bias. To extort attention from time to time, he has swallowed objects from glass to nail polish until his body is a surgery patchwork. The old man crackles with sarcasm about the "system," almost stirring one to say, "That's the way for an old loser to go out!" But Paul's horror at seeing himself a similar loser would prompt middle age to look ahead to its own future. TOPICS: Enmity, Alienation, Courage, Reminiscence.

356. Xin'er, Lu. "The One and the Other" (1987). In *The Serenity of Whiteness: Stories by and About Women in Contemporary China*. Selected and Translated by Zhu Hong. New York: Ballantine Books, 1991, pp. 208-226.
After slavishly devoting three years of her widowhood to the memory of her husband, a woman in her 50s is rejuvenated temporarily by the sudden friendship with a neighbor. Song Huishan was so devoted to her late husband that even in death he controls her life. His grave must be visited, his favorite white roses brought, a place set for him at the table. Then Song meets her neighbor, Hua Qing, who is four years younger, and the latter's charm, openness, and independent ideas win her over. But as their relationship deepens over the next few years, Song becomes possessive of Hua's time and attention, just as, ironically, her husband had been possessive of her. Song cannot accept Hua's capacity to be independent as a woman and defy cultural stereotypes. Song breaks off the friendship when she learns Hua has no interest in ending a love affair with a married man. TOPICS: Culture, Friendship, Disengagement, Loneliness, Widowhood.

357. Yezierska, Anzia. "A Window Full of Sky." In *The*

Open Cage: An Anzia Yiezierska Collection.   New York:
Persea Bks, 1979.   Also in Anthology 5, pp. 284-88.
   Even for an aged woman of shrinking vitality and
means, independence may count for more than the security
of an old people's home.   The speaker of this story is
pressed to explore such a home.   Although the bureaucrat-
ic procedure offends her, she pursues the opening until
she sees the cramped cubicle in which she will have to
exist.   Back in the top floor of her rooming house, she
at least has a window with a magnificent view over New
York city--a "window full of sky" with the light and
spread she will not give up. TOPICS: Housing, Autonomy,
Aging in Place.

358 Yurick, Sol. "The Siege." In *Someone Just Like You*.
New York: Harper, 1972.
   A strange corruption of humanitarian services
occurs when Mrs. Diamond, an old slum welfare case, is
besieged by Miller, the Relief Inspector, and Kalisher,
a social worker. She will not let them see her fourth
room, which they suspect may hold assets that would
disqualify her for aid. Miller's rule is simple. Either
the woman will allow the secret room to be checked or she
will be cut off from relief. Kalisher, by contrast, wants
to win by persuasion and respect. As for Mrs. Diamond,
eking out her life in stench and disorder, Kalisher sees
in her "all of the suffering, the poor, the sick, all the
lonely, old, and deserted in the slums." Her room, when
finally entered in a kind of spiritual rape, contains
only worthless odds and ends. TOPICS: Services, Urban
Aging, Elder Abuse, Mental Health, Aging in Place.

Index of Authors and Their Works

[References are to pages in Parts One and Two.]

Absire, Alain,
    Lazarus (novel), 50, 64, 67, 91
Achebe, Chinua,
    Things Fall Apart (novel), 6, 11, 29, 65, 91
Adams, Alice,
    "The Girl Across the Room" (story), 22, 145
    "Ocracoke Island" (story), 21, 23, 61, 145
Adler, Warren,
    "The Angel of Mercy" (story), 16, 28, 64, 146
Albee, Edward,
    The Sandbox (play), 3, 111
Amis, Kingsley,
    Ending Up (novel), 3, 16, 30, 92
    The Old Devils (novel), 5, 12, 21, 30, 92
Anderson, Jessica,
    Tirra Lirra by the River (novel), 16, 36,
        54, 93
Anderson, Robert,
    I Never Sang for My Father (play), 5, 12,
        19, 26, 73, 111
Angelou, Maya,
    "The Last Decision" (poem), 5, 40, 50, 119
    "Old Folks Laugh" (poem), 42, 119
    "On Aging" (poem), 4, 119
Apple, Max,
    Roommates: My Grandfather's Story (novel), 4,
        5, 11, 25, 40, 93
Ariyoshi, Sawako,
    The Twilight Years (novel), 3, 12, 14, 17,
        27, 35, 94

Aucamp, Hennie,
    "A Bridal Bed for Tant Nonnie" (story), 65,
        146
    "Soup for the Sick" (story), 10, 146
Auchincloss, Louis,
    "The Cathedral Builder" (story), 7, 24, 58,
        63, 66, 147
    "The Double Gap" (story), 12, 19, 147
    "Suttee" (story), 5, 13, 48, 60, 148
Auden, W. H.
    "Doggerel by a Senior Citizen" (poem), 5, 120
    "Old People's Home" (poem), 4, 37, 45, 120

Bahe, Liz Sohappy
    "Grandmother Sleeps" (poem), 5, 11-12, 120
Barker, Pat,
    The Century's Daughter (novel), 7, 9, 25,
        63, 94
    Union Street (novel), 7, 9, 41, 95
Bausch, Richard,
    The Last Good Time (novel), 47, 52, 95
    "Evening" (story), 45, 50, 59, 148
    "Letter to the Lady of the House" (story), 21,
        148
    "Rare and Endangered Species" (story), 18, 21,
        45, 50, 149
    "What Feels Like the World" (story), 25, 149
Baxter, Charles,
    "Fenstad's Mother" (story), 150
    "Horace and Margaret's Fifty-Second"
        (story), 47, 150
Beauvoir, Simone de,
    A Very Easy Death (autobiography), 17, 27, 32,
        35, 53, 79
Bentley, Phyllis,
    "Mother and Daughter" (story), 18-19, 49, 150
Beresford-Howe, Constance,
    The Book of Eve (novel), 13, 21, 23, 40, 96
Berman, Philip, and Connie Goldman, eds.,
    The Ageless Spirit (autobiography), 4, 31, 43,
        44, 52, 59, 79
Bernlef, J.,
    Out of Mind (novel), 20-21, 27-28, 34, 48, 96
Berriault, Gina,
    "The Bystander" (story), 17, 34, 151
    "The Diary of K. W." (story), 6-7, 46, 58, 151
    "Nocturne" (story), 24, 35, 36, 151
Berry, Wendell,
    "Are You All Right?" (story), 3, 41, 152
Blumenthal, Michael,
    "Elegy for My Mother: The Days" (poem), 17,
        60, 62, 68, 120

Blumenthal, Michael (Continued)
    "The Pleasures of Old Age" (poem), 120
    "United Jewish Appeal" (poem), 121
Bly, Robert,
    "A Visit to the Old People's Home" (poem), 20,
        48, 121
Blythe, Ronald,
    The View in Winter (autobiography), 9, 24, 37,
        45, 65, 80
Booth, Philip,
    "Fallback" (poem), 121
    "Old" (poem), 121
Borges, Jorge Luis,
    "The Immortals" (story), 36, 152
Brecht, Bertolt,
    "The Unseemly Old Lady" (story), 5, 13, 20,
        40, 56, 61, 152
Brooks, Gwendolyn,
    "Jessie Mitchell's Mother" (poem), 3, 122
    "Death of a Grandmother" (story), 10, 26, 35,
        36, 68, 153
Brown, Mary Ward,
    "The Amaryllis" (story), 16, 42, 53, 153
Brown, Sterling,
    "Virginia Portrait" (poem), 9, 10, 13, 40, 122
Broyard, Anatole,
    Intoxicated by My Illness (autobiography) 32-
        33, 36, 67, 80

Calisher, Hortense,
    Age (novel), 21, 42, 47, 58, 68, 97
Canin, Ethan,
    "Emperor of the Air" (story), 16, 29, 40, 49,
        154
    "We Are Nighttime Travelers" (story), 23, 154
Carver, Raymond,
    "Happiness in Cornwall" (poem), 16, 61, 122
    "After the Denim" (story), 25, 154
Cather, Willa,
    "Neighbor Rosicky" (story), 9, 11, 18, 20,
        63, 155
    "Old Mrs. Harris" (story), 6, 25, 44, 65, 155
Chekhov, Anton,
    "Grief" (story), 17-18, 60, 155
    "Old Age" (story), 21, 156
Ciardi, John,
    "Matins" (poem), 4, 6, 122
Clifton, Lucille,
    "Miss Rosie" (poem), 10, 123
Coburn, D. L.,
    The Gin Game (play), 22, 29, 37, 56, 112

Collier, Eugenia,
    "Marigolds" (story), 7, 21, 156
Coon, Betty,
    "Daisies" (story), 13, 19, 42, 156
Cooper, Bernard,
    "Picking Plums" (story), 10, 22, 157
Cooper, Susan, and Hume Cronyn,
    Foxfire (play), 9, 17, 21, 43, 60, 112
Cristofer, Michael,
    The Shadow Box (play), 17, 113

Delany, Sarah and Elizabeth,
    *Having Our Say: The Delany Sisters' First
        100 Years* (autobiography) 10, 17, 43-44,
        62, 81
Dodd, Susan,
    "Bifocals" (story), 11, 15, 61, 68, 157
    "Nightlife" (story), 18, 157
    "Sinatra" (story), 4, 157
    "Subversive Coffee" (story), 11, 17, 33, 158
Dokey, Richard,
    "The Autumn of Henry Simpson" (story), 19, 37,
        44, 60, 158
Dorner, Marjorie,
    "Before the Forgetting" (story), 34, 47-48,
        159
    "Tree House" (story), 15, 16, 56-57, 159
Dreiser, Theodore,
    "The Lost Phoebe" (story), 9, 21, 34, 47,
        58, 160
Dumas, Henry,
    "Grandma's Got a Wig" (poem), 123

Eberhart, Richard,
    "Hardy Perennial" (poem), 24, 44, 123
Eiseley, Loren,
    "The Brown Wasp" (autobiography), 62,
        68, 81
Ekström, Margareta,
    "The King Is Threatened" (story), 56, 160
Emerson, Ralph,
    "Terminus" (poem), 39, 59, 63, 123
Ernaux, Annie,
    A Woman's Story (autobiography), 34, 63, 81

Ferber, Edna,
    "Old Lady Mandle" (story), 17, 51, 160
    "Old Man Minick" (story), 8, 9, 19, 27, 38,
        40, 47, 56, 161
Fisher, M. F. K.,
    "The Reunion (story), 67, 161

Forster, E. M.,
    "The Road from Colonus" (story), 44, 56, 59,
        64, 161
Frame, Janet,
    "The Bath" (story), 32, 52, 162
    "Winter Garden" (story), 33, 162
Freeman, Judith,
    Set for Life (novel), 19, 24, 54, 97
Freeman, Mary Wilkins,
    "A Mistaken Charity" (story), 18, 40, 57, 162
    "Two Old Lovers" (story), 46, 163
Frost, Robert,
    "The Death of the Hired Man" (poem), 4, 18,
        46, 123
    "An Old Man's Winter Night" (poem), 32, 48,
        124

Gallant, Mavis,
    "His Mother" (story), 11, 20, 163
Gardner, Herb,
    I'm Not Rappaport (play), 15, 29, 41, 42, 113
Giovanni, Nikki,
    "Legacies" (poem), 26, 66, 124
    "The Life I Led" (poem), 61, 124
Gloag, Julian,
    Only Yesterday (novel), 22, 25-26, 32,
        48-49, 98
Goldman, Connie. *See* Berman, Philip.
Graves, Robert,
    "Nightmare of Senility" (poem), 46, 125
    "The Great-Grandmother" (poem), 26, 29, 125
Gurganus, Allan,
    "Blessed Assurance: A Moral Tale" (story), 10,
        24, 44, 164
    "A Hog Loves Its Life" (story), 25, 42, 56,
        164
    "It Had Wings" (story), 4, 164

Hall, Donald,
    String Too Short to Be Saved
        (autobiography), 8, 25, 42, 44, 31, 55, 82
    "The Day I Was Older" (poem), 6, 125
    "Elegy for Wesley Wells" (poem), 8, 25, 61,
        66, 125
    "The Hole" (poem), 33, 40, 126
    "Ox Cart Man" (poem), 8, 31, 41, 126
Hardy, Thomas,
    "After a Journey" (poem), 61, 126
    "Ah, Are You Digging on My Grave?" (poem), 67,
        126
    "I Look into My Glass" (poem), 22, 33-34, 51,
        126

Hardy, Thomas (Continued)
    "Old Lady Chundle" (story), 33, 165
Harris, Peter,
    "My Father-in-Law's Contract" (poem), 11, 66,
        68, 127
Harrison, Tony,
    "Long Distance II" (poem), 127
Harwood, Ronald,
    The Dresser (play), 22, 31, 42-43, 51, 55, 114
Hemingway, Ernest,
    The Old Man and the Sea (novel), 31, 41,
        65, 98
    "A Clean, Well-Lighted Place" (story), 33,
        46-47, 65, 165
    "Old Man at the Bridge" (story), 5, 32, 48,
        166
Henson, Lance,
    "Grey Woman" (poem), 6, 127
Herman, Michelle,
    Missing (novel), 11, 99
Higgins, Joanna,
    "The Courtship of Widow Sobcek" (story), 11,
        19, 21, 64, 166
Highsmith, Patricia,
    "The Cries of Love" (story), 20, 22, 49, 166
Honel, Rosalie Walsh,
    *Journey with Grandpa: Our Family's Struggle
        with Alzheimer's Disease,*
        (autobiography), 8, 8, 18, 20, 27, 53,
        64, 82
Hughes, Langston,
    "Mother to Son" (poem), 17, 65, 127
Humphrey, William,
    "The Hardys" (story), 47, 61, 167
    "September Song" (story), 23, 167
Hurlimann, Thomas,
    The Couple (novel), 34, 45, 60, 99

Ishiguro, Kazuo,
    The Remains of the Day (novel), 6, 21-22,
        63, 100

Jacobsen, Josephine,
    "Jack Frost" (story), 8, 32, 40, 57, 167
Jacobsen, Rolf,
    "Old Age" (poem), 32, 53, 64, 127
    "The Old Women" (poem), 14, 44, 128
Jarrell, Randall,
    "Aging" (poem), 58, 128
Jenkins, Michael,
    A House in Flanders (autobiography), 5, 13,
        18, 44, 83

Jhabvala, Ruth Prawer,
   "The Man with the Dog" (story), 11, 22, 61,
      168
   "Miss Sahib" (story), 11, 24, 168
Jie, Zhang,
   "An Unfinished Record" (story), 169
Johnson, Josephine,
   "Old Harry" (story), 7, 12, 15, 47, 59, 169
Jolley, Elizabeth,
   "A Hedge of Rosemary" (story), 58, 169
   "A New World" (story), 41-42, 61-62, 170
   "Mr. Parker's Valentine" (story), 4, 16, 170
   "Pear Tree Dance" (story), 55, 170
Joseph, Jenny,
   "Warning" (poem), 13, 29, 52, 128

Kalpakian, Laura,
   "A Christmas Cordial" (story), 46, 57, 171
Kidder, Tracy,
   Old Friends (autobiography), 12, 15, 16, 35,
      37, 45, 83
King, Francis,
   "The Tradesman" (story), 8, 36, 40, 50,
      54, 171
King, Larry,
   "The Old Man" (autobiography), 17, 84
Kinnell, Galway,
   "Goodbye" (poem), 17, 39, 128
Knight, Wallace,
   "The Resurrection Man" (story), 9, 31, 48,
      50, 171
Knopf, Helen,
   "Memories" (poem), 11, 61, 128
Koch, Kenneth,
   I Never Told Anybody: Teaching Poetry
      Writing in a Nursing Home
      (autobiography), 4, 16, 37, 42, 56,
      63, 84
   "The Circus" (poem), 43, 49, 129
Koger, Lisa,
   "Ollie's Gate" (story), 20, 24, 65, 172
Konek, Carol Wolfe,
   Daddyboy: A Memoir (autobiography), 6, 13,
      18, 20, 34, 65-66, 85
Kunitz, Stanley,
   "The Portrait" (poem), 60, 129

Labozzetta, Marissa,
   "Making the Wine" (story), 34, 60, 172
Larkin, Philip,
   "Aubade" (poem), 47, 67, 129

Larkin, Philip (Continued)
    "The Old Fools" (poem), 3, 37, 45, 129
Laurence, Margaret,
    The Stone Angel (novel), 7, 13, 19, 27, 29,
        46, 63, 100
Lawrence, D. H.,
    "Shadows" (poem), 63, 68, 130
Lawrence, Josephine,
    The Web of Time (novel), 20, 55, 101
Lax, Eric,
    "The Death of My Father" (autobiography), 32,
        64, 85
Lessing, Doris,
    The Diary of a Good Neighbour (novel), 4, 6,
        9, 15, 68, 101
    "Casualty" (story), 29, 36, 172
    "Flight" (story), 26, 52, 173
    "The Pit" (story), 13, 41, 52, 173
    "Womb Ward" (story), 13, 43, 173
Lester, Julius,
    Do Lord Remember Me (novel), 9, 20, 41, 62,
        63, 102
Levertov, Denise,
    "A Daughter (I)" (poem), 27, 60, 130
    "A Daughter (II)" (poem), 27, 60, 130
    "The 90th Year" (poem), 17, 53, 130
    "A Woman Alone" (poem), 5, 14, 41, 131

MacDonald, D. R.,
    "Of One Kind" (story), 7, 33, 174
    "Poplars" (story), 26-27, 33, 174
    "Work" (story), 12-13, 15, 47, 174
Maclay, Lise,
    "I Hate the Way I Look" (poem), 4, 24, 34,
        43, 51, 131
    "Infirmities" (poem), 4, 32, 131
    "Occupational Therapy" (poem), 61, 62, 131
MacLeish, Archibald,
    "The Old Gray Couple, I" (poem), 54, 67, 132
    "The Old Gray Couple, II" (poem), 20, 47, 63,
        132
    "The Wild Old Wicked Man" (poem), 45, 58,
        132
    "With Age Wisdom" (poem), 132
Malamud, Bernard,
    "In Retirement" (story), 46, 56, 175
    "The Jewbird" (story), 3, 26, 28, 43,
        175
    "The Mourners" (story), 9, 29, 46, 175
Mann, Thomas,
    "Death in Venice" (story), 23, 176

Mansfield, Katherine,
    "Life of Ma Parker" (story), 45, 50, 176
Marshall, Paule,
    Praisesong for the Widow (novel), 10, 56, 61,
        64, 102
    "Barbados" (story), 6, 9-10, 10, 16, 177
Masters, Olga,
    "You'll Like It There" (story), 19, 48, 177
Matthews, Jack,
    "The Eternal Mortgage" (story), 46, 49, 64,
        177
Matthews, Jack (Continued)
    "First the Legs and Last the Heart"
        (story), 35, 178
    "Storyhood as We Know It" (story), 18, 29, 178
McEnroe, Robert E.,
    The Silver Whistle (play), 24, 37, 42, 50, 114
McFarland, Dennis,
    School for the Blind (novel), 57, 64, 103
McGuane, Thomas,
    "Family" (story), 18, 178
Menaker, Daniel,
    The Old Left (stories), 26, 44, 56, 179
Miller, Arthur,
    Death of a Salesman (play), 3, 17, 50, 114
    The Price (play), 19, 115
Miller, Sue,
    "Appropriate Affect" (story), 13, 20, 33, 45,
        179
Minot, Stephen,
    "Small Point Bridge" (story), 6, 8, 23, 179
    "The Tide and Isaac Bates" (story), 8, 47,
        48, 180
Moffat, Mary Jane,
    "Widow's Supper" (poem), 47, 60, 132
Mori, Toshio,
    "The Man with Bulging Pockets" (story), 12,
        29, 180
Mueller, Lisa,
    "Monet Refuses the Operation" (poem), 35, 43,
        133
Mungoshi, Charles,
    "The Setting Sun and the Rolling
        World" (story), 12, 48, 180
    "Who Will Stop the Dark?" (story), 12, 65, 181
Munro, Alice,
    "Mrs. Cross and Mrs. Kidd" (story), 15, 37,
        181
Murray, Michele,
    "Poem to My Grandmother in Her Death"
        (poem), 26, 133

Myers, Lou,
    When Life Falls It Falls Upside Down
        (novel), 11, 35, 36, 63, 103

Naipaul, V. S.,
    Mrs. Stone and the Knights Companion
        (novel), 103
Niatum, Duane,
    "Old Woman Awaiting the Greyhound Bus"
        (poem), 25, 53, 133
Norris, Leslie,
    "My Uncle's Story" (story), 24-25, 32, 182

O'Brien, Edna,
    "Christmas Roses" (story), 23, 42, 182
O'Connor, Edwin,
    I Was Dancing (novel), 5, 19, 49, 104
O'Connor, Flannery,
    "The Artificial Nigger" (story), 26, 58, 64,
        182
    "A Late Encounter with the Enemy" (story), 51,
        183
O'Connor, Frank,
    "Requiem" (story), 22, 61, 64, 183
O'Hehir, Diane,
    "Home Free" (poem), 133
Olmstead, Alan,
    Threshold: The First Days of Retirement
        (autobiography), 15, 48, 56, 59, 86
Olsen, Tillie,
    "Tell Me a Riddle" (story), 11, 13, 25,
        62, 183
Osborn, Carolyn,
    "Man Dancing" (story), 184
Owen, Howard,
    Littlejohn (novel), 9, 44, 104

P'An Yueh,
    "In Mourning for His Dead Wife" (poem), 47,
        50, 60, 133
Parise, Goffredo,
    "Beauty" (story), 9, 41, 184
    "Fear" (story), 41, 52, 184
    "Memory" (story), 12, 185
Pastan, Linda,
    "Ethics" (poem), 43, 134
    "The Five Stages of Grief" (poem), 45, 60,
        134
    "Funerary Tower: Han Dynasty" (poem), 49, 134
    "My Grandmother" (poem), 11, 26, 134
    "Something About the Trees" (poem), 6, 135

Pitter, Ruth,
    "An Old Woman Speaks of the Moon" (poem), 135
Porter, Katherine Anne,
    "The Jilting of Granny Weatherall"
        (story), 18, 34, 62, 185
Porter, Katherine Anne (Continued)
    "The Last Leaf" (story), 7, 10, 40, 185
    "The Old Order" (story), 10, 22, 186
Powers, J. F.,
    "The Old Man: A Love Story" (story), 3, 6,
        55-56, 186
Pritchett, V. S.,
    "A Trip to the Seaside" (story), 23, 186
Pym, Barbara,
    Quartet in Autumn (novel), 4-5, 34, 41,
        46, 105

Ransom, John Crowe,
    "Old Man Playing with Children" (poem), 25,
        48, 52, 56, 135
Ricci, Julio,
    "The Concert" (story), 3, 43, 187
Robinson, Edwin Arlington,
    "Isaac and Archibald" (poem), 15, 32, 135
Rosner, Anne,
    "Prize Tomatoes" (story), 19, 57, 187
Roth, Philip,
    Patrimony: A True Story (autobiography), 11,
        17, 26, 32, 35-36, 66, 86
Rukeyser, Muriel,
    "In Her Burning" (poem), 22, 135

Sackville-West, Virginia,
    All Passion Spent (novel), 12, 23, 35, 63, 105
Sarton, May,
    After the Stroke (autobiography), 15, 33, 36,
        42, 47, 87
    At Seventy: A Journal (autobiography), 14, 42,
        57, 87
    *Endgame: A Journal of the Seventy-Ninth
        Year* (autobiography), 15, 32, 33, 36, 42,
        50, 88
    As We Are Now (novel), 23, 28, 29, 36, 49,
        52, 106
    "August Third" (poem), 17, 136
    "Der Abschied [The Farewell]" (poem), 23, 47,
        61, 136
    "Gestalt at 60" (poem), 41, 57, 63, 136
    "The House of Gathering" (poem), 41, 53, 137
    "Mourning to Do" (poem), 22, 23, 61, 137
    "On a Winter Night" (poem), 43, 48, 137

Sarton, May (Continued)
  "Who Has Spoken of the Unicorn in Old Age?"
      (poem), 14, 23, 44, 137
Sayles, John,
  "At the Anarchists' Convention" (story), 4,
      11, 16, 29, 43, 52, 187
  "Dillinger in Hollywood" (story), 37, 188
Schwartz, Lynn Sharon,
  Balancing Acts (novel), 23, 24, 29, 37, 59,
      60, 62, 68-69, 106
Scofield, Sandra,
  "Loving Leo" (story), 188
Sexton, Anne,
  "Courage" (poem), 51-52, 67, 137
Shakespeare, William,
  The Tragedy of King Lear (play), 17, 19, 28,
      34, 39-40, 59, 64, 115
Simon, Neil,
  Lost in Yonkers (play), 5, 19, 48, 60, 116
Singer, Isaac Bashevis,
  "The Hotel" (story), 11, 47, 188
  "Old Love" (story), 11, 23, 39, 50-51, 58, 189
Spark, Muriel,
  Memento Mori (novel), 7, 22, 44, 49, 51,
      67, 107
Stanford, Ann,
  "The Fathers" (poem), 66, 137
Stegner, Wallace,
  The Spectator Bird (novel), 4, 46, 49, 62,
      107
  "The Double Corner" (story), 3, 9, 19, 189
Steinbeck, John,
  "The Leader of the People" (story), 20, 25,
      56, 62, 65, 190
Stern, Richard,
  "Arrangements at the Gulf" (story), 39, 45,
      47, 67, 190
  "Dr. Cahn's Visit" (story), 21, 35, 35, 190
  "Packages" (story), 27, 35, 66, 191
Stone, John,
  "He Makes a House Call" (poem), 36, 55, 138
Swift, Jonathan,
  "[The Immortal Struldbruggs]" (story), 34, 34,
      39, 67, 191

Taylor, Elizabeth,
  Mrs. Palfrey at the Claremont (novel), 24,
      52-53, 59, 60-61, 108
Taylor, Nick,
  A Necessary End (autobiography), 8, 17, 27,
      32, 88

Taylor, Peter,
    "Porte-Cochere" (story), 19, 66, 192
Tennyson, Alfred,
    "Ulysses" (poem), 31, 52, 58, 138
Thomas, Annabel,
    "Ashur and Evir" (story), 42, 48, 52, 59, 192
Thomas, Dylan,
    "Do Not Go Gentle into That Good Night"
        (poem), 28-29, 50, 138
Thompson, Ernest,
    On Golden Pond (play), 20, 48, 117
Tolstoy, Leo,
    The Death of Ivan Ilyich (novel), 7, 21, 36,
        51, 55, 64, 68, 108
Trevor, William,
    "Attracta" (story), 53, 192
    "Broken Homes" (story), 8, 24, 28, 57, 193
    "The General's Day" (story), 5, 33, 45,
        56, 193

Uhry, Alfred,
    Driving Miss Daisy (play), 9, 10, 15-16, 33,
        43, 117
Updike, David,
    "Indian Summer" (story), 8, 25, 41, 52, 193

Van Doren, Mark,
    "Bay-Window Ballad" (poem), 6, 45, 138
    "Death of Old Men" (poem), 4, 139
    "The First Snow of the Year" (poem), 20, 27,
        62, 139
    "Nothing but Death" (poem), 51, 61, 139
    "Old Man, Old Woman" (poem), 53-54, 139
    "Sleep, Grandmother" (poem), 18, 139
    "Spirit" (poem), 32, 41, 140
    "The Uncle I Was Named For" (poem), 18,
        66, 140
    "We Were Not Old" (poem), 4, 5, 41, 140
Van Duyn, Mona,
    "Letters from a Father" (poem), 33, 53,
        57, 140
Van Velde, Jacoba,
    The Big Ward (novel), 12, 13, 16, 27, 67, 109
Vining, Elizabeth,
    Being Seventy: The Measure of a Year
        (autobiography), 37, 29, 42, 64, 89
Vivante, Arturo,
    "The Bell" (story), 20, 27, 35, 36, 68, 194
    "A Gallery of Women" (story), 7-8, 12, 27, 194
    "Last Rites" (story), 33, 35, 65, 195
    "The Orchard" (story), 7, 12, 31, 53, 195

Vivante, Arturo (Continued)
    "The Soft Core" (story), 19, 35, 51, 195
Vonnegut, Kurt, Jr.,
    Fortitude (play), 36, 46, 117
    "Tomorrow and Tomorrow and Tomorrow"
        (story), 6, 26, 36, 67, 196

Wagoner, David,
    "Into the Nameless Places" (poem), 34, 46, 141
    "Part Song" (poem), 3, 37, 141
Walker, Alice,
    "Goodnight, Willie Lee, I'll See You
        in the Morning" (poem), 60, 141
    "To Hell with Dying" (story), 10, 24, 33,
        42, 196
    "The Welcome Table" (story), 10, 64, 68, 197
Weaver, Will,
    "From the Landing" (story), 9, 26, 49, 197
    "A Gravestone Made of Wheat" (story), 9,
        57, 197
Welty, Eudora,
    "Old Mr. Marblehall" (story), 5, 45, 58, 198
    "A Visit of Charity" (story), 25, 198
    "A Worn Path" (story), 7, 10, 13, 31, 52,
        53, 198
Wharton, Edith,
    "After Holbein" (story), 7, 62, 199
Wharton, William,
    Dad (novel), 17, 21, 26, 33, 34, 109
Wheelock, John,
    "Dear Men and Women" (poem), 54, 68, 141
    "Song on Reaching Seventy" (poem), 64, 68, 142
Whitman, Walt,
    "Song at Sunset" (poem), 64, 68, 142
Wideman, John Edgar,
    "Presents" (story), 10, 42, 62, 199
Wilder, Thornton,
    The Long Christmas Dinner (play), 18, 53, 58,
        66, 118
Williams, William Carlos,
    "Dedication for a Plot of Ground" (poem), 41,
        66-67, 142
    "Last Words of My English Grandmother"
        (poem), 44, 47, 68, 142
    "To a Poor Old Woman" (poem), 4, 6, 142
    "To Waken an Old Lady" (poem), 31, 143
    "Tract" (poem), 43, 60, 67, 143
    "The Widow's Lament in Springtime" (poem), 60,
        143
Wilson, Angus,
    Late Call (novel), 5, 13, 21, 40, 45, 110

Winslow, Thyra Samter,
    "Grandma" (story), 6, 19, 28, 57, 199
Wiser, William,
    "The Man Who Wrote Letters to Presidents"
        (story), 29, 46, 200

Xin'er, Lu,
    "The One and the Other" (story), 47, 200

Yeats, William Butler,
    "A Prayer for Old Age" (poem), 43, 44, 143
    "Sailing to Byzantium" (poem), 5, 43, 45, 143
Yeats, William Butler (Continued)
    "The Wild Old Wicked Man" (poem), 22, 43,
        45, 144
    "The Wild Swans at Coole" (poem), 44, 49, 144
Yezierska, Anzia,
    "A Window Full of Sky" (story), 8, 40,
        57-58, 200
Yurick, Sol,
    "The Siege" (story), 8, 28, 57, 200

Zuckerman, Marilyn,
    "After Sixty" (poem), 13, 44, 59, 144

Index of Topics in Part One

[Bold-face is used for topics which are main subjects
or main subdivisions of essays in Part One.]

Activity, 31
Adaptation, 5
Adultery, 23
Adventurousness, 31, 52, 58
African-Americans: coping, 41; and courage, 53; and
    intergenerational, 24; Jews, 10; and loss, 60;
    as mentor, 24; poverty, 7; racism, 9-10, and
    religion, 64; and reminiscence, 63
Africans: role loss, 5-6; and transmission of
    values, 65
Afterlife, 68
Ageism, 3
Aging in place, 57-58; motives for, 57; over
    generations, 58; return to old home, 57-58;
    rural, 57
Alcoholism, 33; and leisure, 56; and loneliness, 46-47
Alienation, 45-46; and being out-of-date, 45; and
    grief, 45; and institutionalization, 45;
    lifelong,
    46; of loners, 46; and physical unattractiveness,
    46; and remorse, 46; and sexual desire, 45;
    within
    families, 45
Alzheimer's Disease, 34; and caregiving, 27; effect on
    family, 20; services for, 8
Anxiety, 47-48; and death of parents, 48; and failing
    memory, 47-48; and fear of death, 47; and fear of
    dementia, 47; and intergenerational conflict, 48;
    rejection of, 48
Appalachians, rural, 9

Arson, 49
Aspirations, 58; and final achievements, 58; and
     mentoring, 58
Atonement, 64
Autobiography, as life review, 62
Autonomy, 40-41
Avocation. *See* Leisure

Bereavement: *See* Grief, widowhood, loss
Bird watching, as leisure activity, 57
Blacks. *See* African-Americans, 7
Blindness, 33
Bonds, disengagement from, 39
Bonds, family, 16
Bonds, parent-child, 16-18
Bonds, sibling, 18
Bureaucracy, in medical care, 36

Cancer, 32-33
Career, in decline, 55; and final achievement, 55; as
     main satisfaction, 55; as narcotic, 55;
     second, 59
Caregiving, 26-28; at a distance, 27; and health care
     professionals, 27; Japanese, 27; obstacles to,
     27; by older adult, 27; resistance to
     responsibilities, 27; by son, 26; as symbolic
     activity, 28; by women, 14, 27
Catholicism, 64
Centenarians, 4
Cerebrovascular accident: *See* Stroke
Children, exploitive, 19; hostile, 20;
     manipulative, 19
Coma, 33
Comedy, in treatment of death, 67
Community, 16; supportive, 16; toxic, 16
Companions, in housing, 7-8
Con games, 6
Conflicts, family, 20
Conflicts, parent-child 18-20
Coping, 41-42; through fantasy, 41-42; heroic
     examples, 41; through laughter, 42; with physical
     decline, 41
Courage, 51-52; as adventurous spirit, 52; and death,
     67-68; in everyday tasks, 51-52; as high morale,
     52; in resisting evil, 52; to sacrifice, 52
Creative process, 43
Creative writing, as leisure activity, 56
Creativity, 42-43; gardening, 42; and music, 42; and
     storytelling, 42; and writing, 42
Culture, 12; African, 12; Chinese, 12; Dutch, 12;
     Italian, 12; Japanese, 12

Death, 67-69; and afterlife, 68; awareness of in
    mid-life, 49; and comedy, 67; and courage, 67-68;
    as enhancer of life, 68; and expression of love,
    68; fear of, and anxiety, 47; fearfulness of,
    67; and health-care shortcomings, 68; and
    hypocrisy, 67; and immortality, 67; isolation,
    68; and life review, 68; preparation for, 68; as
    sacrifice, 68; unreadiness for, 67
Dementia, 8, 34-35; and caregiving, 27; and
    embarrassment, 35; fear of, and anxiety, 47;
    first-person accounts, 34; in institutions,
    35; leading to insight, 35; and repulsiveness,
    35; and wandering, 34. *See also* Alzheimer's
    Disease
Depression, 7, 50; and bereavement, 50; in
    retirement, 59; sudden, 50
Deviance, 49-50
Diet, 36
Disability, 33-34
Disease, 32-33
Disengagement, 39; from bonds, 39; and defeat, 40;
    and dying, 40; as giving up living, 40; from
    roles, 39; from late love, 39; as serenity, 40;
    and suicide, 40; from hostility, 40
Diverticulitis, 33
Doctor-patient conflicts, 35
Doctors, insensitivity, 35; routinizing of patients,
    36; sensitivity, 36
Downscaling of activity, 39
Dying. *See* Death

Economics, 6-7
Elder abuse, 28; of relative, 28; in social
    service, 28;
Employment, 6, 55-56
Endurance, 52-53; as carrying on, 52-53; and terminal
    illness, 53
Enmity, 29-30; and elder abuse, 29; as general
    spitefulness, 29-30; as generalized, 29; in
    nursing home, 29; and rivalry, 29; and
    self-mutilation, 29; tenant and landlord, 29
Episcopalianism, 64
Estates, arranging of, 66
Ethnicity, 11-12; immigrant, 11; Japanese-American,
    12; Jewish, 11; Native American, 12
euthanasia, 36, 50

Faith, search for, 64
Family: alienation within, 45; and Alzheimer's, 20;
    extended, 18; as vital institution, 18
Family bonds, 18; African-American, 16-17; after
    suicide, 18; hypocritical, 20

Family conflicts, 20
Fantasy: and loneliness, 46; as coping
     mechanism, 41-42
Farms: California, 9; Indiana, 9; Midwest, 9
fear, of death, 67
Feistiness, as rebellion, 29
Frailty, 31-32; and difficulties of self-care, 31-32;
     resistance to, 32
Friends: loss of, 61; loss of, and loneliness, 47
Friendships, 15-16; cross-gender, 15; lifelong, 15;
     in retirement, 59; women, 15

Gardening: and creativity, 42; as leisure activity, 57
Gay. *See* Homosexual
Gender, men, 12-13; adversarial, 12; autonomy, 40;
     bonding, 12; friendships, 12-13
Gender, women, 13-14; African-American, 13; and
     autonomy, 44; creativity, 14; and final
     achievements, 58; goals, and continued career,
     58; and mentoring, 58; and mid-life crisis,
     48-49; mutual support, 13; new roles, 13;
     resistance to children, 13; resistance to male
     dominance, 13; and self-knowledge, 58; strengths,
     13; and wisdom, 44; working-class, 7
Generation gap, 18-19
Grandchildren, as supportive, 25-26
Grandparenting, 25-26; hostility toward, 26; as role
     models, 25; and story-telling, 25; as
     supportive, 25
Grief, 60; and alienation, 45; anticipatory, 60; and
     death, 68; and depression, 50; duration of, 60;
     exits from, 60; health care, and insanity, 34;
     and reminiscence, 63

Heart disease, 33
Holistic medicine, 36
Home, aging in, 57
Homelessness, 4, 6
Homosexual lovers, loss of, 61
Homosexual relationships, 22
Homosexuality, 23
Housing, 8
Humor, 43; as coping mechanism, 42-43;
     hypocritical, 43

Immigrants, 11
Immortality, 67; and alienation, 46
Insanity, 34; and grief, 34
Institutionalization, and alienation, 45
Intergenerational, 23-25; fear and hostility, 25;
     Native American, 25;

Intergenerational affection, from young, 24
Intergenerational outreach, misguided, 8
Intergenerational support: misplaced, 24; from
    younger, 24
Intimacy, 23; homosexual, 23; incestuous, 23; in lieu
    of marriage, 23; panic at, 23
Irish Catholicism, 64
Isolation, 48; and loneliness, 48; self-imposed, 48

Japanese, caregiving, 27
Jewish life, and reminiscence, 63
Jews: and African-Americans, 10; preparation for
    death, 68

Laughter: as coping mechanism, 42; hypocritical, 43
Legacies, 66-67; as dysfunctional, 66; and estates,
    66; and possessions, 66; of values, 66-67. *See
    also* Transmission of values
Leisure, 56-57; and alcoholism, 56; bird watching, 57;
    creative writing, 56; gardening, 57; and
    playfulness, 56; retirement home activities, 56;
    storytelling, 56; travel, 56
Lesbian relationships, 22
Life span, and medical advances, 36
Life review, 62; through autobiography, 62; and death,
    68; at deathbed, 62; toward final self-knowlege,
    63; as preparation for future, 63
Loneliness, 46-47; and alcoholism, 46-47; and fantasy,
    46; and loss of friends, 47; overcoming, 47; and
    widow(er)hood, 47
Loners, and alienation 46
Long-term care, 37
Loss, 61; and celebration, 61; of child, 60;
    disengagement from, 39; of friends, 61; of
    memories, 60; of parent, 60; of pets, 61;
    through adultery, 61; and love, and death, 68;
    lovers, loss of, 61; of way of life, 61

Madness, 34
Maladjustments, lifelong, 49
Marriage, African-American, 21; and alcoholism, 21;
    dysfunctional, 21; effects of dementia, 21; in
    late years, 21; lost chance for, 21-22; lifetime,
    20-21; and suicide, 21
Matriarchs, 5
Medical advances, and life span, 36
Medical care, bureaucratization, 36
Medical intervention, misguided, 35
Medical staff, overworked, 36
Medicine, holistic, 36
Memory, failure of, and anxiety, 47-48
Men. *See* Gender: men

Mental health, 34
Mentoring, 24, 44-45; as goal, 58; and grandparenting,
    44; 65; uncle, role of, 44. *See also*
    Transmission of values
Mid-life, 48-49; and awareness of death, 49
Mid-life crisis: and generation gap, 48-49;
    resolutions, 49
Multicultural, 10-11; Barbados, 10; India, 11; South
    Africa, 10;
Music, and creativity, 42

Native Americans: and courage, 53-54; loss of culture,
    11; loss of way of life, 61; roles, 5
Neighbors, 16; quarrels, 16; supportive, 16
Neuroses, 34
New England, rural, 9
Nihilism, 65
Nursing homes, 4; as depressing, 37; difficult
    placement in, 37; and elder abuse, 28; positive
    aspects, 37

Obsessive behaviors, 34
Older couples, 20-22

Parent-child bonds, 16-18; children's compassion, 17;
    grieving children, 17; love-hate, 18; Japanese,
    17; reconciliation, 17
Parent-child conflicts, 18-20
Parent-child role reversal, 17
Parental exploitation, 19
Parents, anxiety over death of, 48
Parents: as burdens, 19; as hostile, 19; as role
    models, 17
Patients, reaction to insensitivity, 36
Personal example, and transmission of values, 65
Pets, loss of, 61
Physical appearance, 3-4; as handicap, 33; and
    vanity, 51
Physical vigor, 31
Physical unattractiveness, and alienation, 46
Playfulness, and leisure, 56
Pornography, 49
Poverty, 7

Quarrels, disengagement from, 40

Race, 9-10
Racism, 9-10
Rebellion, 28-29; and cultural change, 29; at death,
    28-29; at established order, 29; as
    feistiness, 29
Reclusiveness, 4, 6-7

Reconciliation, of partners, 23
Religion, 63-64; and African-Americans, 63; and Irish
    Catholicism, 64
Reminiscence, 61-61; as delusive, 63; and grief, 63;
    as obsessive, 63; of others, 63; as pleasure, 63;
    of seminal experience, 63; and serenity, 54. *See
    also* Life review
Remorse, 64; and alienation, 46
Retirement, 59; discontent, 55-56; as disengagement,
    39; and fresh outlook, 59; and new friendships,
    59; and second careers, 59; as shock, 59; as
    traumatic, 59
Retirement homes, 8; activities, 56; as depressing,
    37; drabness of, 24; hostility in, 37; positive
    aspects, 37; and self-improvement, 37
Reunions, supportive, 16
Role reversal, 6; in parent-child relationships, 17
Role loss, 5-6
Roles, 4-5; disengagement from, 39. *See also*
    Adaptation and Role loss
Rural aging, 8-9, 57; Appalachian, 9; English, 9;
    Italian, 9; New England, 8-9; South, 9;
    turn-of-century, 9

Sadism, 49
Second careers, and retirement, 59
Self-care, difficulties, 32
Self-centeredness, 51
Self-knowledge: as goal, 58; through life
    review, 63
Self-reliance, 52
Serenity, 53; as disengagement, 40; in long
    relationships, 54; and memories, 54; and
    resilience, 53; and settling one's affairs, 54;
    and world of nature, 53
Services, 7-8
Sex drive: discontinued, 22; frustrated, 22;
    strong, 22
Sexual love, as goal, 58
Sexuality, 22; and alienation, 45
Siblings, hostile, 22
Slums, 9
Social class, 7
South, rural, 9
Spiritual life, 64-65; and atonement, 64; and joy
    and Serenity, 64
Spitefulness, as enmity, 29-30
Stereotypes of aging, 4
Stoicism, 65
Storytelling: and creativity, 42-43; as leisure
    activity, 56
Street persons, 4, 6

Stroke, 33
Suicide, 50-51; aborted, 50; assisted, 8, 50; as
    disengagement, 40; as escape from intimacy, 23;
    effect on family, 18; impact on others, 51; for
    insurance, 50; and isolation, 48; in marriage,
    21; reaction to new love, 51
Swindles, 6

Tenements, 9
Transmission of values, 65-66; African, 65; and
    mentoring, 65; negative, 66; and personal
    example, 65; resistance to, 65
Travel: as leisure activity, 56; as search for
    roots, 56

Ugliness, 3-4, 33; and vanity, 51
Upper middle-class, English, 7
Upper class, old New York, 7
Urban aging, 9; English, 9; New York, 9

Values, as legacies, 66-67
Values, transmission of, 65-66
Vanity, 51; and death, 51; overcoming it, 51; and
    physical appearance, 51;
Vices, 49

Wandering, in dementia, 34
Widow(er)hood, and loneliness, 47
Widowerhood, grief in, 60
Widowhood, 5, 60-61; grief in, 60; and memories, 60
Wisdom, 43-44; and empathy, 4; and facing mortality,
    44; and problem solving, 44; special insights,
    44; and women, 44
Women. See Gender: women
Writing, and creativity, 42

Index of Topics in Part Two

[References are to topics listed at the end of
annotations in Part Two, pp. 79-202.]

Activity, 80, 82, 99, 115, 117, 137, 138, 140, 144,
167, 174, 185, 187, 198, 202
Adaptation, 94, 112, 116, 119, 140, 153, 161
Ageism, 92, 94, 102, 111, 115, 122, 123, 124, 128,
131, 134, 139, 140, 141, 143, 146, 158, 170, 175,
178, 182, 186, 187, 190, 198
Aging in Place, 83, 87, 88, 95, 95, 98, 105, 113,
118, 150, 152, 157, 162, 170, 171, 172, 177, 188,
193, 194, 197, 200, 201, 201
Alienation, 80, 84, 100, 101, 110, 118, 120, 120, 122,
125, 130, 132, 132, 134, 136, 139, 141, 144, 144,
148, 149, 149, 155, 156, 168, 170, 176, 178, 179,
190, 193, 198, 198, 200
Anxiety, 86, 97, 97, 109, 117, 121, 124, 128, 129,
135, 137, 142, 150, 158, 159, 172, 177, 180, 181,
190, 192, 193
Aspirations, 97, 126, 126, 128, 128, 132, 138, 151,
171, 174, 175, 177, 183, 186, 187, 189, 198
Autonomy, 93, 94, 96, 110, 119, 124, 126, 131, 137,
138, 142, 153, 157, 161, 162, 163, 165, 177, 184,
193, 201

Caregiving, 79, 83, 86, 88, 92, 94, 97, 98, 101,
103, 109, 110, 112, 121, 130, 130, 139, 146, 161,
174, 179, 190, 191, 194, 195, 196
Community, 84, 85, 93, 109, 122, 153, 163, 177, 188,
195
Coping, 95, 99, 102, 105, 113, 119, 136, 140, 140,
143, 145, 152, 164, 170, 171, 173, 174, 180, 182,
185, 194

Courage, 80, 96, 128, 135, 137, 138, 140, 162, 173,
    173, 174, 185, 188, 188, 192, 200
Creativity, 80, 82, 85, 87, 88, 89, 113, 114, 114,
    129, 134, 135, 135, 137, 143, 144, 144, 153, 157,
    160, 164, 182, 192, 199
Culture, 83, 94, 109, 172, 181, 181, 200

Death, 79, 81, 81, 86, 91, 97, 102, 103, 103, 107,
    107, 109, 113, 118, 118, 120, 124, 126, 127, 129,
    130, 130, 132, 137, 138, 140, 141, 142, 142, 143,
    151, 153, 157, 161, 178, 184, 185, 185, 190, 192,
    195, 196, 197
Dementia, 82, 83, 85, 94, 97, 103, 123, 141, 141,
    152, 153, 159, 160, 164, 178, 183, 185, 190, 191,
    191, 194, 196, 199
Depression, 88, 91, 114, 134, 141, 143, 148, 176
Deviance, 104, 106, 107, 154, 167
Disability, 87, 92, 110, 117, 125, 126, 131, 141,
    162, 165, 174, 179, 192
Disease, 81, 86, 86, 88, 126, 155, 158, 166, 176,
    193, 195, 196
Disengagement, 89, 106, 116, 122, 123, 125, 128, 141,
    171, 173, 182, 182, 186, 189, 190, 192, 200
Doctor-Patient Conflicts, 79, 86, 86, 87, 88, 92,
    93, 98, 101, 102, 106, 108, 109, 118, 133, 141,
    158, 171, 173, 179, 191, 194, 195, 196

Economics, 85, 98, 102, 123, 123, 143, 151, 151, 180,
    196
Elder Abuse, 106, 111, 116, 161, 175, 177, 193, 200,
    201
Employment, 100, 101, 104, 109, 114, 115, 126, 148,
    150, 169, 171, 171, 184, 186, 189
Endurance, 79, 81, 83, 99, 108, 118, 163, 191, 193,
    194 199
Enmity, 92, 93, 101, 106, 112, 123, 154, 173, 176,
    180, 200
Ethnicity, 86, 94, 99, 117, 120, 121, 127, 127, 155,
    157, 158, 166, 175, 180, 184, 188, 189, 189

Family Bonds, 83, 83, 94, 103, 118, 124, 140, 140,
    146, 149, 163, 167, 178, 179, 179, 185
Family Conflicts, 83, 99, 101, 167, 172, 179
Frailty, 88, 88, 93, 98, 99, 102, 124, 128, 131, 135,
    139, 140, 166, 168, 182, 188, 197, 197, 199
Friendship, 84, 86, 87, 88, 102, 113, 117, 135, 152,
    157, 160, 169, 175, 182, 187, 190, 200

Gender: Men, 84, 93, 112, 148, 152, 169, 175, 180,
    184, 185, 195

Gender: Women, 81, 87, 93, 94, 95, 95, 96, 101, 106,
    109, 110, 119, 123, 124, 125, 128, 128, 131, 137,
    144, 146, 148, 153, 156, 172, 173, 174, 179, 182,
    184, 199
Grandparenting, 82, 94, 95, 98, 105, 116, 121, 124,
    125, 125, 133, 133, 135, 135, 139, 150, 153, 155,
    164, 173, 175, 181, 183, 184, 190, 194, 196, 197,
    199
Grief, 75, 77, 100, 120, 128, 129, 130, 133, 134, 143,
    156, 176, 180

Housing, 83, 88, 94, 161, 201
Humor, 113, 117, 119, 119, 131, 143, 174, 175, 187,
    188

Intergenerational, 95, 95, 103, 107, 108, 123, 147,
    148, 152, 152, 165, 168, 170, 172, 180, 196, 198
Intimacy, 96, 96, 106, 106, 113, 122, 136, 137, 137,
    146, 148, 149, 160, 163, 167, 176, 180, 182, 185,
    187, 188, 189

Legacies, 84, 86, 115, 124, 125, 127, 142, 147, 164,
    179, 191, 199
Leisure, 84, 84, 85, 88, 93, 101, 102, 108, 112, 117,
    128, 136, 141, 144, 145, 153, 153, 156, 157, 158,
    160, 162, 162, 164, 168, 175, 187, 190, 193, 195,
    195
Life Review, 73, 81, 82, 82, 85, 86, 95, 99, 100, 101,
    102, 102, 103, 103, 105, 106, 108, 113, 115, 115,
    125, 132, 140, 145, 155, 164, 167, 169, 172, 178,
    179, 184, 185
Loneliness, 87, 96, 105, 124, 132, 134, 137, 151, 160,
    161, 163, 164, 166, 169, 169, 170, 171, 174, 175,
    175, 189, 200
Long-term Care, 85, 120, 162, 188
Loss, 80, 87, 92, 113, 124, 126, 126, 129, 136, 137,
    146, 157, 167, 181, 183, 185, 190

Mental Health, 100, 105, 110, 116, 171, 201
Mentoring, 82, 155, 179
Mid-Life, 129, 197
Multicultural, 92, 129, 147, 157, 164, 164, 168, 168,
    177, 186, 186

Neighbors, 87, 146, 154, 170

Older Couples, 93, 96, 97, 97, 98, 100, 100, 102, 108,
    109, 110, 110, 112, 113, 114, 115, 121, 131, 132,
    132, 137, 139, 139, 145, 146, 147, 149, 149, 150,
    154, 155, 156, 156, 160, 160, 163, 166, 167, 167,
    167, 168, 183, 184, 186, 186, 191, 198

Parent-Child Bonds, 79, 81, 82, 84, 85, 86, 86, 88,
    94, 98, 98, 105, 110, 113, 113, 115, 116, 120, 122,
    128, 130, 131, 136, 150, 151, 156, 158, 158, 158,
    161, 178, 179, 191, 197
Parent-Child Conflicts, 85, 86, 98, 101, 102, 104,
    110, 112, 115, 115, 116, 116, 117, 121, 122, 139,
    148, 151, 153, 157, 159, 161, 164, 166, 170, 187,
    190, 190, 191, 192, 194, 196, 200
Poverty, 88, 95, 95, 101, 109, 133, 147, 156, 156,
    169, 192, 195, 199

Race, 81, 102, 102, 117, 119, 122, 122, 123, 123, 124,
    127, 141, 153, 156, 177, 196, 197, 199, 199
Rebellion, 92, 94, 107, 113, 125, 128, 138, 142, 197
Religion, 83, 86, 89, 91, 102, 102, 103, 109, 116,
    123, 130, 133, 136, 141, 146, 147, 162, 164, 166,
    176, 178, 183, 183, 197
Reminiscence, 81, 107, 120, 122, 125, 126, 129, 131,
    159, 190, 199
Retirement, 80, 86, 86, 101, 104, 107, 108, 110, 115,
    115, 116, 123, 144, 148, 150, 154, 160, 169, 184,
    186, 187, 189, 192, 193, 193
Role Reversal, 125, 134, 135
Role Loss, 92, 100, 139, 155, 175, 177, 186, 200
Roles, 83, 104, 105, 120, 120, 131, 144, 148, 160,
    166, 178, 186, 193, 198
Rural Aging, 80, 82, 84, 105, 122, 124, 124, 125, 126,
    155, 160, 164, 168, 172, 180, 180, 190, 194, 197,
    197

Serenity, 93, 98, 122, 124, 128, 132, 133, 135, 137,
    139, 141, 142, 143, 171, 195, 199
Services, 171, 177, 193, 195, 201
Sexuality, 107, 121, 123, 125, 126, 136, 144, 145,
    157, 174, 175, 177, 193
Social Class, 107, 109, 174, 199
Spiritual Life, 80, 99, 128, 141, 142, 142, 142,
    166, 195
Stereotypes, 80, 85, 94, 108, 119, 120, 122, 131,
    165, 188
Suicide, 115, 119, 129, 149, 169, 171, 172

Transmission of Values, 85, 92, 106, 115, 118, 127,
    131, 135, 136, 141, 146, 155, 172, 174, 180, 181,
    190, 192, 193

Urban Aging, 95, 102, 113, 157, 175, 176, 201

Vanity, 107, 109, 114, 126, 131, 139, 186, 187

Widowhood, 102, 113, 116, 122, 125, 131, 132, 134,
    139, 141, 142, 143, 148, 149, 153, 168, 172, 200

Widowerhood, 96, 127, 134, 153, 160, 162, 175, 187
Wisdom, 80, 81, 83, 105, 107, 122, 123, 128, 128,
   132, 137, 139, 142, 143, 144, 144, 159, 162, 164

About the Authors

ROBERT E. YAHNKE, Professor in the General College at the University of Minnesota, has taught courses in film study, composition, literature, and the humanities to entry-level students since 1976. He also teaches graduate-level courses in literature and aging to students in the Department of Family and Social Sciences at the College of Human Ecology. He has presented numerous workshops on the use of educational media in gerontology instruction, and he has presented papers on literature and aging at national meetings of the Association for Gerontology in Higher Education and the Gerontological Society of America. He is the editor of *A Time of Humanities* (1976) and author of *The Great Circle of Life: A Resource Guide to Films and Videos on Aging* (1988) and *Aging in Literature: A Reader's Guide*, with Richard M. Eastman (1990).

RICHARD M. EASTMAN, Professor Emeritus at North Central College, served variously during his years there as chair of English, chair of Humanities, and chair of General Studies, as well as dean of the faculty and vice-president for academic affairs. A writer and music composer, he has also written *Style: Writing and Reading as the Discovery of Outlook* (1984) and a *Guide to the Novel* (1965), together with various articles about aging and literature.

ISBN 0-313-29349-X

90000>

EAN

9 780313 293498

HARDCOVER BAR CODE